THE MYTH OF THE PRESS GANG

THE MYTH OF THE PRESS GANG

VOLUNTEERS, IMPRESSMENT AND THE NAVAL MANPOWER PROBLEM IN THE LATE EIGHTEENTH CENTURY

J. Ross Dancy

THE BOYDELL PRESS

First published 2015
The Boydell Press, Woodbridge

ISBN 978 1 78327 003 3

The Boydell Press is an imprint of Boydell & Brewer Ltd
PO Box 9, Woodbridge, Suffolk IP12 3DF, UK
and of Boydell & Brewer Inc.
668 Mount Hope Ave, Rochester, NY 14620–2731, USA
website: www.boydellandbrewer.com

A catalogue record for this book is available
from the British Library

The publisher has no responsibility for the continued existence or accuracy
of URLs for external or third-party internet websites referred to in this
book, and does not guarantee that any content on such websites is, or will
remain, accurate or appropriate

This publication is printed on acid-free paper

Typeset by Fakenham Prepress Solutions, Fakenham, Norfolk NR21 8NN

For Leslie

Contents

Illustrations

Figures

Tables

Abbreviations

ADM   The Admiralty Papers, The National Archives

HO   Home Office Papers, The National Archives

NMM   National Maritime Museum, Greenwich

PC   Privy Council Papers, The National Archives

PRO   Public Record Office Special Collections, The National Archives

T   Treasury Papers, The National Archives

TNA   The National Archives, London (formerly the Public Record Office)

WO   War Office Papers, The National Archives

Preface

'So you study Nelson?' Over the past several years, I cannot count the times that I have been asked that question, immediately after telling someone that I study the eighteenth-century British Navy. There was a time when this question frustrated me greatly, and I longed to explain how much larger the Royal Navy was than just one man, no matter how successful or heroic. However recently I have come to appreciate Nelson more and more, not only for his feats at sea, but for the attention his legend has brought to the subject of naval history. Nelson's legend has captured the interest of countless individuals and inspired many professional historians, myself included, to commit a career to examining naval history. From that has stemmed an enormous historiography that examines all facets of history, including dockyards, technology, administration, victualling, officers and admirals, and finally the men they commanded. For me, it was these men of the lower deck that captured my interest most. Having enlisted for four years as a US Marine before becoming a historian, and having spent just over twenty-two months at sea, I felt that I could identify with their experiences in ways that many other historians could not.

As this book clearly illustrates, I am certainly not the first to research and write about the seamen of the British Royal Navy. In fact, many of my predecessors have done fantastic jobs shedding light on the world between the wooden decks of the Royal Navy, and I have relied heavily on their work here. However, I am the first to tell their story using statistics, and although the historians that came before me performed admirably, the lack of statistical analysis meant that their work had to rely on educated speculation rather than hard fact. The problem with not using statistics, is that when discussing something as big as the manpower of the Royal Navy, it is difficult to put into perspective the qualitative research used to produce their publications. Essentially, understanding a dozen or even a hundred trees is not understanding the forest, particularly when the nature of the research tends to cause the odd or extraordinary trees to be the ones most likely to be examined. In order to understand the forest we need to study thousands of trees, and that is what this project has attempted to do.

It must also be made clear that this is not the final word on such a large topic, nor is it meant to be. I truly hope this project will provide a new foundation upon which we can re-ask many of the great questions that my predecessors asked in the decades before me. Some of them we will undoubtedly find the same answer to, but some of them may be subtly different, and some will certainly change how we view the subject entirely. Thinking back on this research project, it is clear to me that I have raised many more questions than I have answered, and that makes this book something of an interim report. I hope to continue studying the men of the lower deck, and I hope that my colleagues who study this subject also come forward with new questions and new publications that expand the collective knowledge of our past. If this book can add just a little bit to that knowledge, define perhaps just one piece of the great puzzle that is our history, then I believe it will serve its purpose.

Of course it goes unsaid that a work like this could never be completed without support, and I have countless people to thank, though there is not enough space to fully acknowledge them here. N.A.M. Rodger has probably had the greatest impact on this work, first by allowing me the privilege to read for my doctorate under his tutelage, and also by being a constant source of inspiration and new ideas, even after I left the halls of Oxford. The debt I owe to him cannot be repaid in the pages of a hundred books. There have also been many colleagues who have discussed or read elements of this book along the way, and their input has undoubtedly improved its quality: Roger Knight, Robin Briggs, Michael Duffy, Duncan Redford, Daniel Benjamin, James Davey, Samantha Cavell, Joshua Newton, Paulina Preciado, Nolan Belk, Roberta Staples and especially Evan Wilson and Britt Zerbe. The Boydell Press and Peter Sowden have been particularly helpful throughout the process of publication. The staff at the National Maritime Museum and the National Archives at Kew were most helpful in tracking down hard-to-find documents.

The University of Oxford allowed me the opportunity to enter their magnificent halls and read for a doctorate, and most of the research behind this project was completed beneath those dreamy spires. Also, Lady Margaret Hall at the University of Oxford provided me with funding in the form of the Warr-Goodman scholarship, which allowed me to spend more time in archives than would have been otherwise possible. My service as a US Marine taught me many lessons about life and gave me the work ethic necessary to find success in my career. They also provided me with the GI Bill, which funded a large portion of my education after I left the Corps over a decade ago. Also, I have to thank Sam Houston State University and my fellow members of the History Faculty there. The life of a young academic does not get easier when the doctorate has been completed. From there they are released into a very scary world where finding a job could take them to any corner of the world and after such a journey leave them high and dry. My journey led to Texas where Sam Houston State has provided me with a base of operations and funding to continue researching the subject I love. They have also given me students to teach, which has opened my mind greatly and allowed me to learn so many new things about the history of the world in which we live. I doubt that anything could rekindle my passion for this profession more than introducing it to new young minds.

On a personal note I want to thank my family. My mother and grandparents especially have always pushed me to work hard and their inspiration helped throughout my education and writing this book. My father, though he passed when I was a child, taught me that what mattered was not that you had gotten knocked down, but whether or not you get back up. If it were not for those lessons, I doubt that I would be where I am today. Finally, I want to thank my wife, Leslie. You have followed me all over the world over the past fourteen years, patiently supported me through thick and thin, and I am sure you know more about the British Navy than you ever wanted to know. Thank you from the bottom of my heart, this is for you.

'I heard the voice of the Lord, saying, "Whom shall I send, and who will go for us?" Then I said, "Here am I. Send me!"'

(Isaiah 6:8, King James Version)

Introduction

'Your Lordship is hereby required and directed to give immediate orders to the several Captains, Commanders and Commanding Officers of His Majesty's Ships and vessels under your command, not to enter or impress any more men for the Service of His Majesty's Fleet.'[1] The Admiralty sent this order to Lord Nelson on 10 October 1801. The Treaty of Amiens was being negotiated, peace was on the horizon and the Royal Navy was preparing for the inevitable downsizing that would come with peace. A few more months would see a temporary end to the hostilities that had raged for nearly a decade between Britain and France. However, during the previous nine years, the Royal Navy had grown from the small peacetime number of about 17,000 men to over 130,000 men, the largest navy ever assembled in the Atlantic world. This swell in manpower represented an increase of over 750 per cent. With 150 ships-of-the-line either in ordinary, repairing, or in sea pay in January of 1793,[2] the Royal Navy had a force that could at least equal that of France and any other European nation. Therefore, with the declaration of war in 1793, the Royal Navy's principal problem was not constructing a naval force, but manning the fleet that Britain already had in existence.

Manning the Royal Navy was a problem of colossal proportions, and had grown increasingly throughout the eighteenth century as the Navy along with British sea trade expanded.[3] This resulted in an ever-larger struggle for the scarce resource of skilled manpower, which made itself most evident during the initial mobilisation from peacetime to wartime footing.[4] Recruiting seamen in the eighteenth century was essentially a problem of mathematics, pitting the requirements of the Navy against the population of mariners available to draw upon.[5] Further, naval manning and mobilisation could not be allowed to destroy merchant sea trade through depriving it

[1]   NMM: CRK/16/20, Admiralty to Lord Nelson, 10 October 1801.
[2]   The Royal Navy had 458 vessels, rated and non-rated, as of 1 January 1793, of which 140 were in active service or 'Sea Pay'. By January of 1801 this total had increased to 871 vessels, of which 572 were in active service. TNA: ADM 7/567, 'Admiralty Miscellanea, 1754–1806', ff. 23 & 27.
[3]   John E. Talbott, *The Pen and Ink Sailor: Charles Middleton and the King's Navy, 1778–1813*, Cass Series, Naval Policy and History (London: Frank Cass, 1998), p. 22.
[4]   Michael Oppenheim, *The Maritime History of Devon* (Exeter: University of Exeter, 1968), p. 115.
[5]   Christopher Lloyd, *The British Seaman, 1200–1860* (London: Collins, 1968), p. 112; Roger

entirely of skilled manpower, and Britain simply did not have enough seamen to fully man the Royal Navy and the merchant fleets at the same time.[6] Unlike soldiers, the skills of a sailor were in much demand on both the civilian and military market, and this created an enormous deficit between the numbers of men employed at sea in peace and the number necessary during war.[7] To an extent, this deficiency was made up by the flexibility of the seafaring community, as unemployed and underemployed mariners made their way back to the sea in response to the increase of the wartime labour market.[8] However, the extreme growth of the Royal Navy between peace and war meant that the flexibility of the maritime labour market was taken to its limit well before naval forces reached full mobilisation.

Though the issues involved in finding men to fight in the eighteenth century consisted of recruiting men to fill positions from the youngest boys to the most senior admirals and all those that fell between, this research is primarily concerned with the recruitment of seamen and petty officers who formed the lower deck. Seamen and petty officers made up about 75 per cent of ships' complements at the end of the eighteenth century, and were the most difficult men to recruit. Whereas during wartime the Royal Navy had more officers than they could effectively employ at sea, there were never enough skilled mariners to fulfil the constant demand that naval mobilisation placed on the limited pool of maritime manpower. As we will see, the British Navy relied heavily on volunteers to fill its ships, and used impressment more as a means to improve the skill quality, not quantity, of the men aboard.

Seamen and petty officers formed the core component of a warship's manpower. The officers of a given ship, judging on skill and performance, assigned the men of the lower deck to a rating. Petty officers were the most experienced and competent men of the lower deck and served in positions of authority over seamen, but were subordinate to warrant officers and commissioned officers. Their position was not guaranteed from one ship to another, rather they served in their billet at the behest of a ship's officers. Able seamen were the most skilled of seamen, and had mastered the ability to reef, knot, splice, man a ship's wheel, as well as work aloft in the ship's rigging, among other duties. Essentially, these men could work efficiently at any of the duties aboard ship that required 'sea skills'. It took several years of experience, generally five or more, to acquire enough skill to rise to this level in their

Morriss, *Naval Power and British Culture, 1760–1850: Public Trust and Government Ideology* (Aldershot: Ashgate, 2003), p. 18.

[6]   N.A.M. Rodger, *The Wooden World: An Anatomy of the Georgian Navy* (New York: W.W. Norton & Company, 1996), p. 153.

[7]   Jan Glete, *Navies and Nations: Warships, Navies, and State Building in Europe and America, 1500–1860*, vol. I (Stockholm: Almqvist & Wiksell International, 1993), p. 173; N.A.M. Rodger, "'A Little Navy of Your Own Making": Admiral Boscawen and the Cornish Connection in the Royal Navy', in *Parameters of British Naval Power, 1650–1850*, ed. Michael Duffy (Exeter: University of Exeter Press, 1998), p. 83.

[8]   David J. Starkey, 'War and the Market for Seafarers in Britain, 1736–1792', in *Shipping and Trade, 1750–1950: Essays in International Maritime Economic History*, ed. Lewis R. Fischer and Helge W. Nordvik (Pontefract: Lofthouse Publications, 1990), pp. 30–31.

profession. Ordinary seamen were semi-skilled men who knew, though had yet to master, the skills of able seamen. They proved useful on ship by working alongside able seamen in most aspects of daily life aboard a wooden warship, leaving the most difficult duties, such as working on the highest spars, to able seamen alone. Often ordinary seamen had many years of sea experience in the coasting trade under their belts. They served in small 'fore and aft' rigged ships, rather than the large square rigged ships, like those that made up the bulk of the Royal Navy, as well as in the deep-sea trading fleets. Landsmen, as their title implies, were men with little or no skills at all aboard ships at sea, and could not perform the basic tasks of a seaman. Generally, it took at least two years for a landsman to gain enough experience to become an ordinary seaman; however this depended on the ability of the individual. Although they lacked sea-based skills, landsmen were not useless aboard warships. The majority of the heavy work in trimming and shifting sails and spars was performed via ropes that ran to deck, where strength rather than skill was needed. Unskilled men, who simply needed an experienced able seaman or petty officer to direct their work, performed these tasks from the relative safety of the deck.

Seamen and petty officers' primary compensation was pay, and for skilled seamen that rate remained the same from 1653 until 1797, at £1.4.0 for able seamen and £0.19.0 for ordinary seamen per lunar (28-day) month. Landsmen, known as grommets before 1700, were paid £0.14.3 from 1653 until 1700, then £0.18.0 from 1700 until 1797. In 1797, largely as a result of the great mutinies at Spithead and the Nore, seamen's pay increased to £1.9.6 for able seamen, £1.3.6 for ordinary seamen, and £1.1.6 for landsmen. A further pay increase in 1801 changed pay to £1.13.6 for able seamen, £1.5.6 for ordinary seamen, and £1.2.6 for landsmen.[9] Pay for petty officers varied greatly depending on the type of petty officer, as well as the size of the ship on which they served. For example, on the 1797 pay scale, a gunner's mate serving on a first rate ship-of-the-line received £2.0.6 per lunar month, while a gunner's mate serving on a sixth rate or smaller vessel received £1.11.6. On the 1797 scale, a petty officer could make as little as £1.10.6 in the case of a quarter gunner on a sixth rate frigate, or as much as £3.11.6 in the case of a master's mate serving on a first rate ship-of-the-line.[10]

The essential quality in all positions of the lower deck was the ability to work in unity, as sailing a large warship was an extremely complicated task that involved the most technologically advanced and expensive components of the day, just as today's naval ships are the most sophisticated and costly mechanisms of our time. No matter the skill of the individuals aboard, this teamwork could only be gained by working together at sea as a crew, and just

---

[9]   N.A.M. Rodger, *The Command of the Ocean: A Naval History of Britain, 1649–1815*, 1st American edn (New York: W.W. Norton, 2005), pp. 618–628.

[10]   After 1798, lesser petty officers, captains of the forecastle, foretop, maintop, afterguard, and waist, became defined as separate from able seamen and received pay equal to a quarter master's mate. However, for continuity, this database continued to count them as able seamen.

like well-trained military units of today, the crew had to be able to anticipate in depth the actions required of an order, as well as how orders carried out by one portion of the crew would affect the others.

For the purposes of this book, the term 'seamen' will refer to able seamen, ordinary seamen, and landsmen, while 'skilled seamen' will refer to able and ordinary seamen. 'Highly skilled men' will refer to petty officers and able seamen, who formed the most skilled portion of the lower deck, while 'semi-skilled seamen' will refer to ordinary seamen alone. References to the 'lower deck' refer only to petty officers and seamen, and exclude boys and idlers, as this research is not primarily concerned with their recruitment.

The historiography of the eighteenth-century European navies is dominated by studies of great men, great battles and great technology. This can clearly be seen when looking on the shelves in any library. However, amongst the administrative and social histories that fall outside of that category, naval manning, particularly in Britain, is a subject that has received its share of attention over the course of the past two centuries. The historiography, for the most part, has been written around the concept of a navy that was primarily manned by impressment, and has assumed that most men in the Royal Navy served against their will. However, recent historians, notably N.A.M. Rodger, have challenged that perception and called for a new study of the subject, using statistics rather than speculation to define naval manpower and lay a new groundwork for the social history of the lower deck. Over the last fifty years, works by Michael Lewis,[11] Stephen Gradish,[12] Christopher Lloyd[13] and N.A.M. Rodger,[14] amongst others, have opened our eyes to life at sea in the eighteenth century. The insight that these historians have provided has been invaluable and this book relies heavily on the works of many such historians that came before and blazed new trails for historians like myself to follow.

As is evident in the historiography, naval manning is an extremely complex subject, and it is unlikely that any single monograph will prove the definitive tome on the subject. In fact, the opposite is true: any serious study of naval manning, especially a statistical study, will be expected to unearth more questions than it answers. Though scholarly study of naval manning has been relatively rare, most of the research done thus far has produced valuable information. Nonetheless, in the light of recent statistical research it is time to re-visit the questions masterfully asked by Gradish, Lewis, Lloyd and Rodger, amongst others. Answering these questions will not, however, entail an end to the subject, but hopefully inspire new questions as it prompts us to re-examine our past and how we view our present. Uncovering new questions and areas that require further research is one of the key goals of this project.

---

[11] Michael Lewis, *A Social History of the Navy, 1793–1815* (London: Allen & Unwin, 1960).
[12] Stephen Gradish, *The Manning of the British Navy During the Seven Years' War* (London: Royal Historical Society, 1980).
[13] Lloyd, *The British Seaman, 1200–1860*.
[14] Rodger, *The Wooden World*.

The backbone of this study is a database that examines naval recruitment and was compiled from sampling Royal Navy muster books of ships commissioned between 1793 and 1801. This research tests the current observations, most of which claim that the Royal Navy was a dismal and undesirable working environment for seamen, and therefore few men voluntarily entered naval service, and thus the primary method of manning warships was impressment. Using statistical methods, this research revisits contemporary and modern interpretations of the success of British naval manning methods, the flexibility of Britain's maritime labour market, and the disposition of the seamen and petty officers of the lower deck in the ever-turbulent climate of eighteenth-century warfare.

The database constructed for this study utilises ships' muster books as the primary source, which list data on the individual seaman or petty officer's rating, age, form of recruitment, date of entry, place of birth, and discharge, and the list continues. For the Royal Navy, muster books formed a bi-monthly account of all men serving aboard a warship, and were therefore an important source of information for naval administration at the lowest end. Once a ship was decommissioned, the muster books were stored, and today they can be found in the National Archives in London, along with a vast amount of Admiralty records.

The database samples ships that commissioned and manned at Chatham, Portsmouth and Plymouth, and samples the time period of 1793 to 1801. The database covers three ships from each port in each year; thus nine ships in each year, and a total of eighty-one ships over the nine years of the sample. The three ships from each port, in each year, consist of one ship-of-the-line, one frigate, and one sloop. Third rate ships-of-the-line to first rates, armed with 64 to over 100 guns, were manned with between 491 and over 850 men. Fifth and sixth rate frigates were armed with between 22 guns for the smallest example, and 44 guns for the largest frigates, and were manned with between 145 and 310 men. Sloops were armed with between 14 and 20 guns and manned with anywhere from 76 to 125 men.[15] For this sample, Chatham included ships out of the Thames and at the Nore, Portsmouth included Spithead, and Plymouth included Torbay. Ships had to commission from one of these ports to be considered for the database, and further had to remain there until they received 80 per cent or more of their authorised complement before sailing to another location. Thus a ship that commissioned at Portsmouth, and then a few weeks later, with only half its total

---

[15] It is notable that these numbers reference ships' authorised complements as defined by the Admiralty; the ships may have had more or fewer men aboard at any given time. Further, numbers of guns do not define a ship's firepower as much as the weight of the shot fired by those guns. For example a thirty-two gun frigate armed primarily with eighteen-pounder cannon was drastically more powerful than a twenty-eight gun frigate armed with twelve-pounder cannons, even though in the first instance the ship carried only four more guns than in the latter, due to the fact that a broadside fired from the thirty-two gun ship was more than 50 per cent heavier than that fired from the other.

crew, sailed to Plymouth where it finished manning, was disqualified from the database.

Ships included in the database also had to be commissioned to serve in 'home waters', or European waters excluding the Mediterranean and Baltic. Essentially this means that the ships in this survey were in the Channel fleet, by far the largest fleet at the time. The reasons for excluding other ships include the fact that ships serving on other stations, especially the Mediterranean, often sailed with less than their full complements and finished manning on station. Further, including other fleets, and getting a fair sample that represented all stations equally, proved to be very difficult without drastically expanding the size of the database, or creating separate databases for each station. However, it should be noted that some ships commissioned for Channel service did, at the last minute, receive orders that sent them to other stations, and those ships were not disqualified from this data set.

The primary tool for choosing ships for this database was the Admiralty List books,[16] which contain monthly returns compiled by the Admiralty Office entitled 'The present Disposal of His Majesty's Ships and Vessels in Sea Pay', and show the disposition of ships, the name of the commanding officers and lieutenants, and the date of commission. The entire collection housed at the National Archive covers the years from 1673 to 1909. The ships in the books are listed geographically and organised by the station to which the ship was assigned. From these books, a list was compiled of all of the ships that commissioned out of each of the three ports during each year, 1793 to 1801.[17] Once the lists were compiled, twenty-six pieces of paper, each with a letter of the alphabet on them, went into a bag and from that one letter representing each year was drawn. Using these letters as starting points, ships were chosen in alphabetical order in each year beginning with the letter designated to that particular year.

Table (a) Letters assigned to years

1793 = J	1794 = L	1795 = S
1796 = H	1797 = E	1798 = M
1799 = P	1800 = B	1801 = C

The ships used in the database had to be commissioned and have begun sea-pay in a given year, though the musters used occasionally bled over into the next year. For example, a ship that commissioned in November of 1796 would likely not have first gone to sea until the beginning of 1797; thus the

---

[16] TNA: ADM 8/69 to TNA: ADM 8/82 cover the years 1793 to 1801. TNA: ADM 8/83 to TNA: ADM 8/100 cover the years 1802 to 1813, and TNA: ADM 8/101 covers the years 1814 to 1821.

[17] Ships commissioned in 1802 were not used, as after brief examination of the muster books, it was obvious that peace and demobilisation had drastically affected statistics in that year, including the fact that few ships commissioned in that year.

muster used for the database was from the first of the following year. Once the initial list of ships, including back-ups, had been assembled, muster books for the given ships were inspected.[18] The muster during which a given ship first went to sea was chosen, as this was likely the first opportunity that a ship's officers had to observe the men at work and rate them properly.[19] Once the desired muster had been located, it was imaged with a digital camera. Each image contained one sheet of the muster book, and each sheet contained the details of as many as twenty men. The sample contained over 2,000 images, each showing one sheet, which contained two pages of the muster.

Table (b) Ships' musters used in the database[20]

Year	Ship type	Chatham	Portsmouth	Plymouth
1793	Ships-of-the-line	*Minotaur* (74)	*Leviathan* (80)	*London* (90)
	Frigates	*L'Aimable* (32)	*L'Oiseau* (36)	*Melampus* (38)
	Sloops	*Lady Taylor* (16)	*Swift* (16)	*Chapman* (20)
1794	Ships-of-the-line	*Polyphemus* (64)	*Prince* (90)	*Blenheim* (90)
	Frigates	*Seahourse* (38)	*La Babet* (24)	*Magnanime* (44)
	Sloops	*Petterell* (16)	*L'Espiegle* (14)	*La Trompeuse* (16)
1795	Ships-of-the-line	*Vengeance* (74)	*Sans Pareil* (90)	*Standard* (64)
	Frigates	*St. Fiorenzo* (38)	*La Topaze* (38)	*Castor* (32)
	Sloops	*Swallow* (16)	*La Victorieuse* (16)	*Spy* (16)
1796	Ships-of-the-line	*Montague* (74)	*Impetueux* (74)	*Overyssel* (64)
	Frigates	*Janus* (32)	*Thames* (32)	*La Nymphe* (36)
	Sloops	*Harpy* (16)	*Arrow* (16)	*Scourge* (16)
1797	Ships-of-the-line	*Vanguard* (74)	*Intrepid* (64)	*Veteran* (64)
	Frigates	*Ethalion* (38)	*Solebay* (32)	*Amelia* (38)
	Sloops	*Pylades* (16)	*Tribune* (32)*	*Eugenie* (16)
1798	Ships-of-the-line	*Northumberland* (74)	*Tigre* (74)	*Magnificent* (74)
	Frigates	*Amphion* (36)	*Alarm* (32)	*Volage* (24)
	Sloops	*Selby* (14)	*Pheasant* (16)	*Raileur* (14)

[18] In a few cases different ships had to be substituted, as time and deterioration had rendered some muster books illegible.

[19] TNA: ADM 36 is the location of Royal Navy muster books between 1688 and 1808 and contains 17,471 volumes.

[20] Ships marked with an asterisk were substituted in cases where the appropriate ship for that port and year could not be found, or the muster was unusable. For example, in 1801 in Plymouth, no frigates commissioned that then remained there for the manning process, so the sixteen-gun sloop *Imogen* had to be used in place of a frigate.

Year	Ship type	Chatham	Portsmouth	Plymouth
1799	Ships-of-the-line	*Ruby* (64)	*Resolution* (74)	*Windsor Castle* (90)
	Frigates	*Severn* (44)	*Quebec* (32)	*La Constance* (24)
	Sloops	*Shark* (16)	*La Sophie* (16)	*Renard* (16)
1800	Ships-of-the-line	*Leyden* (64)	*Belleisle* (74)	*San Josef* (114)
	Frigates	*Deseree* (36)	*Jason* (36)	*Bourdelois* (28)
	Sloops	*Gannet* (14)	*Déterminée* (22)*	*Raven* (16)
1801	Ships-of-the-line	*De Ruyter* (64)	*Dreadnought* (98)	*Donegal* (74)
	Frigates	*Narcissus* (36)	*Resistance* (36)	*Imogen* (16)*
	Sloops	*Hunter* (14)	*Carysfort* (28)*	*Wasp* (14)

Once the muster books had been imaged, the data found in them were manually entered into the database. Each man listed had twenty-six points of data, which, if available, were listed. These data points included name, age, recruitment, bounty received, town, county, and nation of birth. Further data points were used for sorting purposes, such as ship name, type, document number, date of commission, date of muster, and the list goes on.[21] All in all, the data entry process took twenty-two weeks to complete and resulted in a database that lists 27,174 men, and contains 706,524 data entries, which once assembled provided a statistical sample that stretches across all nine years of the French Revolutionary Wars.[22] In comparison to the whole of the Royal Navy, approximated at about 250,000 men who served during the French Revolutionary Wars, this database results in roughly a 10 per cent sample of men recruited into the Royal Navy.[23]

A second, much smaller, database was constructed from the Port Quota Act returns of London.[24] This database only covered 3,894 men recruited under the Port Quota Act in London in 1795, and recorded only each man's age, previous occupation and rating. Unlike ships' muster books, which were generally recorded by ships' pursers, the records of Port Quota Act recruitment in London were recorded by the officials charged with carrying out the Act, and not by the pursers of ships.

It is important to note that the information contained in this database does have limitations. As it examines ships relatively recently after they were

21 The twenty-six data points used to construct the database are: Record Number, Name, Age, Age Group, Rating, Rating Detail, Promotion or Demotion, Rating Type, Recruitment Type, Recruitment Specifics, Bounty Received, Discharged or Run, Birthplace, County of Birth, Nation of Birth, Domestic or Foreign, Ship's Name, Guns Carried, Ship Rate, Ship Type, Date of Commission, TNA Document Number, Beginning of Muster, End of Muster, Port of Commission, and Year of Commission.
22 Note that all figures and tables found within this work, unless otherwise noted, come from this database.
23 See Chapter 2 for further details on the approximated size of the Royal Navy.
24 TNA: ADM 7/361, 'Account of Men Raised … Port of London by Virtue of the Act 35th Geo III, Cap 9'.

commissioned, it cannot provide insight into the wastage of manpower due to sickness, injury, death or desertion that certainly occurred over the length of any ship's commission. It also cannot examine how officers dealt with the continuous need to maintain manpower levels throughout the length of commissions. Further, it does not examine ships assigned to foreign stations, nor the manpower problems that existed there. These important issues, along with others, were not addressed by this database because doing so and ensuring that the data was applicable to the Royal Navy as a whole would have drastically expanded the size of the overall project.

This book analyses British naval manpower during the French Revolutionary and Napoleonic Wars. As such, it has been broken down into five chapters. The first chapter lays out the complicated structure and history of naval administration between 1660 and 1793. The emphasis of this chapter is on naval manning, both the difficulties that arose as naval warfare evolved, as well as the changes that were made to administration to cope with the ever-greater manpower problem, particularly the centralisation of naval recruiting efforts with the development of the Impress Service. This chapter provides an understanding of naval administration necessary to get the most out of the statistical analysis found throughout the rest of the book.

The second chapter looks at overall statistics of the Royal Navy, and the lower deck, as a whole. It examines the skill levels, ages, nationality and recruitment of the men, among other things. Crucially, it also discusses the statistical dilemma of dealing with men turned over, and explains in detail the factoring process that was developed to handle this issue. This chapter forms an important point of reference, as it is the only chapter that engages the lower deck as one large group, rather than breaking them down by manner of recruitment.

Chapter 3 examines the largest body of men, the volunteers, and is correspondingly the longest chapter. This chapter defines the average volunteer including his age, skill level, where he came from, and more. Further it questions the motivations that persuaded men to volunteer, such as naval pay, conditions of service, and prize money. It also details how volunteer seamen were essential to naval manning, and, as the Admiralty understood this fact, what efforts were made to encourage volunteerism among seamen. It also examines the maritime labour pool, and compares British efforts in attracting volunteers to the recruitment policies of other European nations.

Chapter 4 investigates what is probably the most volatile topic of naval manning, impressment. This chapter provides a statistical analysis of pressed men similar to that of the previous chapter; however it goes on to determine the success of naval impressment and the Impress Service, as well as defining the actual form and function of impressment. Statistics revealed in this study strongly disagree with much of what has been said thus far in the historiography, and challenge many current views on the subject.

Chapter 5 specifically examines the Quota Acts of 1795 and 1796, which formed the only new and innovative manner of naval manning to be put into action during the French Revolutionary and Napoleonic Wars. Much of the infamy of the Quota Acts comes from the blame placed upon them for the great mutinies of 1797, a concept addressed in this chapter. The Quota Acts, both praised and hated by contemporaries and historians alike, placed the burden of naval manning onto the shoulders of local authorities in counties, parishes and ports across England, Wales and Scotland. Though the success or failure of these Acts can be argued equally, based on one's interpretation of their objective, they did provide an influx of manpower at a time when the maritime labour pool was beginning to be stretched desperately thin.

Throughout the eighteenth century, the size and ability of Europe's navies was determined as much by manpower as it was by the number of ships they had available, for without men to sail the great ships of war, they posed little threat to an enemy at sea. The British Royal Navy saw great victories at sea throughout the eighteenth century, which culminated in the successes of the French Revolutionary and Napoleonic Wars. These victories stemmed from the success of naval manning, and this book aims to explore how Britain manned its naval forces, and question the historiography thus far on the subject. Throughout the age of sail, with the exception of finance, there was no aspect of naval warfare that exhibited as much difficulty and anguish as manning the fleet. Finding the necessary skilled seamen to man its ships was the alpha and omega of problems for the Royal Navy, as in wartime it was the first to appear with mobilisation and the last to be overcome.[25]

---

[25] Rodger, *The Wooden World*, p. 145; Rodger, *The Command of the Ocean*, p. 205.

1

British Naval Administration

Beyond financing the naval war, the manning problem was the greatest hurdle that British naval administrators faced at the opening of the French Revolutionary Wars, and continued to be one of the most controversial and difficult obstacles over the twenty-two years of conflict that followed. By the end of the French Revolutionary Wars, the Royal Navy had grown into a force of over 130,000 men. Less than a century and a half earlier, Charles II's wartime Navy had consisted of only about 20,000 men. The English Navy of the 1660s was designed to fight in the North Sea, close to its own support facilities, while the Navy of 1801 had spread its influence well outside of the North Atlantic, into the Indian and Pacific Oceans. These changes required an efficient and effective infrastructure and administration more than ever before. All aspects of naval support, including construction, repair, victualling, manning, and more, had to grow in size and efficiency to cope with expanding naval commitments. By the end of the eighteenth century, this growth had produced a fleet capable of harassing, and in some cases nearly halting, communication between continental Europe and its colonies, while British merchants carried trade across the globe. The strength of the Royal Navy allowed George III and his government ministers to sit behind Britain's 'wooden walls' with relative confidence while attrition took a heavy toll on their enemies. The English Navy of the Restoration never afforded such luxuries.

The objective of this chapter is to trace British naval administration as it applied to manning, from the Restoration of 1660, through to the opening of the French Revolutionary Wars in 1793. It is not an attempt to re-write administrative history, but to provide a background for better understanding the history behind the manpower problems that faced naval administrators when war broke out in 1793.

The Restoration and Naval Advancement

When Charles II came to power in 1660, the English Navy was the strongest element of his newly inherited government.[1] The crumbling

---

[1] Rodger, *The Command of the Ocean*, p. 65.

Commonwealth had left the fleet largely in disrepair and the Navy was deep in debt. Even though it was in poor condition, the fleet still existed. It would have taken more than a decade to rebuild the fleet from scratch. However, the infrastructure backing the fleet was more important. The system of dockyards and administration that backed the English Navy was its greatest asset. Over the next three decades the English Navy would be built into a solid and professional fighting force backed by an ever improving administrative system. To a great extent this was due to the attention that the Navy received from both Charles II and his brother and successor James II. Unlike other English and British monarchs, before and after, they had a keen interest in the Navy, which they translated into expert knowledge of their seaborne forces, and were fully capable of transacting technical and detailed naval business themselves.[2] James, while Duke of York and Lord High Admiral, even became a capable fleet commander. Such leadership and patronage allowed new advances in naval administration. A new generation of naval administrators, not least among them Samuel Pepys, used the power of this leadership and patronage to streamline naval administration, making it more effective at all levels, from construction and repairs to victualling and finance. This ensured that ships were not left in disrepair but rather kept in a state of readiness during peacetime, and further that when commissioned for service they were properly supplied and serviced.

The Restoration Navy was primarily based in the Thames and the Medway. This was a strategic asset, as the major threat to English security and trade during the reigns of Charles II and James II was the Dutch Republic. With the predominant winds coming from the west or southwest, the main concentration of the English Navy was windward of the Dutch threat, meaning that it had the ability to get ships underway and meet threats without having to fight against the wind. It also meant that the Navy could keep its fleet concentrated rather than having to be dispersed to cover multiple threats. Another key advantage was the fact that the Thames was the primary base for English deep-sea trade. Though it was concentrated close to England's most likely adversary, the proximity to the primary port facilities for the English Navy made trade easier to protect. It also meant that mariners could be found locally to man the Navy, and during the Second and Third Dutch Wars the majority of fighting seamen came from the towns and villages of the Thames and Medway.[3]

The English Navy of the Restoration was also a seasonal navy, only being mobilised during the major campaign season, almost exclusively during the summer months. Winter weather in the North Sea was not conducive to fleet battles, so typically the fleet was manned in the spring, campaigned in the summer, and was then paid off in the autumn. This provided many

---

[2] Ibid., p. 96.
[3] J.D. Davies, *Gentlemen and Tarpaulins: The Officers and Men of the Restoration Navy* (Oxford: Clarendon Press, 1991), p. 68.

advantages. The first was that the crews only had to be paid for about half of the year. Paying the men was one of the major naval expenses in the age of sail; by manning the ships with only skeleton crews in the winter months the Crown saved large sums of money. Another advantage, assuming finances were in order, was that seasonal deployment allowed for ships to be kept in good repair, as they spent several months each year in port without the prospect of sailing at short notice. There was also an economic advantage to seasonal warfare, as it allowed seamen to work aboard merchant ships during winter months. This reduced the impact of warfare on merchant trading and allowed men to serve for only a few months at a time in the Navy. Subsequently, this made naval manning a less demanding affair. However, mobilising the fleet each year was not an easy task, and placed great financial strain on the Crown. The failure to mobilise a fleet in 1667, due to a lack of finances, resulted in the disastrous Dutch raid on the Medway.[4]

One advantage held by the administration of the Restoration Navy was the relatively small size of naval forces between 1660 and 1688, when compared to a century later. During the Seven Years' War, the American War, and the French Revolutionary Wars the size of the Royal Navy expanded to over 86,000 men, 105,000 men, and 130,000 men respectively in each conflict.[5] There are no reliable manning statistics for the years preceding 1688 and the Glorious Revolution;[6] however estimates suggest that during the Dutch Wars the English Navy consisted of just over 20,000 men during war, and only about 4,000 men during peace.[7] Essentially, the small size was dictated by the fact that the Dutch threat was contained to the North Sea, which the naval facilities of the Thames estuary were ideally suited to cover. The Glorious Revolution caused a shift in international politics which resulted in peace with the Dutch Republic and a rivalry with France that lasted for two centuries. The result forced British naval expansion to cover the new threat.

These factors, however, did not mean that manning the Restoration Navy was a simple process. Finding enough men to man the English Navy had been a problem long before Charles II re-established the monarchy. Just as was the case in the eighteenth century, merchant pay was higher during wartime, due to the shortage of skilled seafarers, and provided stiff competition for the limited number of seamen available.[8] The primary encouragements for volunteers, as in the eighteenth century, were the offer of a bounty and an opportunity for prize money.[9] The bounty was a simple monetary sum paid to a volunteer seaman, often equal to several months' pay, and was thought to offset the fact that pay in the Navy was lower than in merchant ships during

---

[4]   Rodger, *The Command of the Ocean*, pp. 67–77.
[5]   Ibid., pp. 638–639.
[6]   Ibid., p. 636.
[7]   Peter Earle, *Sailors: English Merchant Seamen, 1650–1775* (London: Methuen, 1998), p. 187.
[8]   Gijs Rommelse, *The Second Anglo-Dutch War, 1665–1667* (Hilversm: Verloren, 2006), p. 128.
[9]   See Chapter 3 for a more detailed discussion of bounties and prize money.

war. Sailors were also entitled to a percentage of prize money that came from the capture of any enemy vessel. The amount of prize money received was based on an individual's rating, and for seamen the percentage per man was minute. However, the value of a homeward-bound Dutch East Indiaman could be substantial and allow a sailor the opportunity to make more than a year's pay in an afternoon. The sailors could also profit from essentially plundering a ship. Under the Commonwealth in 1652, the Rump Parliament established a method of valuation for ships taken in war, which was the value of the ship and cargo in the hold, thus allowing sailors to take anything stored either on or above the gun deck that they could carry.[10] Sailors also received a portion of the 'head money', which was awarded on the basis of prisoners captured. Though rich prizes were rare, the slight possibility of becoming wealthy was used heavily to encourage volunteers.[11]

The Restoration Navy relied mainly upon ships' officers to man the fleet. However, manning the Navy solely with volunteers was never possible, even during the seventeenth century. Many seamen sought employment in the merchant service during wartime, which caused a shortage of skilled manpower in the Navy. The result was that the Navy had to rely on impressment, a medieval prerogative of the Crown that played a role in supplying the Navy with men all the way through the Napoleonic Wars.[12] Press gangs worked both ashore and afloat. On land, they patrolled the streets of the urban centres in and around London searching for seamen. At sea, they waited in the English Channel aboard tenders and sought incoming merchant ships, which they boarded looking for seamen to man the fleet.[13] Sometimes these efforts were not enough and naval manning had to be supplemented by placing embargoes on outward-bound shipping until the fleet was manned.[14] Such embargoes encouraged merchants to produce men for the Navy, as they lost money sitting idle. However, this policy was devastating to the maritime economy and unpopular with merchants and Members of Parliament alike.

The Glorious Revolution and Naval Stagnation

The fall of James II from power ended three decades of the Crown having a keen interest in naval affairs, and Pepys resigned soon thereafter, and was not effectively replaced.[15] In 1689, England entered into a new conflict, the War of the Grand Alliance. With the ascension of William III, France, with its greater size, population, and numerous seaports along the Atlantic and in the

---

[10] Bernard Capp, *Cromwell's Navy: The Fleet and the English Revolution, 1648–1660* (Oxford: Clarendon, 1989), p. 260.

[11] Richard Hill, *The Prizes of War: The Naval Prize System in the Napoleonic Wars, 1793–1815* (Stroud: Sutton Publishing Ltd, 1998), pp. 7–10.

[12] Roland G. Usher Jr., 'Royal Navy Impressment During the American Revolution', *The Mississippi Valley Historical Review* XXXVII, no. 4 (1951): p. 679.

[13] For a detailed account of impressment refer to Chapter 4.

[14] Capp, p. 263.

[15] Rodger, *The Command of the Ocean*, p. 181.

Mediterranean, became the new enemy of England and would remain so for well over a century. With this change, many of the advantages that the English Navy had while fighting the Dutch Republic became weaknesses. War with France was fought throughout the year, in distant waters, with substantial fleets, and over long periods of nine or ten years.[16] War with France meant that England's primary docking and victualling facilities based around the Thames estuary were suddenly leeward of the French threat, importantly their primary Atlantic base at Brest. English warships now had to wait for favourable winds to transit the Channel. Once in the open Atlantic they had no facilities within close proximity capable of victualling or servicing large ships, much less a fleet. Naval engagements were no longer fought in the North Sea, but in the Atlantic and further abroad, such as in the West Indies. To cover these new threats, the English fleet had to increase the number of ships in commission, as well as the facilities to support them. The failure to cope with these changes was evident in 1693, when a combined English and Dutch fleet barely managed to stay at sea for two weeks before returning to port, leaving the massive Smyrna convoy virtually defenceless. Ultimately, only a quarter of the convoy was captured or sunk. This was largely due to two gallant Dutch captains who sacrificed their ships in a delaying action, combined with good English luck and a timid French Admiral. Otherwise, the devastation might have been catastrophic. Even so, French prizes from the action sold for more than thirty million *livres*, more than the annual French naval budget of 1692. Most of the ships taken or destroyed were Dutch; however damage to London merchants equalled that of the Great Fire of 1666.[17]

The War of the Grand Alliance ended the concept of seasonal naval warfare. During the winters of 1691 to 1694, the English government decided to keep the fleet manned in an attempt to avoid having to re-recruit seamen in the spring.[18] Thus, men were not being released after the traditional campaign season, and as the War of the Grand Alliance lasted nearly a decade, volunteering or impressment involved several years of service. There were seldom enough volunteers to man the service, and the Navy was forced to rely upon compulsion to man the fleet.[19] At the same time, the Royal Navy was growing in size and required more seamen. Rather than paying off ships when they came in to be refitted, men were turned over to another ship, which made recruiting new men even more difficult. A large portion of a warship's crew often came from a small area, possibly a captain's hometown. Turning the men over meant they were put into strange surroundings with men they did not know or trust, which further damaged sailors' willingness

[16] Daniel A. Baugh, *British Naval Administration in the Age of Walpole* (Princeton: Princeton University Press, 1965), pp. 147–148; Rodger, *The Command of the Ocean*, pp. 205–206.

[17] Rodger, *The Command of the Ocean*, pp. 153–154.

[18] Ibid., p. 206.

[19] John Ehrman, *The Navy in the War of William III, 1689–1697: Its State and Direction* (Cambridge: Cambridge University Press, 1953), p. 113.

to serve.[20] However, volunteers still made up the nucleus of naval crews, and retained privileges over pressed men. These privileges included the fact that volunteers could not be removed from their ship and placed into another without consent. Further, they had to be discharged at the end of the season, unless they volunteered again.[21] These factors not only made the task of impressing skilled mariners more difficult, but also increased the likelihood that pressed men would desert.

During peacetime, naval service was just another job for mariners, as naval and merchant pay were roughly equal; the Navy paid twenty-four shillings per lunar month and the merchant service paid about twenty-five shillings for able seamen.[22] However, this changed completely during war. Naval expansion placed a severe drain on the number of available seamen for merchant ships. Merchants were forced to offer high wages to obtain mariners; otherwise they were destined to sit in port while their cargoes spoiled, possibly forcing the owners into bankruptcy.[23] Therefore, merchant wartime wages were more than double peacetime wages, at forty-five to fifty-five shillings per month between 1690 and 1740, placing the Royal Navy at a disadvantage when in competition with merchants for manpower.[24]

The manning problem in William III's reign was a serious issue. Few men volunteered and impressment was necessary to locate and fill warships as quickly as possible. The manpower shortage meant that every mariner that the Navy could employ was a precious commodity that could not be wasted. The manpower issue produced a three-way battle between the merchants, who needed men for trade, the Navy, which needed men for war, and the Privy Council, which produced policy that often reconciled the differences.[25] Evidence of this can be seen in an Order in Council to port counties that asked officials to ensure that pressed men arrived aboard warships unharmed.[26] The tone of the document lends the impression that men recruited by civil authorities were arriving aboard their ships in poor condition, possibly beaten and starving, and were maybe not found useful enough to be retained. Producing men who were too badly abused or not skilled enough to be of use to the Navy was an obvious waste of manning resources. Further, poor treatment of men harmed morale and did little to attract volunteers. Retention was also a problem, as high merchant wages tempted men to flee if the occasion arose, especially when considering

---

[20] Rodger, *The Command of the Ocean*, p. 206.
[21] Ehrman, p. 120.
[22] Earle, *Sailors: English Merchant Seamen, 1650–1775*, p. 186; Rodger, *The Wooden World*, p. 113.
[23] James Edward Oglethorpe, 'The Sailors Advocate (1728)', in *The Manning of the Royal Navy: Selected Public Pamphlets, 1693–1873*, ed. J.S. Bromley, Publications of the Navy Records Society (London: Navy Records Society, 1974), p. 74.
[24] Earle, *Sailors: English Merchant Seamen, 1650–1775*, p. 188; Marcus Rediker, *Between the Devil and the Deep Blue Sea: Merchant Seamen, Pirates and the Anglo-American Maritime World, 1700–1750* (Cambridge: Cambridge University Press, 1987), pp. 32–33.
[25] Ehrman, p. 113.
[26] NMM: HSR/H/1, 'Whitehall Council Chamber Letter to Port Counties, 7 April 1692'.

that naval pay was often years in arrears. Ironically, administrators often defended withholding wages as a way to ensure seamen did not desert. Pay was rarely less than six months behind during wartime and seamen occasionally even found their wages three years in arrears. The Royal Navy's justification was that mariners were less likely to desert if they were owed large sums of money.[27] However, this destroyed naval morale. Though many excuses were made, the real reason for seamen not being paid was that the Navy was underfunded, and for naval administrators of the time, paying seamen fell far below the necessity of building and maintaining ships and purchasing powder. The English Navy of William III faced many problems, some of which were created by the changes that occurred to naval warfare at the end of the seventeenth century and continued to plague the Royal Navy throughout the eighteenth century. After finance, manning was the major issue that faced William III's fleets, and this problem was never truly solved throughout the age of sail.[28]

The manning problem under Queen Anne appeared to fare a little better than it had under William III. There were fewer complaints and impressment was better regulated.[29] The burden of recruitment fell less on civil authorities and more on the Navy, which found more suitable men. Further, fast-growing English and Scottish sea trade provided more seamen to fulfil the Navy's need.[30] A 1706 Proclamation granted constables twenty shillings a head for able-bodied seamen brought to the Navy, gave them the right to 'break open the doors of any house where they shall suspect any such seamen to be concealed', and declared a fine of five pounds for harbouring seamen from the press.[31] This Proclamation illustrates that even though improvements were made, extreme measures were still occasionally taken to man the Navy.

With the Glorious Revolution and William III, came a new era of naval administration. Having the monarchy actively manage the Navy had advantages as long as the Crown maintained a professional interest in the fleet. However, financial security became a major problem, and proved a direct cause of the disastrous Dutch raid on the Medway in 1667, when a lack of money in the King's coffers prevented naval mobilisation. The long-term financial solution was for Parliament to take control, which required the Crown to withdraw from active management of the Navy. The change of naval administration that followed, combined with the change of naval focus, from the Dutch to the French, produced new difficulties that took time to

[27] R. Pares, 'The Manning of the Navy in the West Indies, 1702–63', *Transactions of the Royal Historical Society* XX (1937): pp. 38–39.

[28] Rodger, *The Command of the Ocean*, p. 205.

[29] 'Admiralty to the Captains appointed to regulate the Press on the River Thames', in *Queen Anne's Navy: Documents Concerning the Administration of the Navy of Queen Anne, 1702–1714*, ed. R.D. Merriman, Publications of the Navy Records Society (London: Navy Records Society, 1961), pp. 201–201.

[30] Rodger, *The Command of the Ocean*, p. 211.

[31] NMM: PBB/7521, 'Proclamation for the Encouragement and Increase of Seamen, 1706'.

sort out. However, with new administrative measures, more secure finances, and growing merchant trade, the manpower problem began to improve with the War of Spanish Succession.

Foundation, Finance and the Mid-Eighteenth Century

By the War of Austrian Succession, the wartime Navy had grown by nearly 50 per cent over that of Queen Anne, to over 58,000 in 1747.[32] The merchant trade had also grown, however not to the same extent as the wartime Navy, and this was reflected in pressure on naval administration. New administrative measures had been put into place, the most significant being the paying of bills 'in course', which essentially allowed the Royal Navy to run its own short-term borrowing scheme, where Navy Bills bore interest after six months. Between 1714 and 1748 the interest was 5 per cent and from 1748 to 1787 it fell to 4 per cent.[33] Essentially, this made investors out of anyone who was paid in course by the Royal Navy. For the Navy, this provided the ability to access money when it was needed, whether it was for mobilisation, victualling, or repair and maintenance. Further, paying ships' crews in arrears allowed access to vital funds for the Navy. This also made the men, collectively, the largest naval creditors. For naval administration, this provided the stability needed to improve the system and ensure that the Royal Navy could cope with the ever-growing operational commitments it faced during war.[34]

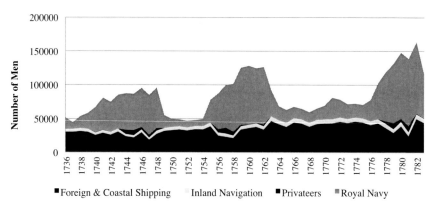

Figure 1.1 British men employed at sea, 1736–1783
Source: TNA: ADM 7/567, 'Admiralty Miscellanea, 1754–1806', ff. 22, 27; Rodger,
Command of the Ocean, pp. 636–639; Starkey, 'War and the Market for Seafarers'
pp. 40–41.

---

[32] Rodger, *The Command of the Ocean*, pp. 637–638.
[33] Ibid., pp. 292–293.
[34] Ibid., pp. 292–294.

The War of Austrian Succession again meant the Royal Navy sent a larger force to sea than before. Manning was always a problem during the age of sail, and the campaigns of 1739 to 1748 proved to be no different. By 1745, the manning crisis grew to the point that the Admiralty revoked the protections it had issued to the trading companies and claimed one in six men from merchants to man warships.[35] During this conflict, two Regulating Captains were introduced in London, who inspected men taken by press gangs before they were sent to ships. The introduction of Regulating Captains streamlined impressment in the London area and ensured that men being conscripted were actually seamen and not vagrants or criminals.[36] This was a major step in simplifying the process of naval manning, which by the French Revolutionary Wars had all but taken manning out of the hands of officers aboard warships.

The evolution of naval administration was necessary for the Royal Navy to maintain its ability to control home waters and defend British interests abroad. By the 1740s, naval warfare had changed in comparison to half a century earlier. The fleet was truly mobilised year around for the duration of the war and, for the first time, major campaigns were fought in foreign waters, requiring large fleet deployments to the West Indies to defend British interests and harass enemy lines of trade and communication. During the eighty years that separated the Second Dutch War and the War of Austrian Succession, the Royal Navy had grown nearly threefold. These factors had an effect on fleet manning and made recruiting the required number of men more difficult than it had ever been before. Long deployments in foreign waters also made manpower retention an issue that had to be addressed, not only in preventing desertion but also by ensuring that fleets were not struck down with disease. However, this war also reaffirmed the importance of a powerful and sound navy to policy makers, as campaigns in foreign waters could not be fought without strong naval support and superiority. Whether fought on land or at sea, any campaign abroad required transportation of forces and well protected lines of communication and supply. The Royal Navy of the mid-eighteenth century had become more than 'wooden walls' that defended the British Isles from invasion; it had also become the lifeline of support for British operations overseas. The Seven Years' War again expanded naval warfare further than before. The numbers of men on the books exceeded 84,000 in 1762, making the Royal Navy 45 per cent larger than during the previous war.[37] This war was also increasingly fought in foreign waters. However, it was in the Seven Years' War that the Royal Navy rose to dominate the seas as never before, and decisively defeated Britain's enemies in a war that spanned the North Atlantic.

---

[35] 'Admiralty Memorial to the Lords Justices, 1 August 1745', in *Naval Administration, 1715–1750*, ed. Daniel A. Baugh, Publications of the Navy Records Society (London: Navy Records Society, 1977), pp. 137–138.

[36] Lloyd, *The British Seaman, 1200–1860*, p. 128.

[37] Rodger, *The Command of the Ocean*, p. 638.

During the mid-eighteenth century, increased seaborne trade produced an expansion of the maritime population of Britain. One source of evidence available to determine this is the records from the Sixpenny Office, which recorded the amount of money withdrawn from sailors' pay per annum to support the Royal Hospital at Greenwich. This entailed every mariner having sixpence of his monthly wage deducted to support this facility. From these records, it can be observed that the Sixpenny Office collected £5,481 in 1707, £5,985 in 1747 and £10,550 in 1777.[38] This represents 18,270 mariners in 1707, 19,950 in 1747 and 35,167 in 1777. These records cannot be used to accurately calculate how many seamen Britain had at its disposal, as some men escaped paying into the fund, either from corruption or negligence. Using the fund to depict the maritime population directly assumes that seamen worked year round, even though this was not the case, as many seamen spent weeks or months ashore between long voyages. However, the figures from the Sixpenny Office do show an expansion of the merchant marine. During the thirty years between 1747 and 1777 it is clear to see that numbers of men paying into the fund nearly doubled, which coincides with a great expansion of British trade both within its colonies and in foreign territories.[39]

The expanding number of mariners during the third quarter of the eighteenth century was due to the escalation of maritime trade. Although it did provide a larger number of men for the Royal Navy to pull from during wartime, the ever-growing naval force in return threatened the merchant fleet's existence.[40] Expanding seaborne trade combined with the need for a larger navy added up to a grander struggle for the scarce resource of skilled manpower during the Seven Years' War. Initial mobilisation, the transition from peacetime to war, was the Navy's biggest problem. The immense size of the fleet made it more challenging to find seamen to man the ships, even with supplementing the skilled force with unskilled landsmen. During 1755, the first year of mobilisation, the Royal Navy was only able to recruit three-quarters of the men needed to fill the ships commissioned that year.[41] Impressment was still needed as a means of ensuring the fleet received the necessary manpower to achieve supremacy at sea. However, the use of impressment brought naval manpower requirements into direct conflict with the seaborne trade and fishing industries. An embargo was attempted in 1756, but met with outrage from merchants who claimed they were being ruined by foreign shipping that took their cargoes while British merchants were forced to remain in port.[42] The embargo had to be lifted to prevent

---

[38] Lloyd, *The British Seaman, 1200–1860*, p. 117.

[39] Ralph Davis, 'English Foreign Trade, 1700–1774', in *The Growth of English Overseas Trade in the Seventeenth and Eighteenth Centuries*, ed. W.E. Minchinton (London: Methuen & Co., Ltd, 1969), pp. 107–111.

[40] Larry Neal, 'The Cost of Impressment During the Seven Years' War', *The Mariner's Mirror* LXIV, no. 1 (1978): p. 45.

[41] Stephen Gradish, 'Wages and Manning: The Navy Act of 1758', *English Historical Review* XCIII, no. 366 (1978): p. 46.

[42] Gradish, *The Manning of the British Navy During the Seven Years' War*, pp. 64–65.

damaging the maritime economy any more than was necessary during the time of war.

The Seven Years' War established a new innovation to naval manning, the Impress Service, which found its roots in the previous war with the introduction of Regulating Captains. The Impress Service became a permanent fixture at the beginning of the war and Regulating Captains were posted in several coastal cities including Bristol, Liverpool, Whitehaven, Newcastle, Yarmouth and Edinburgh. Further expansion in 1756, 1759 and 1762 placed Regulating Captains in many other cities, such as Gloucester, Winchester, Reading, Southampton, Aberdeen, Exeter and Cork.[43] The innovation of making the Impress Service a permanent fixture was an attempt to make naval recruiting practices more streamlined and effective by taking the responsibility of manning ships away from ship's officers and making it into an administrative function. The Regulating Captains supervised lieutenants who ran individual press gangs and occasionally even the rendezvous.

One advantage to the Impress Service was the fact that press gangs no longer needed to be operated by mariners. Press gangs that originated from warships generally found their men from within the ship's crew, and this proved a waste of valuable manpower that could be otherwise employed readying the ship for sea. However, lieutenants of the Impress Service generally chose local men to employ in the gangs who were usually not seamen. These men were less expensive, as they did not need to be paid a seaman's wage, and did not possess the valuable skills that the Royal Navy desperately needed aboard warships. An exception to this was in tenders employed by the Impress Service, as these small craft needed to be operated by skilled men. However, seamen from the coasting trade, rather than men with deep-sea square rigged sailing experience, were capable of manning small press tenders. Though it took a substantial portion of the manning burden, the Impress Service did not fully take the recruiting responsibility away from officers aboard warships, and the captains of ships were still issued with press warrants in order to man their vessels.

By far the largest number of pressed men came from impressment at sea, where captains served their warrants on board merchant ships as they returned from voyages abroad. These ships were prime targets for naval recruiting, as they proved a prime location for finding experienced sailors. Some historians suggest as much as 40 per cent of all mariners who served in the Royal Navy during the Seven Years' War were pressed from ships at sea.[44] This practice was strictly regulated to ensure that pressing from merchants did not cripple the maritime economy. The Royal Navy was only allowed to press from ships returning to Britain. Not only did this ensure that outgoing ships were not harassed, it also allowed the opportunity for merchants to evade the press, especially if they were not going into the Thames estuary, the area of heaviest recruiting.

---

[43] Ibid., p. 57.
[44] Rodger, *The Wooden World*, pp. 145–146.

Another major achievement in naval manning administration during the Seven Years' War was the Navy Act of 1758, arguably the single most important piece of legislation that addressed the manning problem during the eighteenth century.[45] The Bill, introduced and pushed by the treasurer of the Navy, George Grenville, addressed one of the major grievances that mariners had with the Royal Navy, irregular pay. The Act granted regular pay to seamen employed in the Royal Navy. This was accomplished by ordering the Navy Board to find the money necessary to pay seamen. The Act stated that seamen had to be paid either two months' wages every six months or a year's wages every eighteen months.[46] This changed the previous standard where seamen often spent years in the Royal Navy without receiving their wages. The Act also included provisions for seamen to have a portion of their wages sent to either their mothers or wives, allowing their families to benefit from their employment. Although this Act addressed a fundamental grievance that mariners had with the Royal Navy, it still did not increase seamen's low wages, which remained unchanged between 1653 and 1797.[47]

The Seven Years' War was a time of adjustment for naval manning. The rapidly increasing size of the Royal Navy resulted in new problems across the board for naval administrators, and with a better financial foundation, the Navy was in a position to focus its attention on finding a more efficient means of manning. Naval administration also made advances that indirectly improved manning by fixing problems that negatively affected morale, such as victualling and supply. At the end of the seventeenth century the Royal Navy had barely been able to stay at sea for two weeks at a time. During the Seven Years' War, Hawke managed to blockade Brest by keeping his fleet at sea for six months, while he continued to be well supplied and his men remained healthy.[48]

Nearly all of Europe and North America was involved in the Seven Years' War, making it larger than any prior conflict in the Atlantic World. The Royal Navy played a key role in British victory. To a great extent, this was due to Britain's ability to mobilise a large and well-manned naval force that dominated the North Atlantic, in turn straining communication between continental powers and their colonial possessions, and deprived Britain's enemies of income produced by their colonies. By denying European rivals the finances and tools they needed to wage war, the Royal Navy became the strategic centrepiece of British military might.

The War of American Independence

Britain's victory during the Seven Years' War placed it on a pedestal as the dominant power in Europe, while at the same time leaving the nation with few friends. The War of American Independence started as a small colonial

---

[45]   Gradish, 'Wages and Manning', p. 46.
[46]   'An Act for the Encouragement of Seamen employed in the Royal Navy...' 31 Geo. II c.10
[47]   Gradish, 'Wages and Manning', pp. 46–47.
[48]   Rodger, *The Command of the Ocean*, p. 291.

rebellion and erupted into worldwide warfare in which Britain found itself almost alone against the rest of Europe. During the Seven Years' War, the Royal Navy had dominated the world's oceans by controlling European waters. The nature of the American War stretched Britain to its limits to man the Navy, while the lack of quick mobilisation and the need for large fleets in the North American theatre kept the Royal Navy from gaining control of home waters during the opening years of the conflict.[49] The end result was not the great victory of the previous war, but a difficult compromise that provided thirteen of Britain's North American colonies with independence.

The American War was a different conflict from any fought before. It began as a rebellion of British colonies seeking independence. The early stages of the war saw large numbers of transport ships being conveyed back and forth across the Atlantic to move troops and supplies into the North American theatre. Initially this caused some manning problems as ships used for transport competed with warships for skilled seamen, even though during the early phases of the war the manning problems were not as serious as those faced in the Seven Years' War. The rebelling colonial 'navy' was little more than privateers and small vessels, with no ability to fight a fleet action. However, colonial success in 1777 prompted France to recognise American independence, and in the summer of 1778, Europe exploded into war as first France and later Spain declared war on Britain, followed by Britain declaring war on the Dutch Republic.

At this point the manning crisis in the Royal Navy became more severe than ever before.[50] Britain needed a fleet capable of fighting France, Spain and the Dutch Republic simultaneously and was not prepared. With many British mariners tied up in the supply lines that conveyed across the Atlantic, there were simply not enough men to mobilise the Navy quickly. This problem was further compounded by the fact that Britain was facing serious internal social conflicts.[51] Many parts of Britain sympathised with the American colonies and the war became increasingly unpopular as it progressed. This increasing dislike by the public has been blamed for the estimated number of desertions, which ranged from 42,000 to 79,000.[52] Despite this large number, at the end of the conflict the Royal Navy employed over 105,000 men, dwarfing the number reached in the previous war.[53]

Such overwhelming growth for the Royal Navy was not an easy problem to handle. By 1779, the manning crisis had stripped Britain of nearly all of her skilled mariners. Evidence of this can be seen in correspondence between the Treasury and the Commission of Excise and Customs asking for help to raise

[49] N.A.M. Rodger, *The Insatiable Earl: A Life of John Montagu, Fourth Earl of Sandwich, 1718–1792* (London: HarperCollins, 1993), pp. 235–237.
[50] Rodger, *The Command of the Ocean*, p. 395.
[51] Stephen Conway, 'The Politics of British Military and Naval Mobilization, 1775–83', *English Historical Review* CXII, no. 449 (1997): p. 1179.
[52] Usher Jr., 'Royal Navy Impressment', pp. 682–683.
[53] Rodger, *The Command of the Ocean*, p. 638.

seamen and enquiring to the Collectors and Comptrollers of Ports requesting them to 'take the most prudent measures to produce discoveries of such seamen'.[54] Though finding men for naval service was difficult, the Impress Service proved its value and raised 116,357 of the 230,000 to 235,000 men that served in the Navy throughout the war.[55] However, this was not done cheaply. The official report stated that the total cost of the Impress Service in the American Revolution was £1,603,438.[56] This equalled an average cost of about £13.15.0 per man recruited by the Impress Service at a time when a year's wage for an able seaman was £15.12.0. This figure includes both volunteers and pressed men. However, as the majority of manpower in the Impress Service, and the expense of maintaining it, was tied to pressing men into service, the cost per pressed man therefore greatly exceeded £13.15.0. Impressment on a mass scale was expensive for the British government, but it was a necessary evil, as there was no other way to effectively ensure enough highly skilled men were employed aboard Navy warships.

The Royal Navy had to work hard to produce the mariners needed to man the ships required for fighting the European war that erupted from the American Revolution. One of the reasons for this constant need for men was the high turnover rate within the Navy.[57] Generally, when ships did come in for major repairs, they were paid off, and the largest portion of the men were retained aboard hulks and turned over to other ships. However, some men were paid and released from naval service, and many of them went their own way, many likely to be pressed again.[58] However, this meant that each year, thousands of men were being turned out of the Royal Navy rather than being turned over. Undoubtedly this was advantageous to seamen, as they saw it as a chance to join a merchant ship if they were so inclined, or to volunteer and receive the bounty again. For the Impress Service, it was a nightmare and inflated the cost of keeping the Navy fully manned. The fact that the ships' companies were paid off or released from naval service, and ultimately required replacing, meant that thousands of pounds were spent finding new seamen. Had this practice been revoked and all men simply turned over from ship to ship, fleet morale would probably have plummeted, and may possibly have caused even further problems, such as mutiny.

At the end of the War of American Independence, Britain remained as Europe's dominant naval power, though it required a lot of hard work and resulted in a compromised peace in which thirteen of the American colonies were granted independence. Britain had produced the largest naval force in its history and managed to successfully conduct the naval campaign that led to the end of the conflict. Producing such a large naval force hinged on recruiting, and the unique conditions of the war resulted in an even grander

[54] NMM: MEL/5, 'John Robinson Letter to Commission of Excise and Customs, 25 June 1779'.
[55] Rodger, *The Command of the Ocean*, p. 396.
[56] NMM: MID 7/3/2, 'Expense of the Impress Service in the American War of Year 1775 to 1783'.
[57] Rodger, *The Command of the Ocean*, p. 398.
[58] Nicholas Rogers, *The Press Gang: Naval Impressment and Its Opponents in Georgian Britain* (London: Continuum, 2007), pp. 4–6.

struggle for the limited number of British seamen. The American War took the administrative systems developed during the Seven Years' War and stretched them to new limits; however the true test of naval administration was yet to come.

A New and Grander Struggle

The French Revolutionary and Napoleonic Wars proved to be the greatest conflict faced by Britain throughout its history, and it was not surpassed until the twentieth century. From the Restoration Navy of Charles II the Royal Navy had become increasingly larger with each progressive conflict, as had the British maritime population.[59] During the American War the Royal Navy exceeded 105,000 men; however the decade of relative peace saw the naval numbers continually reduced, and on the eve of war with France, Parliament only voted funds for 16,000 men in the Royal Navy; and though just over 17,000 men were borne on the books, only about 15,000 were mustered.[60]

The years following the American Revolution were filled with unrest in Britain. British radicals celebrated the French Revolution as a 'triumph of liberty' in 1789, as many Britons celebrated the centennial of their own revolution. However, conservatives viewed the humiliation of the French king as a mockery of the fundamental principles of the Glorious Revolution of 1688.[61] To many people, the French Revolution was welcomed, as it was viewed as a weakening of the 'old enemy'.[62] As time progressed, the 'reign of terror' that engulfed France in blood quickly drove many British sympathisers away from the French cause. By 1792, what had begun with the storming of the Bastille had placed all of Europe on the brink of a war that lasted over two decades and plunged the Atlantic World into a conflict greater than any before.

At the opening of the French Revolutionary Wars, Britain's naval strength was superior to any other in Europe. Two brief mobilisations, one against Spain over Nootka Sound in 1790 and another against Russia over Turkey the following year, had left the Royal Navy's ships in relatively good condition.[63] However, as the outbreak of hostilities became imminent in late 1792, the Royal Navy found itself unprepared in one crucial area, manning the fleet.[64] As the American War came to an end, the Royal Navy was heavily in debt, especially after thousands of seamen were paid off and ships were laid up in ordinary. Paying seamen off quickly and releasing them from service became a priority. This saved the Crown money and was further required by law. Administrators also did not want the lack of pay to prove a disincentive

---

[59] Richard Harding, *Seapower and Naval Warfare, 1650–1830* (London: Routledge, 1999), p. 138.

[60] TNA: PRO 30/8/248, 'Account of Seamen …', f. 29.

[61] Nicholas Rogers, *Crowds, Culture, and Politics in Georgian Britain* (Oxford: Clarendon Press, 1998), pp. 188–190.

[62] Clive Emsley, *British Society and the French Wars, 1793–1815* (London: Macmillan, 1979), p. 13.

[63] W.M. James, *The Naval History of Great Britain During the French Revolutionary and Napoleonic Wars, 1793–1796*, vol. I (London: Conway Maritime, 2002), p. 48.

[64] Harding, p. 259.

for future manning drives.[65] Further, the peacetime Navy was downsized as much as possible in order to reduce naval expenses, and only 16,613 men were employed in the Royal Navy at the beginning of 1792, nearly 4,000 fewer men than on the eve of the American Revolution.[66] There was still no large-scale naval reserve and the idea of compulsory registration had been dismissed as 'French and tyrannical'.[67] With only a few guard-ships as a reserve to call upon, the Royal Navy was forced to expand threefold in the first year,[68] and the opening years of the French Revolutionary Wars stretched the Navy's manning capabilities to their limit.

Summation

Between the Restoration of Charles II and the dawn of the French Revolutionary Wars the Royal Navy evolved from a seasonal wartime force of about 20,000 men designed to fight in the North Sea, into a perpetually mobilised force, capable of fighting in home and foreign waters, and expanded to more than 100,000 men. The progression of the Royal Navy over this period resulted in the advancement of naval manning strategies. Recruiting large numbers of men required a refined and streamlined administrative system that raised large numbers of men quickly and tied down the least amount of naval resources. This allowed Britain to float a naval force equal to or greater than any two European nations combined throughout most of the eighteenth century. This in turn afforded Britain the ability to increasingly deprive the rest of Europe from reliably being able to use the sea during wartime, cutting off communication and supply to overseas territory, while increasing British strength abroad.

However, this progression can be difficult to gauge. The primary goal of this work is to obtain a statistical understanding of naval manning during the French Revolutionary and Napoleonic Wars, and to use this knowledge to draw new concepts and conclusions on naval manning at the end of the age of sail. Many of the findings are surprising and pull into question many of the claims made across the historiography of the subject. It stands to reason that a similar study that examined earlier periods, if records allowed, would find similar discrepancies. At present all we can accurately claim to know is the number of men voted by Parliament. We can find, with reasonable accuracy, the number of men that were borne on ships' books, and at least

---

[65] Clive Wilkinson, *The British Navy and the State in the Eighteenth Century* (Woodbridge: The Boydell Press, 2004), p. 107.

[66] R.J.B. Knight, *The Pursuit of Victory: The Life and Achievement of Horatio Nelson* (London: Allen Lane, 2005), p. 142.

[67] David Aldridge, 'The Navy as Handmaid for Commerce and High Policy, 1680–1720', in *The British Navy and the Use of Naval Power in the Eighteenth Century*, ed. Jeremy Black and Philip Woodfine (Leicester: Leicester University Press, 1988), pp. 56–57; J.S. Bromley, 'The British Navy and Its Seamen after 1688: Notes for an Unwritten History', in *Charted and Uncharted Waters*, ed. Sarah Palmer and David Williams (Queen Mary College, London: Trustees of the National Maritime Museum, 1981), p. 150.

[68] Rogers, *The Press Gang: Naval Impressment and Its Opponents in Georgian Britain*, pp. 5–6.

for the American War, the amount of money that was spent on land-based recruitment.

However, even with the shortcomings in our statistical knowledge of most of the eighteenth-century Royal Navy, we can clearly see the evolutionary trajectory outlined, ever so briefly, in this chapter. By the end of the eighteenth century, the Navy was a driving force behind Britain's advancing economy. The sheer size of the naval administration and infrastructure was like nothing seen before. Britain's naval support system, from ship construction and repair to victualling and manning, was driven to advancement, as the only means of successfully fielding such a large naval force depended upon efficiency. Understanding the evolution of naval manning across the eighteenth century is key to understanding the problems faced by the Admiralty on the eve of the French Revolutionary Wars. Parliament and the Admiralty, which attempted to solve this problem in the 1790s, did so from a standpoint of their experiences and the experiences of administrators before them. Understanding this problem in its contemporary light is necessary to appreciate the actions taken in order to man the Royal Navy during the French Revolutionary and Napoleonic Wars.

2

Manning Statistics

Critical to the success of every European navy in the eighteenth century was the ability to acquire men with seafaring skills. Without skilled men to handle sails, both in good and bad weather, any ship would find itself in peril. The Royal Navy drew its manpower from a world-leading mercantile and fishing fleet,[1] which had increased in size, power and prosperity during the eighteenth century.[2] Manning the fleets during wartime was one of the largest problems faced by the Royal Navy, a problem that grew increasingly throughout the eighteenth century, as the Navy, along with British sea trade, expanded.[3] This resulted in a struggle for the resource of skilled manpower, made most evident during the mobilisation from peace to wartime footing.[4] In the French Revolutionary Wars the problem was greater than ever before, as the Royal Navy expanded from 17,000 men

---

[1] Jeremy Black, *Naval Power: A History of Warfare and the Sea from 1500* (Basingstoke: Palgrave Macmillan, 2009), p. 104; Peter Earle, 'English Sailors, 1570–1775', in *'Those Emblems of Hell?' European Sailors and the Maritime Labour Market, 1570–1870*, ed. Paul van Royen, Jaap Bruijn and Jan Lucassen, Research in Maritime History (St John's, Newfoundland: International Maritime Economic History Association, 1997), p. 91; Glete, pp. 173–174; N.A.M. Rodger, 'Mobilizing Seapower in the Eighteenth Century', in *Essays in Naval History, from Medieval to Modern*, ed. N.A.M. Rodger (Farnham: Ashgate Publishing, 2009), pp. 5–6; A.T. Mahan, *The Influence of Sea Power upon the French Revolution and Empire: 1793–1812*, vol. I (London: Sampson Low, 1892), p. 70; Margarette Lincoln, *Representing the Royal Navy: British Sea Power, 1750–1815* (Aldershot: Ashgate, 2002), p. 78.

[2] John Brewer, *The Sinews of Power: War, Money and the English State, 1688–1783* (London: Unwin Hyman, 1989), p. 12; Sarah Palmer and David M. Williams, 'British Sailors, 1775–1870', in *'Those Emblems of Hell?' European Sailors and the Maritime Labour Market, 1570–1870*, ed. Paul van Royen, Jaap Bruijn and Jan Lucassen, Research in Maritime History (St John's, Newfoundland: International Maritime Economic History Assoication, 1997), p. 97; Starkey, 'War and the Market for Seafarers in Britain, 1736–1792', p. 28.

[3] David Starkey's study of maritime labour at the end of the eighteenth and beginning of the nineteenth century has revealed that in 1793 there were around 81,225 men employed in merchant shipping, inland navigation, and private ships-of-war. By 1801 that number had risen to around 102,704, and in 1812 it reached approximately 131,161 men. David J. Starkey, 'Quantifying British Seafarers, 1789–1828', in *Maritime Labour: Contributions to the History of Work at Sea, 1500–2000*, ed. Richard Gorski (Amsterdam: Aksant Academic Publishers, 2007), p. 102.

[4] Oppenheim, p. 115.

in 1792 to over 130,000 in 1801. By 1810, British naval manpower had reached over 145,000 men, about 2.7 per cent of Britain's male population.[5] Recruiting seamen in the eighteenth century was essentially a problem of supply, pitting the requirements of the Navy and merchant sea trade against the population of mariners available.[6] In the end there were not enough seamen to fully man the Royal Navy and the merchant fleets at the same time.[7]

Analysing eighteenth-century naval manning has always been challenging. The main problem is a lack of statistical data on the subject, without which the actual outcome of naval manning efforts is difficult to determine. Without solid numbers, obtaining an accurate understanding of the men that the Royal Navy recruited is nearly impossible. Examining primary source material, such as letters or Admiralty instructions, allows for a basic understanding of naval manning and how it was received by both officials and the public; however it does little to show anything about the men who actually served in Royal Navy ships. Without statistical evidence, there is little that can be said about the men of the lower deck. Without quantitative research we cannot determine how most men were recruited, their skill levels, their ages, their nationalities, and the list goes on.

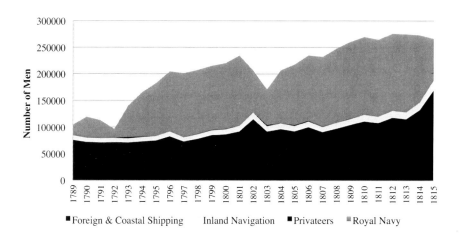

■ Foreign & Coastal Shipping   Inland Navigation   ■ Privateers   ■ Royal Navy

Figure 2.1 British men employed at sea, 1789–1815
Source: TNA: ADM 7/567, 'Admiralty Miscellanea, 1754–1806', ff. 22, 27; Rodger, *Command of the Ocean*, pp. 636–639, Starkey, 'Quantifying British Seafarers', p. 102.

5 Nicholas Blake and Richard Russell Lawrence, *The Illustrated Companion to Nelson's Navy* (London: Chatham Publishing, 1999), p. 64.
6 Lloyd, *The British Seaman, 1200–1860*, p. 112; Morriss, p. 18.
7 Rodger, *The Wooden World*, p. 153.

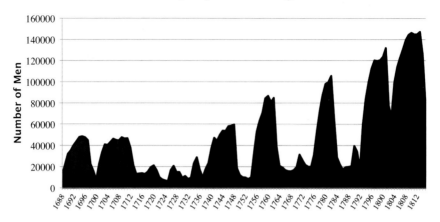

Figure 2.2 Royal Navy manpower in the eighteenth century
Source: TNA: ADM 7/567, 'Admiralty Miscellanea, 1754–1806', ff. 22, 27; Rodger,
Command of the Ocean, pp. 636–639.

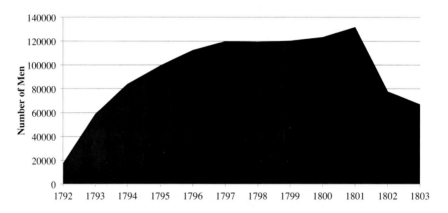

Figure 2.3 Royal Navy manpower, 1792–1803
Source: TNA: ADM 7/567, 'Admiralty Miscellanea, 1754–1806', ff. 22, 27; Rodger,
Command of the Ocean, pp. 636–639.

The centre of the debate over naval manpower across the last two centuries has consistently dealt with recruitment, and has generally been geared toward the issue of impressment. This is a topic where the value of statistical data is clear. Speculation on naval recruitment has varied widely, and many historians have given estimates of how many men they believed were impressed or volunteered. Michael Lewis,[8] Steven Gradish,[9] and Nicholas Rogers,[10] among others, all gave estimates as to the proportion of pressed

---

[8] Michael Lewis, *A Social History of the Navy, 1793–1815* (London: Chatham Publishing, 2004), p. 139.
[9] Gradish, *The Manning of the British Navy During the Seven Years' War*, p. 62.
[10] Rogers, *The Press Gang: Naval Impressment and Its Opponents in Georgian Britain*, pp. 3–5.

and volunteer men aboard Royal Navy ships during the eighteenth century; however none of these estimates were based on statistical data, but rather came from the historiography of the subject, which is based more on conjecture than factual data. Only N.A.M. Rodger has used statistics, when he examined the muster books of five ships that commissioned during the Seven Years' War,[11] though the small size of the sample, and the variation within the sample, meant that his findings could only be used as a suggestion of what may have been, rather than being able to statistically argue that they were applicable to the Royal Navy as a whole. More importantly, they exposed the need for an in-depth study of naval manning, based on statistical fact.

This work is not a call-to-arms against historians who have written on the subject, nor does it call their research inadequate. To the contrary, many historians writing on the subject did a superb job of deciphering the data they had with the resources available to them. Large-scale statistics, of the nature needed in this type of project, are only practical when combined with computer technology that is able to produce usable numbers from databases. Realistically, only historians publishing from about the mid-1990s onwards would have had access to computers, programs and training that allowed them to attempt this type of study. Without this technology, a statistical study of naval manning, with enough depth and breadth for the findings to be considered statistically sound, would be so labour-intensive that it would be impractical.

As explained at length in the introduction, the core of this project has been to collect and analyse statistics dealing with naval manpower. The data come from the muster books of eighty-one ships commissioned into the Royal Navy between 1793 and 1801. Though the rest of this work examines the three major forms of naval recruitment – volunteering, impressment, and the Quota Acts – it does little to examine the men of the Royal Navy as a whole. This chapter, therefore, provides raw statistics about the men who served on British warships. In particular, this chapter examines the lower deck of Royal Navy warships, essentially those men who were rated as seamen or petty officers. The ships' muster books that were used in constructing the database behind this project offer the best information available for these men, as they generally provide information for each individual, including their means of recruitment, age, place of birth, whether or not they received a bounty and if so the amount, as well as other valuable information that allows for large-scale statistical examination. The size of this database, which covers 27,174 men, equates to approximately 10 per cent of the men who served between 1793 and 1802, and thus these findings are statistically applicable to the Royal Navy as a whole during the period. Thus, this chapter does not present the same in-depth analysis of recruitment that is made available throughout the rest of this project; however it does provide an overarching look at the statistics of naval manning.

[11]   Rodger, *The Wooden World.*

The Recruitment of Petty Officers and Seamen

Recruiting statistics produced by this data sample, which examines 17,859 seamen and 2,354 petty officers, show the basic ways by which the men of the lower deck arrived aboard newly commissioned warships. Between 1793 and 1801, the majority of seamen either arrived as new volunteers (42 per cent) or had been turned over from other ships (41 per cent). Only 10 per cent of seamen were newly pressed, a surprisingly low statistic when considering the historiography. A further 5 per cent of men were recruited as volunteers via the Quota Acts, all of whom entered naval service between 1795 and 1797. A very small number of men were recorded as having entered as former members of the Army or Militia, recruited as former POWs, come from civil prison, or entered as substitutes for pressed men. These four categories added together consisted of only 123 seamen and made up less than 1 per cent of the total. For simplicity, all four of these groups have been placed in a common recruitment group in the database, listed collectively as 'other'. Finally, there are 176 seamen from this sample whose recruitment remains unknown, due to their entries in muster books being either unreadable or simply left blank.

There were only nineteen men who were listed as having joined as former members of the Army or Militia. This is an exceptionally small number of men for such a large data sample, and is an oddity, as they were all out of one ship. All nineteen entered HMS *Vengeance*, a seventy-four gun ship-of-the-line, in 1795. Of these men, sixteen came from the Surrey Militia, all of whom were landsmen. Of the remaining three, able seaman David Barrington and ordinary seaman William Buddie came from the Chatham Barracks, while ordinary seaman Richard Holmes was from the Yeomen of the Guard. The fact that these men were listed only on one ship suggests two possibilities. The first is that they existed in greater numbers than realised

Total: 17,859 men   Total: 2,354 men

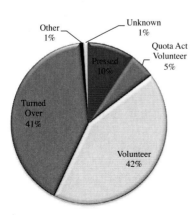

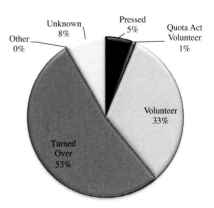

Figure 2.4 Seamen recruitment   **Figure 2.5** Petty officer recruitment

from this data, and that the general practice when entering them into ships' muster books was to list these men as volunteers. The alternative is that there was some particular personal connection between these men and HMS *Vengeance*, which in turn means that naval recruiting from Army or Militia units was even more rare than depicted in this database. It does not appear that their joining of the navy was treated in the same way as turned over men, as most turned over men had annotations that recorded their previous posting, and there is no mention of Army or Militia service among turned over seamen.

Forty-three seamen were recorded as having joined as former prisoners of war, and were found on seven of the eighty-one ships covered in this survey, all from frigates and ships-of-the-line. Thirty of the seamen who came as former prisoners of war were rated as landsmen, while eleven were rated ordinary seamen, and only two were able seamen. Thirty of these men were twenty-five years old or younger, and the rest were under forty. Fifteen of these men were Dutch, all found aboard the seventy-four gun *Montague* in 1796. All but five of these men were European. The five non-Europeans were from North America, two from America, two from Canada, and one was listed as being from the West Indies.

There were also four seamen in the survey who were listed as having been from a French prison, all aboard the sixty-four gun *Veteran* in 1797. Two were ordinary seamen: John Drake was twenty-five and from Dublin, and John Trennon was twenty and from Halifax, West Yorkshire. The other two were able seamen: Samuel Clements was twenty-two and from Belfast, and George Dawson was forty-four and from Falkirk, Scotland. As they were all found aboard one ship, it suggests other men that joined after spending time as French prisoners were likely only recorded in the usual way.

Nineteen men from this sample were recorded as being recruited from civil prison, five of whom were landsmen, twelve ordinary seamen, and two able seamen. Fourteen of these men were found aboard HMS *Dreadnought*. This again suggests that rather than being a reliable statistic, they were in fact an anomaly of record keeping. However, it is interesting that three-quarters of the men listed here as being from civil prisons were recognised by the Royal Navy as seamen. It is important to point out that while criminals, especially thieves, were not recruited into the Navy, as they clearly posed a threat to morale aboard ship, minor offenders, such as for riot, drunkenness, and debt, were sometimes allowed to volunteer, especially if they had the seagoing skills that were so highly prized aboard warships.[12]

Thirty-eight men were listed as being substitutes for pressed men, of whom eleven were rated able seamen, eight ordinary seamen, and nineteen landsmen, and all but five were less than thirty years of age. These thirty-eight

---

[12] Clive Emsley, 'The Recruitment of Petty Offenders During the French Wars, 1793–1815', *The Mariner's Mirror* CXVI, no. 3 (1980); Rodger, *The Command of the Ocean*, pp. 397, 444.

men were found on fifteen different ships; thus the recording of substitutes was most likely standard practice. Substitutes were essentially men who joined in the place of a man who had been pressed, resulting in the release of the pressed man from naval service. The process of getting someone to take the position of a pressed man most likely meant some type of compensation was provided by the friends and family of the pressed man for the substitute; however as each case was different and there is not any known documentation of these events, the exact 'price' of a substitute is not known. Though providing a substitute in lieu of a pressed man was a possibility, the very low number of substitutes found in this database suggests that it was not a very common practice.

Examining these statistics on a year-by-year basis for 1793 to 1801 shows a very high number of volunteers during 1793 and 1794, which drops during 1795 and 1796, likely due to the Quota Acts. In 1797, the number of volunteers spiked, possible due to both the end of the Quota Acts recruiting scheme, and the changes the Navy made as a result of the great mutinies of 1797, which made naval service more attractive to seamen. However, from 1798 to 1801 volunteer seamen were replaced by turned over seamen as the primary source of manpower coming aboard newly commissioned ships. Notably this was after a full five years of war, and corresponds with the slowing of naval growth that began in 1798, as the Royal Navy became fully mobilised.[13] It is also notable here, though it will be covered in detail later, that pressed seamen made up a relatively steady number of men each year, except during 1795.

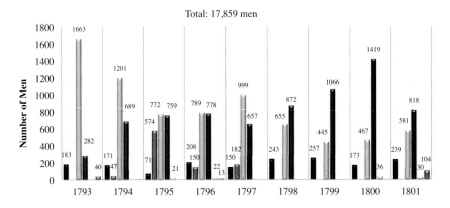

Figure 2.6 Seamen recruitment, 1793–1801

---

[13] See Figure 2.3.

Total: 2,354 petty officers

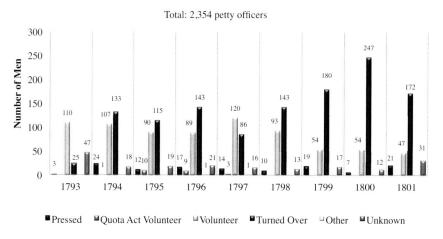

Figure 2.7 Petty officer recruitment, 1793–1801

This survey included the recruiting information for 2,354 petty officers, and the basic statistics for their recruitment show similar trends to the statistics for seamen. The key difference is the higher rate of turned over petty officers, 53 per cent in comparison to only 41 per cent amongst seamen.[14] Thirty-three per cent of petty officers were volunteers and a further 1 per cent volunteered under the Quota Acts. Pressed men accounted for only 5 per cent of petty officers in the raw statistics. Unlike seamen, a full 8 per cent of petty officers' recruitment remains unknown.

Only two petty officers were not covered by one of these five categories and were assigned to the category labelled 'other'. David Roberts, a twenty-nine year old Welshman, joined the sloop *Harpy* in 1796 as a substitute for a pressed man. He came aboard as an able seaman and by the time the ship put to sea for the first time he was promoted to gunner's mate. The other anomaly was Robert Burke, a forty-seven year old quartermaster's mate from Cork, Ireland. He joined the sixty-four gun *Veteran* in 1797 after being returned from a French prison, along with four seamen discussed earlier.

The real difference between petty officer and seaman recruitment can be observed when looking at the recruitment returns over the nine years covered by this database. Volunteer petty officers only outnumbered those that were turned over during the first year of the war and again in 1797. For every other year of the conflict, men turned over from previous ships were the primary source for petty officers who joined newly commissioned ships. This trend increased throughout the war, and in 1799, 1800 and 1801 turned over men accounted for 67, 77 and 64 per cent of petty officers found aboard newly commissioned warships. This illustrates the fact that men with naval experience were more likely to be rated as petty officers than men who were entering into the Royal Navy without naval experience. It is also important to

---

[14] See Figure 2.5.

note that there is no way of knowing how many of the volunteers had volunteered again after being discharged from another ship, or even deserting. It is certainly possible that after being paid off, experienced seamen would have recognised the value of finding another berth in a Royal Navy ship, and receiving the volunteer bounty, possibly for the second or third time.

A further point of interest with petty officers serving aboard Royal Navy ships is their promotion from seamen. As this database concerns itself with ships' musters from when a given ship was first commissioned, to the time when it first put to sea with, more or less, its full complement, it only shows promotions that occurred during the first weeks or months of a ship's service. Notably, when a ship first put to sea it was the first real opportunity to see the men at work under sail and judge their actual skills and ability; generally this was when the first lieutenant or captain would rate the men. From this data we can see that 61 per cent of petty officers remained at the same rating that they were listed as when they first joined the ship. Two per cent of petty officers moved from one petty officer rating to another during this time period. Thirty-two per cent of petty officers were promoted from able seamen, 2 per cent were promoted from ordinary seamen, 1 per cent were promoted from landsmen, 1 per cent were promoted from midshipmen, and finally less than 1 per cent were promoted from idlers. This trend was fairly steady across all nine years covered by the database, with the highest rate of promotion to petty officer being in 1796 when 46 per cent of petty officers were newly promoted, and the lowest rate of promotion to petty officer coming in 1800 when only 25 per cent of petty officers were newly promoted. However, in all other years, between 60 and 65 per cent of petty officers listed on the muster books remained in the same position that they filled when they first joined their respective ships.

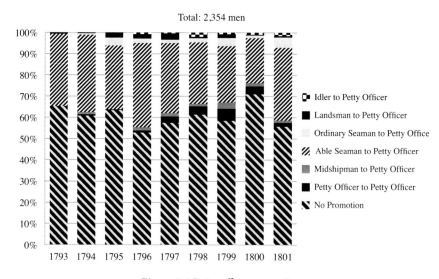

Figure 2.8 Petty officer promotion

Factoring Turned Over Men

When examining this data, one of the key problems of researching naval manning quickly surfaces: determining the original recruitment of turned over men. Men who were marked as 'turned over' were, for the most part, men who had previously served on another Royal Navy ship; however when that vessel was paid off for repairs or storage, rather than being released from naval service, these men were assigned to another ship. As these men had previously served aboard different warships, their original recruitment is difficult to determine without the time-consuming process of tracking them from ship to ship, a process nearly impossible when considering the scale of the task. However, there is a way to factor the original recruitment of these men.

In January 1793, the men already in the Royal Navy were virtually all volunteers, as they were recruited during peacetime, and naval conscription was only used during war. Between then and 1801 the Royal Navy grew by almost 120,000 men. All of this growth had to come from sources other than men turned over. A turned over man, as he was moved from one ship to another, served only to keep the Royal Navy at the same size. Therefore, as the Navy had such a large net growth, and as the men already serving at the beginning of 1793 were virtually all volunteers, the men who were turned over necessarily had to be recruited in approximately the same proportions of volunteers and pressed men as observed throughout the data sample. If, for example, 70 per cent of the non-turned over men were volunteers, it stands to reason that 70 per cent of turned over men had volunteered when they were originally recruited into naval service. The overall process is more complex than this example; however this illustrates the basic principle.

To ensure that the factoring process is as accurate as possible, the factoring procedure has been applied to each individual year. To do this, it has been presumed that turned over men were likely recruited during the three previous years, as the rate of turnover within individual ships averaged about 50 per cent per year; thus statistically the entire crew of a ship would be renewed every two years, the men either discharged from the Navy or turned over to another ship.[15] Further, an average of 41 per cent of seamen were turned over in each ship, suggesting that a large portion were in fact paid off rather than being turned over. Therefore, to factor the turned over men, this project uses an average of proportions of volunteers and pressed men observed over the previous three years. For turned over men in 1793, it was assumed that the men turned over would have all been volunteers, as they would have come from the peacetime fleet. To factor 1794, an average of the pre-1793 all-volunteer estimate and the data returns for non-turned over men recruited during 1793 was used to produce recruitment estimates for turned over men joining newly commissioned ships in 1794. Factoring for turned over men in 1795 is based on the averages of non-turned over

---

[15] Rodger, *The Wooden World*, p. 359.

recruitment from 1793 and 1794. Finally, for 1796 to 1801, the average statistics for non-turned over men from the previous three years were used. For example, factoring the turned over men from 1800 involved averaging the recruitment statistics of non-turned over men for 1797 to 1799.

In order to explain the process, a simplified example can be used involving four fictitious years, 'A' to 'D'. If in year 'D' 200 men were recruited, and of those 70 were volunteers, 30 had been pressed, and 100 had been turned over, then the task would be to find out the original recruitment of those 100 that were turned over. Then, during the years 'A', 'B' and 'C' the average percentages of non-turned over men were 80 per cent volunteer and 20 per cent pressed. Therefore, we can assume that of the men turned over in year 'D' 80 per cent would have been recruited as volunteers, and 20 per cent had been pressed, as they were most likely to have been recruited during the three previous years. Thus, of those 100 turned over men, 80 would be counted as volunteers and 20 as pressed. This would then be added to the original number of volunteers and pressed men for that year and the final factored statistic for year 'D' would stand at 150 volunteers and 50 pressed men. Performing this exercise produces factored statistics for the original recruitment for turned over men entering warships during each year of the war and gives a more accurate estimate of original recruitment statistics than anything yet produced in the historiography. By using this factoring process, we can look beyond how turned over men simply arrived aboard subsequent Royal Navy warships, to how they were originally recruited; eliminating much of the guesswork that has come before and replacing it with viable statistics.

This exercise produces a set of statistics that is very different from the historiography that has developed over the last two centuries. Rather than volunteers accounting for as little as a quarter to as much as half of seamen,

Total: 17,859 men   Total: 2,354 men

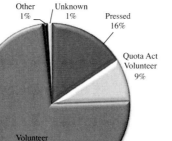

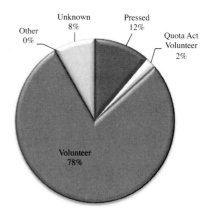

Figure 2.9 Factored seamen recruitment   **Figure 2.10** Factored petty officer recruitment

statistics show that volunteers accounted for approximately 73 per cent of seamen, and a further 9 per cent were Quota Act volunteers. Combined, volunteers and Quota Act volunteers made up roughly 82 per cent of seamen aboard warships when examining 1793 to 1801 as a whole, while pressed men only accounted for 16 per cent. Similarly with petty officers, volunteers made up approximately 78 per cent, and Quota Act volunteers accounted for 2 per cent, totalling 80 per cent voluntary service for petty officers.

Examining factored statistics during each year illustrates how volunteers made up the vast majority of men aboard British warships throughout the French Revolutionary Wars. Impressment never came close to outpacing volunteer recruitment as a source of naval manpower for either seamen or petty officers. However, as the war progressed, especially after 1798, the numbers of pressed men did slowly grow and accounted for a significant portion of seamen in 1798 (19 per cent), 1799 (26 per cent), 1800 (25 per cent), and 1801 (27 per cent). However, these percentages, which were the highest of the war, present a picture of naval recruitment that is nearly the polar opposite of what has been portrayed in the historiography thus far. Similarly, the impressment rate amongst petty officers was highest at the end of the war. From 1794 to 1798, around 10 per cent of petty officers were pressed; however this rose in 1799 (15 per cent), 1800 (14 per cent), and 1801 (18 per cent).

Dividing the recruitment returns by the rating of the men reveals how different forms of recruitment had distinctive levels of effectiveness amongst various skill levels. From the outset we can observe that men of higher skill were more likely to be turned over. Not only would officers be interested in keeping skilled men as opposed to unskilled men, but men gained skill over time. Thus, a completely green landsman, after about two or three years at

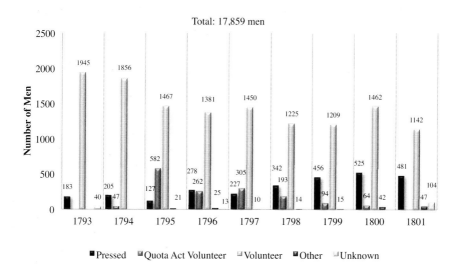

Figure 2.11 Factored seamen recruitment, 1793–1801

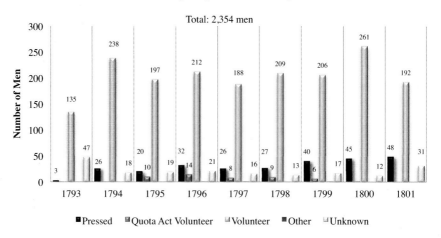

Figure 2.12 Factored petty officer recruitment, 1793–1801

sea, the length of a normal commission for a warship, would have likely obtained enough time and skill to become an ordinary seaman. The same is true with ordinary seamen, who by time and experience became able seamen. Though not all able seamen became petty officers, virtually all petty officers were once able seamen, whether in naval or merchant service. With petty officers, naval experience would have been an important quality, as they were expected to lead less experienced men.

By examining the factored manning returns, we can clearly see that volunteerism was the dominant form of recruitment for all ratings on the lower deck, with the lowest percentage of volunteers belonging to ordinary seamen, at 70 per cent. Impressment also accounts for a significant number of skilled men, 23 per cent of able and ordinary seamen, but only 7 per cent of landsmen, which demonstrates that press gangs sought skilled men, rather than scraping the dregs of society for anyone they could find. The Quota Acts had a clear trend toward recruiting unskilled men, as almost exactly twice as many landsmen were recruited under the scheme, as were ordinary seamen, able seamen and petty officers combined. The one notable anomaly in the database is that petty officers were more likely not to have their recruitment information recorded than any of the seamen classes. This may be the result of officers, especially captains, bringing a select following of men with them from previous commands, and their recruitment, being turned over in this case, was simply not listed. If this is in fact the case, then the men were not likely to have been turned over against their will, but had elected to follow their officers. There is a trend in the muster books for these 'unknown' petty officers to be listed as having joined ships as they commissioned, rather than during the following weeks as most of the crew did, which supports such a hypothesis. However, without further data, this is simply conjecture.

Table 2.1 Manning returns, 1793–1801

	Pressed	Quota Acts	Volunteer	Turned over	Other	Unknown	Total
Petty officers	127 (5%)	23 (1%)	764 (33%)	1,244 (53%)	2 (<1%)	194 (8%)	**2,354**
Able seamen	763 (10%)	65 (1%)	2,341 (32%)	4,024 (55%)	18 (<1%)	116 (2%)	**7,327**
Ordinary seamen	635 (13%)	150 (3%)	1,929 (39%)	2,155 (44%)	35 (<1%)	27 (<1%)	**4,931**
Landsmen	297 (5%)	738 (13%)	3,302 (59%)	1,161 (21%)	70 (1%)	33 (<1%)	**5,601**
Total	**1,822 (9%)**	**976 (5%)**	**8,336 (41%)**	**8,584 (42%)**	**125 (<1%)**	**370 (2%)**	**20,213**

Table 2.2 Factored manning returns, 1793–1801

	Pressed	Quota Acts	Volunteer	Other	Unknown	Total
Petty officers	267 (12%)	50 (2%)	1,838 (78%)	3 (<1%)	194 (8%)	**2,352**
Able seamen	1,726 (23%)	147 (2%)	5,297 (72%)	41 (<1%)	116 (2%)	**7,327**
Ordinary seamen	1,133 (23%)	268 (5%)	3,441 (70%)	62 (1%)	27 (<1%)	**4,931**
Landsmen	375 (7%)	932 (17%)	4,172 (74%)	88 (1%)	33 (<1%)	**5,600**
Total	**3,501 (17%)**	**1,397 (7%)**	**14,748 (73%)**	**194 (<1%)**	**370 (2%)**	**20,210**

Ship Complements and Seamen Skill

Though investigating British naval recruitment was the key concern behind creating this database, its uses extend beyond whether men were simply volunteer or pressed. Statistics from the database show the division of men aboard ship. Not surprisingly, the majority, 66 per cent, of men aboard Royal Navy warships were seamen, whether able seamen, ordinary seamen, or landsmen. Nine per cent of the men were petty officers and 2 per cent were warrant officers, while 3 per cent were commissioned officers. Though they did not have commissions, midshipmen were counted amongst commissioned officers for the purposes of this database, as they were officers in training. Idlers, men who occupied specialist jobs aboard ships, made up 1 per cent of the crew. Boys, essentially being trained to become seamen, made up 5 per cent, and marines made up 13 per cent.[16] One final category, marked as 'other' for the purposes of this survey, accounted for 1 per cent of ship's crews. The men of this category were generally officers' servants, such as the captain's cook, steward, or secretary. Eighty per cent of the ship's crew – the seamen, petty officers, and boys – were considered to be part of the lower deck, and essentially performed the manual labour involved in sailing a warship, while 5 per cent – warrant and commissioned officers – held leadership positions over various portions or even the whole of the ship, and were considered a part of the 'quarter deck'. Further the men of the quarter deck occupied positions of permanent employment within the Royal Navy, while the men of the lower deck were only employed for the length of a given ship's commission, after which they might be paid off and put ashore or turned over to another warship.

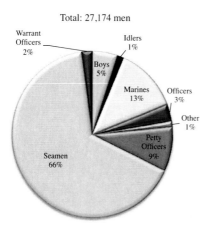

Figure 2.13 Ship complements, 1793–1801

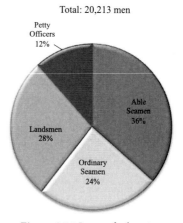

Figure 2.14 Lower deck ratings

[16] Note that marines also provided an additional source of 'unskilled' labour aboard warships. For more information on marines aboard warships see Zerbe, *Birth of the Royal Marines*.

The lower deck of Royal Navy warships, excluding the boys, consisted of petty officers and seamen. Able seamen, ordinary seamen and landsmen, together, made up 88 per cent of the lower deck, and petty officers accounted for the remaining 12 per cent. The largest portion of men on the lower deck was made up of able seamen, who accounted for over a third of the men (36 per cent), followed by landsmen (28 per cent) and ordinary seamen (24 per cent). Combining petty officers and able seamen shows that 48 per cent of the men of the lower deck were highly skilled, and adding ordinary seamen illustrates that 72 per cent of the labour force aboard British warships had sea skill and experience.

Looking at the men of the lower deck as the war progressed we can see that over the first four years of the war, able seamen substantially outnumbered ordinary seamen and landsmen.[17] In 1793, able seamen outnumbered ordinary seamen and landsmen combined on British warships. However, as the war continued, the number of able seamen in comparison to ordinary seamen and landsmen fell, and from 1798 to 1801, the three classes of seamen were in roughly equal proportions in the Royal Navy. Notably, there was a spike in ordinary seamen in 1797, which may have coincided with changes made to the Royal Navy as a result of the great mutinies of that same year. At the same time there was a drop in landsmen, which may have coincided with the good harvest of 1796, which also negatively affected the 1796 Quota Acts, as agricultural labourers were not as badly in need of work as they had been the previous year when harvests had not done well and much of the lower peasant class faced difficult times with high unemployment and shortages of food.[18]

When viewing the average of all nine years of the survey, petty officers made up 12 per cent of the men of the lower deck; however examining recruitment statistics for each year reveals an interesting manning problem. In 1793, petty officers made up only 8 per cent of the lower deck; however in 1794 this increased to 12 per cent and fluctuated between 10 and 12 per cent up to 1797. From 1798, the year that naval expansion slowed, to 1801, petty officers made up a steady 13 per cent of the lower deck population. A change of 5 per cent may not seem like much, especially when examining these graphs; however, the increase from 8 per cent to 12 per cent between 1793 and 1794 was a full 50 per cent increase. As the percentage of petty officers aboard Royal Navy warships levelled off during the final four years of the war at 13 per cent, we can conclude that this was the proportion of petty officers necessary for the most efficient running of a warship. This also means that ships that commissioned in 1793 only had about two-thirds of the necessary petty officers on board. The reason for this was undoubtedly that most able seamen needed some naval experience before they could fill a petty officer billet, and therefore it was 1794 before there were enough able seamen available with the necessary skill to be promoted to petty officer. It

[17]   See Figures 2.15 and 2.16.
[18]   Rodger, *The Command of the Ocean*, pp. 443–444.

Total: 20,213 men

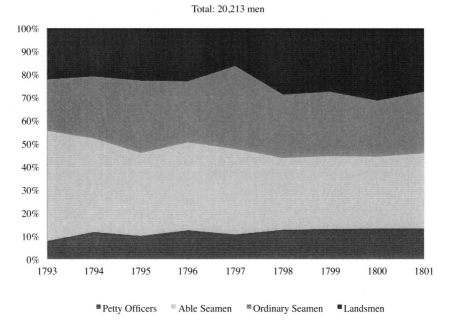

Petty Officers   Able Seamen   Ordinary Seamen   Landsmen

Figure 2.15 Seamen and petty officers

Total: 20,213 men

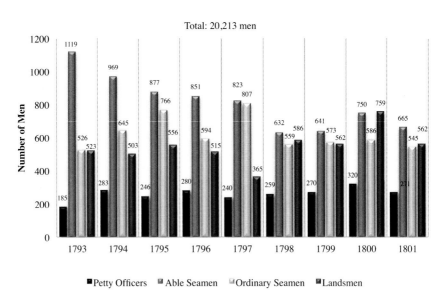

Petty Officers   Able Seamen   Ordinary Seamen   Landsmen

Figure 2.16 Seamen and petty officers

is also notable that between 1793 and 1794 there was a sharp increase in the number of petty officers who had been turned over, from 14 to 47 per cent. Further, as ships that commissioned in 1793 had less than the necessary petty officers, it must have meant that the petty officers that were serving had heavier workloads. This was most likely balanced by the fact that during the same year there was a high percentage of able seamen in comparison to other years. The fact that a larger percentage of the men aboard were highly skilled meant that not as much direction was needed from petty officers. However, it seems certain that officers would have been motivated to ensure that experienced able seamen were being promoted, especially when considering the rapid expansion of the Navy.

Ports and Recruitment

Examining recruitment for each of the three naval ports covered in this database, Chatham, Portsmouth and Plymouth, reveals that the statistics for each varied.[19] Ships that were manned at Chatham, for instance, had a higher percentage of pressed men than did ships commissioned at either Portsmouth or Plymouth. Sixteen per cent of the seamen aboard ships manned at Chatham were pressed into service, compared to only 6 per cent in both Portsmouth and Plymouth. Chatham also had the lowest percentage of turned over seamen, with only 28 per cent, while 53 per cent of seamen at Portsmouth and 42 per cent of seamen at Plymouth were turned over. Nearly half of the seamen who joined ships at Plymouth (49 per cent) were new volunteers, while only 43 per cent of seamen at Chatham and 36 of the seamen at Portsmouth were fresh volunteers.

The Quota Acts made up a substantial number of men recruited between 1795 and 1797. In Chatham, Quota men made up 47 per cent of seamen recruited in 1795, 20 per cent recruited in 1796, and about 9 per cent of men recruited in 1797. Although the Quota Acts went into effect in 1795 and 1796, the 1796 Quota Acts did not take effect until November and therefore the recruitment returns bled over into 1797. The effect of the Quota Acts in Plymouth was not nearly so great, as Quota men made up only 22 per cent of men in 1795, and 6 per cent of seamen recruited in 1797. Notably, only one seaman out of the 626 covered in this data set from Plymouth in 1796 was listed as having been a product of the Quota Acts. In Portsmouth, the Quota Acts accounted for 9 per cent of men in 1795, 2 per cent in 1796, and 12 per cent in 1797.

Examining recruiting statistics by port shows trends for each port. In every year except 1793, 1794 and 1798, Portsmouth had the highest percentage of turned over men, exceeding 80 per cent of seamen in 1796, 1799 and 1800. As mentioned, Chatham received the majority of men recruited by the Quota Acts, and also had the highest percentage of pressed men in every year except 1793. This shows the importance of London for naval recruiting efforts. Seamen

---

[19] It is important to note that during the eighteenth century the vast majority of warships commissioned at one of these three ports.

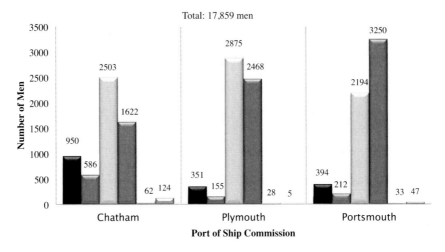

Figure 2.17 Seamen recruitment by port, 1793–1801

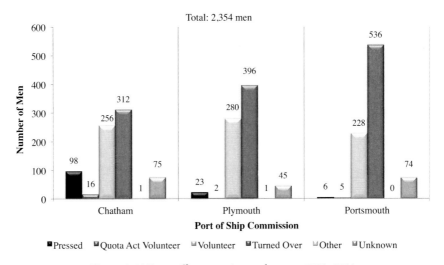

Figure 2.18 Petty officer recruitment by port, 1793–1801

recruited by the Quota Acts made up 47 per cent of seamen recruited into Chatham-based ships in 1795, and 20 per cent in 1796. Under the Port Quota Act of 1795, London had to produce 5,704 men,[20] far more than any other port. The high quota for London was due to its importance as a hub of international trade and thus the large maritime population that could be found in the city. Further, ships commissioning at Chatham were also likely to receive the Quota men from the east coast of England and Scotland, as well as those from

[20] 35 Geo. III c.9.

the Midlands. This was the reason behind Chatham ships receiving such a high number of Quota men in comparison to Portsmouth and Plymouth. This importance also extended to impressment. Though impressment certainly took place across Britain, the fact that ships that manned near Chatham had a higher percentage of pressed men is an indication that more men were pressed in the maritime centres in and around London than anywhere else. Logically this makes sense, as London was undeniably the largest centre of overseas trade in Britain, and therefore was always host to a multitude of seamen. Ships that commissioned out of Chatham also benefited from impressment activities all along the east coast of Britain, as the naval facilities near London were closer than either Portsmouth or Plymouth.

As far as division of skill was concerned, petty officers were spread roughly equally across all three ports, making up 11 or 12 per cent of the lower deck. However, ships that commissioned at Portsmouth statistically had a higher percentage of able seamen, 41 per cent, compared to 33 per cent at Chatham and 34 per cent at Plymouth. This is concurrent with the fact that Portsmouth also consistently had the highest percentage of turned over men. Therefore, as men turned over were statistically more skilled than men newly recruited, it makes sense that ships commissioned at Portsmouth had the highest percentage of skilled men on the lower deck. The larger percentage of turned over men, as well as the resulting higher skill level, was most likely the result of Portsmouth being the home of the Channel Fleet, the largest of all British fleets. Chatham, most likely due to its location near the densely populated area of London, received the highest percentage of landsmen. It is interesting that despite its close proximity to London, the largest centre of seaborne trade in Britain, Chatham ships had the lowest percentage of able and ordinary seamen, when compared to ships commissioned at Portsmouth and Plymouth.

Table 2.3 Skill by port, 1793–1801

	Chatham	Portsmouth	Plymouth	Total
Petty officers	758 (12%)	849 (12%)	747 (11%)	**2,354**
Able seamen	2,211 (33%)	2,855 (41%)	2,261 (34%)	**7,327**
Ordinary seamen	1,539 (23%)	1,646 (24%)	1,746 (27%)	**4,391**
Landsmen	2,097 (32%)	1,629 (23%)	1,875 (28%)	**5,601**
Total	**6,605 (100%)**	**6,979 (100%)**	**6,629 (100%)**	<u>**20,213**</u>

The Age of the Lower Deck

The men of the lower deck were young. Seventy per cent of seamen were twenty-nine years of age or younger, and 44 per cent were under the age of twenty-five. The peak age for landsmen and ordinary seamen joining ships of the Royal Navy was twenty, while for able seamen the peak age was twenty-two and for petty officers it was thirty. However, it should be taken into account that for seamen and petty officers there is a spike in the number of men who were reported as being thirty years old; there is also another spike, although less pronounced, at the age of forty. In both cases, this is likely due to men not knowing their actual age. Thus, men who were actually in their late twenties or early thirties, though did not know exactly, ended up being listed as thirty. For petty officers, this is significant, because the spike at age thirty is the high point. However, taking a closer look shows a relatively stable plateau of petty officers that joined between the age of twenty-four and twenty-eight, after which, if the spike at thirty is omitted, a slow and steady decline begins between the ages of twenty-nine and thirty-nine.

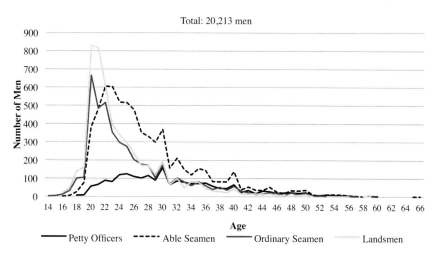

Figure 2.19 Age line chart for seamen and petty officers

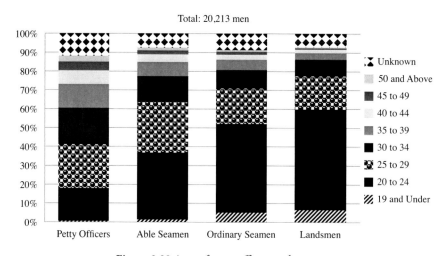

Figure 2.20 Ages of petty officers and seamen

Breaking up the returns into age brackets of five years gives a better illustration of how age and skill corresponded on the lower deck of British warships. Naturally, as they had no experience, landsmen were statistically the youngest men on the lower deck. Seventy-seven per cent of landsmen were under the age of thirty. The largest portion of these men, 53 per cent, fell between twenty and twenty-four years old. Six per cent of landsmen were under the age of twenty, the largest percentage of any single group, excluding boys. Further, only 13 per cent of landsmen were between the ages of thirty and thirty-nine, and only 3 per cent were forty or above.

Ordinary seamen were statistically older than landsmen, but only slightly. Seventy-one per cent were twenty-nine years of age or younger. Five per cent were nineteen or younger, 47 per cent were between twenty and twenty-four years old, and 19 per cent were between twenty-five and twenty-nine. Fifteen per cent were between thirty and thirty-nine, while only 6 per cent were above forty years old. Generally speaking, the age difference between landsmen and ordinary seamen was almost negligible. The general difference was that ordinary seamen most likely grew up in the maritime world, and had experience of the sea from a young age. However, with time and experience, landsmen became ordinary seamen, and ordinary seamen, with more time experience, progressed to become able seamen.

Though the age difference between landsmen and ordinary seamen was small, the difference between ordinary seamen and able seamen was significant, which corresponds with the considerable increase in skill necessary to become an able seaman. Only 2 per cent of able seamen were nineteen or under; young men who had obviously been at sea since childhood. Thirty-five per cent of able seamen were between twenty and twenty-four years old, and again to achieve that amount of skill by such a young age, they must have first gone to sea as teenage boys. Twenty-seven per cent were between twenty-five and twenty-nine years old, making the portion that were less than thirty years old a full 64 per cent. Twenty-one per cent were between thirty and thirty-nine, while 8 per cent were above forty years old. The major difference between able seamen and their ordinary seamen and landsmen counterparts was that significantly more of them were in their late twenties rather than their early twenties. Similarly, as the necessary experience made able seamen noticeably older than ordinary seamen and landsmen, so too petty officers were older than seamen. Less than half (41 per cent) of petty officers were under thirty. Only 1 per cent of petty officers were nineteen or under. Seventeen per cent were twenty to twenty-four years old and 23 per cent were aged twenty-five to twenty-nine. Thirty-two per cent of petty officers were in their thirties, while 12 per cent were in their forties, and 3 per cent were fifty or older.

Nationality of Men in the Royal Navy

English seamen, naturally, dominated the nationality of the lower deck and comprised 51 per cent of all seamen and petty officers. This is not unexpected when considering that all three of the major naval centres, the areas surrounding Chatham, Portsmouth and Plymouth, were deeply rooted in England. Rather surprising was the relatively low number of Irishmen found on the lower deck of British warships. Historians and contemporaries have claimed that in excess of 25 per cent of the men of the lower deck of Royal Navy warships were Irish.[21] Theobald Wolfe Tone, an Irish revolutionary of the 1790s, believed that two-thirds or more of the Royal Navy were Irish.[22] However, this database shows that between 1793 and 1801, only 19 per cent of the men of the lower deck were Irish. A further 10 per cent were Scottish, and only 3 per cent were Welsh. Eight per cent of seamen and petty officers were from outside of the British Isles and marked as foreign,[23] and 9 per cent of seamen and petty officers recorded in this database were marked as having an unknown nationality, either due to the data not having been recorded, or being indecipherable.

Viewing the nationality of the lower deck as it related to the skill of the men has revealed some interesting new facts. Englishmen were represented fairly evenly across the different skill levels, making up approximately half of petty officers (54 per cent), able seamen (52 per cent), ordinary seamen (47 per cent) and landsmen (52 per cent). Welshmen in the Royal Navy were also very stable across the skill ratings of the lower deck, and made up 3 per cent of each of the four ratings. However, this is also an exceptionally small percentage. Although there were no Welsh ports heavily involved in international trade, Bristol was certainly close enough to facilitate Welshmen finding berths for such voyages. Wales, like Ireland, also had a healthy coasting trade, especially across the Bristol Channel with southwest England. Notably, 57 per cent of Welsh seamen and 56 per cent of Welsh petty officers serving in British warships came from the four Welsh counties that bordered the Bristol Channel: Pembrokeshire, Carmarthenshire, Glamorganshire and Monmouthshire.

However, when it comes to Irish and Scottish mariners the ratios are not so stable in regard to skill. The Irish representation was far lower within the highly skilled positions than it was within the unskilled. Irishmen made up about a quarter of landsmen (25 per cent) and ordinary seamen (22 per cent), but made up only 15 per cent of able seamen and only 9 per cent of petty officers. To some extent, this is likely due to the fact that outside the ports of Dublin and Cork, Ireland did not play a large role in international trade, which produced men with deep-sea, square rigged experience – men with the necessary experience and skill to be rated as able seamen or even petty officers. However, Ireland did have a thriving coasting trade, which produced ordinary seamen, who had experience on smaller ships with fore-and-aft

---

[21] Roger A.E. Wells, ed. *Insurrection: The British Experience 1795–1803* (Gloucester: Alan Sutton, 1983), p. 82.

[22] Marianne Elliott, *Partners in Revolution: The United Irishmen and France* (New Haven: Yale University Press, 1982), pp. 331–332.

[23] Note that men from the Isle of Man and the Channel Isles were marked as foreign in the database.

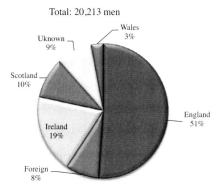

Total: 20,213 men

Figure 2.21 Seamen and petty officer nationality

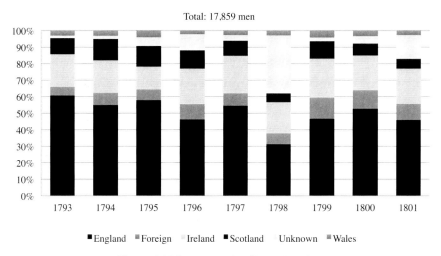

Total: 17,859 men

■England ■Foreign Ireland ■Scotland Unknown ■Wales

Figure 2.22 Seamen nationality, 1793–1801

rigging. Ireland also had a lot of agricultural labourers, and the fact that harvests did not do as well as expected across the British Isles throughout most of the French Revolutionary and Napoleonic Wars meant that there were plenty of young men without enough work to keep themselves housed and fed.

Scottish influence on the lower deck shows a nearly opposite trend to that of the Irish. Scotsmen made up only 7 per cent of landsmen and 9 per cent of ordinary seamen. However, they made up 12 per cent of able seamen and 14 per cent of petty officers. Though the variance in skill and nationality was not as extreme in Scotsmen as it was for Irishmen, it still represents a significant change, as the percentage of Scottish petty officers is double that of Scottish landsmen.

Foreign men also followed a trend similar to that of Scotsmen. Foreigners made up only 5 per cent of landsmen; however they made up 9 per cent of ordinary seamen, 11 per cent of able seamen, and 8 per cent of petty officers. The lower number of foreign landsmen can be easily explained by the fact that the Royal Navy did not actively recruit men in foreign countries. So naturally, fewer foreign landsmen made their way into British naval service. Additionally, the Navy had no need of more unskilled men, as plenty of men without experience at sea could be found across the British Isles, but rather they actively sought skilled men. The increased representation of foreigners amongst ordinary and able seamen was due to international trade. Experienced foreign seamen were found on trading vessels that called at the same British ports as domestic merchant ships, and such places were naturally the focus of British recruiting efforts. Further, foreign seamen were often found on British merchant ships, especially during times of war. The international nature of the sea trade meant that seamen, regardless of their nationality, found berths aboard whatever ships they could. Thus, any foreign seamen inclined toward British naval service had ample opportunity to volunteer. The drop in foreign petty officers is noticeable, and to some degree inexplicable at present. Though, as petty officers were in charge of much of the work on the lower deck, it is logical that the officers who rated men as petty officers, based on skill, trust and language skill, were more likely to rate British seamen as petty officers than foreigners. However, before such conclusions can be drawn, we need a more detailed study of foreigners in the Royal Navy.

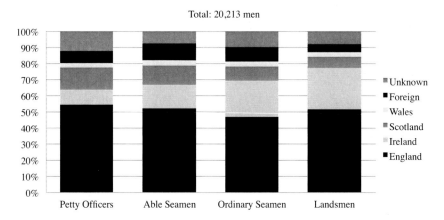

Figure 2.23 Seamen and petty officer rating and nationality

The statistics of nationalities recruited in each port also show how geography played a role in naval recruiting. English seamen, 9,044 of whom were included in this database, were evenly spread between the three major naval centres, as close to a third entered ships commissioned at each: Chatham (34 per cent), Portsmouth (36 per cent), and Plymouth (30 per cent). Similarly, of the 1,281 English petty officers in this sample, about a third entered ships in each: Chatham (32 per cent), Portsmouth (34 per cent), and Plymouth (34 per cent). This comes as no surprise as all three are English ports. However, the ratios are not so even for other nationalities. Irish and Welsh seamen and petty officers disproportionately joined ships commissioned at Plymouth. Forty-five per cent of Irish seamen, and 41 per cent of Irish petty officers joined ships commissioned at Plymouth, whereas only 21 per cent and 24 per cent of Irish seamen and petty officers joined ships at Chatham, and only 34 and 35 per cent respectively joined ships out of Portsmouth. Welsh seamen and petty officers display similar statistics. Fifty-three per cent of Welsh seamen and 41 per cent of Welsh petty officers in the Royal Navy entered ships at Plymouth; 29 per cent of Welsh seamen and 33 per cent of petty officers joined ships at Portsmouth; and only 18 per cent of Welsh seamen and 26 per cent of Welsh petty officers joined ships at Chatham. For both Irish and Welsh seamen, a geographic trend is clearly seen, and resulted in Plymouth receiving the most men from each nationality. Similarly, Chatham ships, which were the furthest away, received the smallest proportion of Irish and Welsh men. Scottish seamen showed a similar but less drastic trend; however it favoured Chatham (37 per cent) over Portsmouth (33 per cent) and Plymouth (30 per cent). Scottish petty officers favoured Portsmouth (39 per cent) over Chatham (35 per cent) and Plymouth (26 per cent).

These statistics show that recruitment feeding into each port was geographically based. More importantly it was based on transportation by sea, which can be seen more clearly with Scottish seamen, who came to Chatham in a slightly higher proportion than to Portsmouth and Plymouth, based on the heavier volume of east coast naval activity and merchant traffic than that of the west coast. Similarly, Irish and Welsh men went to Plymouth in larger volumes than to Portsmouth or Chatham. Essentially, it appears that these men were not moving via road, but in Royal Navy tenders that transported them to the nearest naval port where they entered aboard ships that were manning.[24]

Summation

Examining ships' muster books is crucial to the study of the lower deck of the Royal Navy during the eighteenth century, and as of yet no serious study of naval manning has been completed.[25] However, without computer technology, a serious statistical study of ships' musters would have proved labour-intensive, and further, the results that could have been produced from them would have been limited in comparison to what can be done today. The

---

[24] A case study of naval recruiting in Devon by N.A.M. Rodger, which examined twelve ships commissioned at Plymouth during the American War, found similarly that 24 per cent of petty officers, seamen and idlers found aboard those ships came from Devon. N.A.M. Rodger, 'Devon Men and the Navy, 1689–1815', in *The New Maritime History of Devon*, ed. Michael Duffy *et al.* (London: Conway Maritime Press, 1992), pp. 211–213.

[25] Rodger, *The Command of the Ocean*, p. 442.

Total: 17,859 men

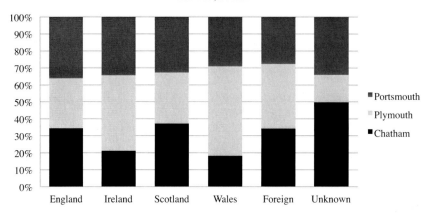

Figure 2.24 Seamen nationality and port

Total: 2,354 men

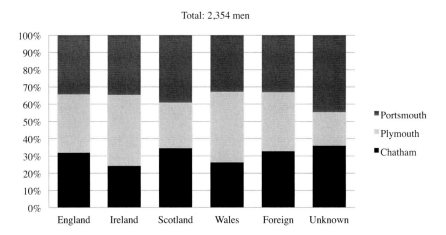

Figure 2.25 Petty officer nationality and port

lack of a statistical study of naval manpower has played havoc with the historiography of the subject, as historians have had to base their conclusions on the opinions of naval officers and civilians as recorded in public debates and private correspondence. The problem with this approach is twofold. First, only the extraordinary was recorded and required any debate, as everyday and mundane events, as happens today, simply were not recorded. Secondly, much of what has been said about naval manning, mainly concerning impressment, came from the politically charged 1830s, when naval manning procedures were vilified in order to support the arguments of radical politicians that dealt with corporal punishment and the treatment of the men serving in naval warships.[26] Most of the historians who dealt with the subject, Michael Lewis and Steven Gradish especially, did exemplary jobs with the information available to them. However, understanding how the Royal Navy manned its warships or who the men of the lower deck actually were without such data is virtually impossible; and this chapter has illuminated the basic statistics that have resulted from a large-scale study of ships' muster books during the French Revolutionary Wars.

Examination of recruiting through statistics exposes the problems found within the historiography, especially when considering the low percentage of men who were impressed, when compared to what history has told us. The extremity of this can be further seen when factoring the recruitment of men who were turned over, which illustrates that approximately four out of five men of the lower deck were in fact there as a result of volunteering, not conscription. Further, we can clearly see that the men of the lower deck were young; seamen were generally in their early twenties and petty officers were in their late twenties or early thirties. More than half of the men were English by birth, and only 19 per cent were Irish. This data calls into question many of the conclusions drawn throughout the historiography, especially those made concerning pressed men. Statistics also draw attention to problems faced by the Royal Navy during its rapid expansion from peacetime to wartime footing, particularly the shortage of petty officers.

The data produced in this chapter only scratches the surface of what can be done with a serious statistical study of the Royal Navy, and further research will certainly produce results that will challenge our current perception of the historiography to date. The significance of statistics to the study of any large group of people is imperative, and with modern computer technology there is little excuse for ignoring the potential of such a study, especially for a social historical subject such as naval manpower where the documentation exists to provide the necessary data. Such data also draw into question how the findings of historians of the past might have changed had they had access to the technology that we do today; and perhaps most of all, it calls for a new social history of the Royal Navy.

[26]   Ibid., p. 492.

3

Volunteers

Your fleet and your trade have so near a relation, and such a mutual influence
upon each other they cannot be well separated; your trade is the mother and
nurse of your seamen; your seamen are the life of your fleet, and your fleet is
the security and protection of your trade, and both together are the wealth,
strength, security and glory of Britain.[1]

Military volunteering during the French Revolutionary and Napoleonic Wars
was likely the greatest popular movement in Georgian Britain.[2] Though Lord
Haversham's quote from the House of Lords is in reference to the strength of
the Royal Navy at the beginning of the eighteenth century, he took the opportunity to specifically mention seamen as the 'life' of the fleet. For the Royal
Navy, seamen were of vital importance for success at sea, and as no formal
system of naval training existed, the vast majority of those men gained their
experience from merchant seafaring. This ensured, as Henry Dundas wrote
in 1800, that 'the present strength and pre-eminence of this country is owing
to the extent of its resources arising from its commerce and its naval power
which are inseparably connected'.[3] The skills required by navy seamen were
virtually identical to those of merchant seamen.[4] There was no way to tell
one from another; there was no distinctiveness between a merchant sailor
and naval seamen. They were simply seamen, who at a given point worked
for one employer or another, whether it be the King's service or a merchant.[5]

---

[1] Spoken in House of Lords by Lord Haversham, 1707, quoted in Linda Colley, *Britons: Forging
the Nation, 1707–1837* (London: Pimlico, 1994), p. 65; P.K. O'Brien and S.L. Engerman, 'Exports
and the Growth of the British Economy from the Glorious Revolution to the Peace of Amiens',
in *Slavery and the Rise of the Atlantic System*, ed. Barbara L. Solow (Cambridge: Cambridge
University Press, 1991), p. 189.

[2] J.E. Cookson, 'The English Volunteer Movement of the French Wars, 1793–1815', *The Historical
Journal* XXXII, no. 4 (1989): p. 867.

[3] H. Dundas, *Memorandum for the Consideration of His Majesty's Ministers*, 31 March 1800, quoted
in John B. Hattendorf *et al.*, eds, *British Naval Documents, 1204–1960*, Publications of the Naval
Records Society (Aldershot: Ashgate, 1993), pp. 344–350.

[4] Usher Jr., 'Royal Navy Impressment', p. 674.

[5] Rodger, *The Wooden World*, p. 113.

Without a large supply of such men, any naval force was disadvantaged.[6] The most severe limitation on every navy was manpower, as it limited the number of ships that could be put into service, even when the ability to construct and support larger numbers of ships existed.[7]

Volunteers were the basic source of manpower for the Navy, just as they were for the Army.[8] These men formed the first and fundamental means of naval manning.[9] It is clear, at least in Britain, that eighteenth-century naval administrators understood that the quickest manner of sending ships to sea was by manning them with skilled and experienced volunteers.[10] Seamen, unlike naval officers whose skills eroded during peacetime, honed their skills in the merchant sea trade, both at times of war and peace.[11] The key to naval manpower was topmen, who formed the youngest, most agile, and highly experienced able seamen.[12] Skilled seamen took years to train, and thus there was no quick way to produce them.[13] Soldiers were certainly not seamen, and could not be trained to be seamen. Even at the time of the Spanish Armada, at the end of the sixteenth century, it had been realised that it was far easier to teach mariners to fight, rather than to teach soldiers to sail.[14] These were the men most sought by the infamous press gangs, and thus getting them to volunteer was doubly advantageous. The Royal Navy did not hire large numbers of foreign men, essentially mercenaries, to fulfil its operational requirements.[15] It did accept foreign volunteers; however these men did not make up large proportions of the fleet and were spread thinly throughout the Navy.

For the Royal Navy, volunteers were exceptionally valuable as the primary source of manpower. The value of volunteers can be seen in the bounties they received. Throughout the French Revolutionary and Napoleonic Wars, the King's bounty for volunteer seamen generally remained the same, £5.0.0 for an able seaman, £2.10.0 for an ordinary seaman, and £1.10.0 for a landsman, each amount representing the skill level expected of the individual. As

---

6   Daniel Baugh, 'Maritime Strength and Atlantic Commerce: The Uses of "a Grand Marine Empire"', in *An Imperial State at War: Britain from 1689 to 1815*, ed. Lawrence Stone (London: Routledge, 1994), p. 186.

7   N.A.M. Rodger, 'Mobilizing Seapower in the Eighteenth Century', in *Essays in Naval History, from Medieval to Modern*, ed. N.A.M. Rodger (Farnham: Ashgate Publishing, 2009), pp. 4–5.

8   The majority of the ranks of the British Army were filled with volunteers, most of whom were obtained by small parties dispatched to raise men by beat of drum. Alan J. Guy, *Oeconomy and Discipline: Officership and Administration in the British Army 1714–63* (Manchester: Manchester University Press, 1985), p. 123.

9   Rodger, *The Wooden World*, p. 163; Rodger, *The Command of the Ocean*, p. 397.

10 Gradish, 'Wages and Manning', p. 46; Gradish, *The Manning of the British Navy During the Seven Years' War*, p. 70.

11 Mahan, p. 70; Rodger, 'Mobilizing Seapower in the Eighteenth Century', pp. 3–4.

12 Rodger, '"A Little Navy of Your Own Making": Admiral Boscawen and the Cornish Connection in the Royal Navy', p. 83.

13 Rodger, 'Mobilizing Seapower in the Eighteenth Century', p. 4.

14 Geoffrey Callender, *The Naval Side of British History* (London: Christophers, 1925), pp. 63–64.

15 Jeremy Black, *The British Seaborne Empire* (New Haven, Conn.: Yale University Press, 2004), pp. 121–122.

able seamen had more skill and experience and were thus of more value to the Navy, they earned a higher volunteer bounty. However, for the British government, volunteers were worth their bounty. Pressed seamen had to be compelled to serve, and they cost much more as a result of the large administrative mechanisms put into place to seek them out for naval service. Estimates from the eighteenth century claimed that pressed seamen cost the Royal Navy in excess of £20.0.0 each.[16] In his study of British naval administration during the American War, Roland Usher calculated that men pressed by the Impress Service cost nearly £34 each.[17] Further, these men took time to acquire, whereas volunteers sought out opportunities to enter naval service, and did so in vast numbers at the very onset of war.

For Britain to mobilise a sound fleet more quickly than its opponents was advantageous in the early stages of war.[18] Many of the problems facing eighteenth-century navies arose from the fact that they were demobilised during peacetime.[19] The fact that the Royal Navy was demobilised during peacetime meant that it took two or three years to mobilise, more so at the end of the eighteenth century as the British Navy exceeded 120,000 men at the height of the French Revolutionary Wars and 140,000 during the Napoleonic Wars. The greatest cost was missed opportunity, as even a small squadron could cause an enemy immense problems if put to sea before the enemy could deploy an opposing force.[20] With the onset of hostilities, the greatest difficulty facing any eighteenth-century navy was not how to use, but how to realise its naval power.[21] Production of a naval force that inspired the confidence necessary to keep the British public, and importantly seaborne trade, in good standing required volunteering in vast numbers. Volunteers were exceptionally important during the early stages of war, as they helped to speed up mobilisation. In 1755, 13,000 men had joined during the first six weeks of mobilisation, which effectively doubled the peacetime size of the Royal Navy.[22] At the opening of the French Revolutionary Wars, it was hoped that the initial mobilisation would take place with purely volunteer crews, and though recruiting began on 1 December 1792, press warrants were not issued until the following February.[23] The initial mobilisation went relatively easily, and volunteers made up the largest proportions of warship crews.[24] Though

---

[16] Henry Baynham, *From the Lower Deck* (London: Hutchinson & Co., 1969), p. 6.

[17] Roland G. Usher Jr., 'The Civil Administration of the British Navy During the American Revolution' (University of Michigan, 1942), p. 243.

[18] Michael Duffy, *The Younger Pitt* (Harlow: Longman, 2000), p. 169.

[19] Rodger, *The Insatiable Earl: A Life of John Montagu, Fourth Earl of Sandwich, 1718–1792*, p. 62; Rodger, '"A Little Navy of Your Own Making": Admiral Boscawen and the Cornish Connection in the Royal Navy', p. 83.

[20] Rodger, 'Mobilizing Seapower in the Eighteenth Century', p. 9.

[21] Ibid., p. 1.

[22] Richard Middleton, 'Naval Administration in the Age of Pitt and Anson, 1755–1763', in *The British Navy and the Use of Naval Power in the Eighteenth Century*, ed. Jeremy Black and Philip Woodfine (Leicester: Leicester University Press, 1988), p. 110.

[23] Emsley, *British Society and the French Wars, 1793–1815*, p. 34.

[24] Rodger, *The Command of the Ocean*, p. 442.

the pressures of enemy activity and missed opportunity drove the Navy to man quickly, care had to be taken not to destroy merchant trade by draining it of all available manpower, a concept understood by naval administrators.[25]

During wartime, manning was always the most intractable problem faced by the Royal Navy.[26] Between 1793 and 1815, the Royal Navy's manning situation was more serious than it had been during previous wars.[27] For Britain, no prior conflict had approached the scale of mobilisation experienced during the French Revolutionary and Napoleonic Wars. Between 1800 and 1812 in England, Scotland and Wales the number of adult males involved in military service of some form was never less than one in six, and between 1803 and 1805 that proportion swelled to one in five.[28] There were, further, places in Britain where more than a quarter of adult males were serving King and country in one manner or another.[29] This was a substantial increase over the American War, when even at the height of the conflict only about one in eight adult males were involved in military service.[30] However, it is also important to note that throughout the eighteenth century the British population had much less contact with military forces than did other European populations. Though men were recruited in high numbers for military service, British forces, mainly the Army, were not stationed in civilian areas on the same scale as witnessed in the rest of Europe, and needless to say England, Scotland and Wales were not subject to an enemy invasion or occupation during the eighteenth century.[31] Further, even when British civilian populations were exposed to military forces *en masse*, they were protected from military excess by civil law.[32]

The volume of military involvement in Britain, coupled with relatively low contact between the civilian population and military units, added to the value of the naval volunteer. First off, as seamen were a specially sought after class of manpower, it is likely that the ratio of military participation among seamen was higher than one in four throughout the war. This resulted in a supply and demand problem between naval and merchant service which the Admiralty countered with press gangs that sought out skilled seamen, but at great expense. Thus the volunteer was a valued commodity, as it allowed the

[25]   Michael Duffy, ed. *Parameters of British Naval Power, 1650–1850* (Exeter: University of Exeter Press, 1998), p. 7.

[26]   Talbott, p. 22.

[27]   N.A.M. Rodger, 'Shipboard Life in the Georgian Navy, 1750–1800: The Decline of the Old Order?', in *The North Sea: Twelve Essays on Social History of Maritime Labour*, ed. Lewis R. Fischer *et al.* (Stavanger: Stavanger Maritime Museum, 1992), p. 30.

[28]   Linda Colley, 'Whose Nation? Class and National Consciousness in Britain, 1750–1830', *Past and Present*, no. 113 (1986): p. 101.

[29]   Cookson, 'The English Volunteer Movement of the French Wars, 1793–1815', p. 870.

[30]   Conway, 'The Politics of British Military and Naval Mobilization, 1775–83', p. 1180.

[31]   Brewer, p. 46. Note that Spanish forces landed in Scotland in 1719, and French forces repeated the action in 1746. France also landed forces in Wales in 1797; however none of these 'invasion' attempts, which sought to produce popular uprisings, were of a large scale, and needless to say, none were successful.

[32]   Ibid., pp. 47–48.

Royal Navy to expand during mobilisation without further increasing the size and cost of impressment operations. Additionally, as British civilians were not used to heavy or oppressive contact from military forces, the intrusiveness of press gangs, as they searched for seamen, became all the more prominent, causing great social friction. Again, forthcoming volunteers minimised the need for impressment, and though press gangs were commonplace in areas with maritime traffic, they could have been substantially worse, and their inefficiency at gathering men made them a more bearable burden for seamen as well as civilian populations in maritime centres.

Volunteers formed the backbone of an ever-expanding naval force.[33] British naval strategy was based on pushing opponents to peace by outbuilding them in terms of seaborne strength, not a strategy based on expanding empire.[34] The primary concern was destroying French and French allied naval and commercial strength, and this required an immense naval force. Such a force had to be large enough to counter any French naval presence that might threaten invasion or action against British commerce in home waters and over trade routes, while further being powerful enough to take the battle to enemy trade and deny them the ability to utilise overseas wealth and supplies. This became even more prevalent as French forces began to invade and take over other European naval forces that could be used against Britain. To counter this threat the Royal Navy deployed large numbers of warships, which were divided into seven classes or rates based on the numbers of guns carried. First, second and third rate ships formed the line of battle, while fourth, fifth and sixth rate ships took up various duties, from scouting for the fleet and relaying communication to cruising in search of enemy merchant shipping. Finally, smaller 'non-rated' ships, performed many duties, from transporting supplies and men to carrying communications, escorting convoys, and even interdicting enemy shipping. All but sixth rates and non-rated ships were generally of greater than 1,000 tons, with first rates exceeding 3,500 tons. These ships carried immense expanses of canvas in order to drive them as fast as possible before the wind. In comparison, the average East Indiaman was 707 tons, and the average West Indiaman was 233 tons.[35] These ships required skilled men with experience in blue water square rigged Atlantic sailing. Though much larger than merchants, warships required the same skills. Such ships, with their vast size and increased complexity, could not be manned primarily with inexperienced men from land-based trades. Though Britain could claim a dominance of skilled manpower, manning the Royal Navy for war was its most difficult problem, and it seriously affected naval readiness and ability in the early stages of war.[36] Though Britain was able to produce a

[33] Davies, *Gentlemen and Tarpaulins*, p. 69.

[34] Michael Duffy, 'World-Wide War and British Empire, 1793–1815', in *The Oxford History of the British Empire: The Eighteenth Century*, ed. P.J. Marshall (Oxford: Oxford University Press, 1998), pp. 184–191.

[35] Michael Duffy, *Soldiers, Sugar and Seapower: The Expeditions to the West Indies and the War against Revolutionary France* (Oxford: Clarendon Press, 1987), pp. 20–21.

[36] Daniel Baugh, 'The Eighteenth-Century Navy as a National Institution, 1690–1815', in *The Oxford*

very large and effective naval force through most of the eighteenth century, it is important to note that it was not until the very end of the seventeenth century that England could stand behind its 'wooden walls' as a confident defence.[37] By the eighteenth century, however, it was in the area of skilled sea labour that Britain had its most marked advantage over its continental counterparts.[38] It is important to remember that seamen, though professional sailors, could not be considered professional fighters until they had spent some time aboard a warship.[39]

Manning Problems throughout Europe

Britain was not alone in its struggle for naval manpower; rather it was a problem that affected all nations that fielded large wartime fleets. The French Navy also suffered manning problems, and with the opening of the French Revolutionary Wars, they could not have manned a fleet of eighty or more capital ships, even if they had that ability to construct them. For France, this was not just a problem of naval expansion during the 1780s, but one that had been constant throughout the eighteenth century.[40] After Trafalgar, Napoleon was able to rebuild the French fleets, and by 1809 the Toulon fleet was nearly as large as the British fleet blockading the port; however it was crippled by a lack of skilled manpower.[41] The French *Inscription Maritime* enrolled seamen into a system that rather than being fair and rotating men through naval service, simply turned into a more repressive form of conscription during wartime that took in every mariner they could possibly find.[42] The advantage of the system was quick mobilisation, as with the onset of war French naval authorities simply went through the list and recruited all of the men on it.[43] Relatively quick French mobilisation and the remoteness of the Toulon Squadron from Britain meant that during the initial months of three successive wars, in 1740, 1756 and 1778, the Toulon Squadron proved a French wild card that could be played almost anywhere in the world, and remained virtually unchecked by the British.[44]

In the 1790s, French recruitment legislation provoked attacks on the gendarmes and officials responsible for its introduction, as well as sparking

---

Illustrated History of the Royal Navy, ed. J.R. Hill and Bryan Ranft (Oxford: Oxford University Press, 1995; reprint, 2002), p. 133.

[37] Brewer, p. 10.

[38] Black, *Naval Power: A History of Warfare and the Sea from 1500*, p. 104; Harding, p. 138; A.T. Mahan, *The Influence of Sea Power Upon History, 1660–1783* (Gretna: Penguin Publishing Company, 2003), pp. 45–46.

[39] Glete, p. 174.

[40] William S. Cormack, *Revolution and Political Conflict in the French Navy, 1789–1794* (Cambridge: Cambridge University Press, 1995), p. 24; Harding, p. 137.

[41] Black, *The British Seaborne Empire*, p. 155.

[42] Lloyd, *The British Seaman, 1200–1860*, p. 175.

[43] Ibid.

[44] N.A.M. Rodger, 'Sea-Power and Empire, 1688–1793', in *The Oxford History of the British Empire: Vol. 2, The Eighteenth Century*, ed. P.J. Marshall (Oxford: Oxford University Press, 1998), p. 177.

off uprisings in Brittany and the Vendée.[45] It seems the major problem for the French Navy, in getting volunteers as well as making the *Inscription Maritime* work, was not one of naval administration, but of uncertain finances. The French Navy constantly had problems paying its crews and therefore French seamen did what they could to avoid naval service.[46] Though crippled by a lack of manpower, many French officers and administrators sympathised with the men and hardly felt that the full weight of punishment could be imposed for desertion if seamen did not get regular pay.[47] However, France's naval manpower problem did not come solely from recruitment and retention. Further loss of manpower to the British in the form of casualties and men taken prisoner was devastating. At the Battle of the Glorious First of June, in 1794, France lost over 5,000 men to the British, as both casualties and prisoners.[48] Much of the problem that France faced was due to a basic shortage of seamen, in part due to the fact that though French trade had greatly increased over the eighteenth century, it was largely carried out in foreign ships.[49] Though faster to man ships during the outset of war, France did not have as many seamen to draw from as Britain, and in wartime the Royal Navy could always commission more ships.[50] The result was that France looked to overcome its naval shortcomings by coercing other continental powers to add their fleets and overseas bases to the French war effort.[51]

Spain also faced naval recruitment problems throughout the eighteenth century, and saw the advantage of voluntary recruitment in naval manning.[52] Like France, Spain had a similar system of maritime inscription, where men who worked in the merchant and fishing fleets placed their names on a list for military service during times of war. The entire recruitment process in Spain was generally more decentralised in comparison to France, as local authorities were responsible for gathering men for the Navy, though the entire process was directed from the centre.[53] However, like the French system it did nothing to solve the problem of a basic shortage of seamen.[54] During the American War, it is estimated that France had about 46,000

---

[45] Clive Emsley, James Walvin and Gwyn A. Williams, 'The Impact of War and Military Participation on Britain and France', in *Artisans, Peasants and Proletarians, 1760–1860: Essays Presented to Gwyn A. Williams*, ed. Clive Emsley, James Walvin and Gwyn A. Williams (London: Croom Helm Ltd, 1985), p. 68.

[46] Cormack, p. 26.

[47] Ibid., p. 27.

[48] Black, *The British Seaborne Empire*, p. 150.

[49] Adam Smith, *An Inquiry into the Nature and Causes of the Wealth of Nations*, 2nd edn (London: Encyclopaedia Britannica, Inc., 1990), p. 207.

[50] Rodger, 'Mobilizing Seapower in the Eighteenth Century', pp. 5–6.

[51] Duffy, 'World-Wide War and British Empire, 1793–1815', p. 189.

[52] Carla Rahn Phillips, 'The Life Blood of the Navy: Recruiting Sailors in Eighteenth-Century Spain', *The Mariner's Mirror* LXXXVII, no. 4 (2001): p. 421.

[53] Ibid., p. 423.

[54] Rodger, *The Insatiable Earl: A Life of John Montagu, Fourth Earl of Sandwich, 1718–1792*, pp. 62–63; Rodger, 'Mobilizing Seapower in the Eighteenth Century', p. 5.

to 62,000 seamen, while Spain's register listed about 47,000 names.[55] Both France and Spain used systems of register for maritime recruitment; however they could never match the number of British seamen.[56] Though their systems of naval manning were generally based around systems of seamen registration, both nations had administrative problems with enforcing them, not the least of which were to do with paying men for their service. It would seem only logical that both systems actually discouraged volunteers, at least those with the necessary skill, as legally they were required to serve.

A similar look at the Dutch Navy reveals that they manned their fleets by placing embargoes and quotas on merchant shipping. However, they were able to provide a generous wage, and they generally only manned their fleet seasonally, which helped to encourage men into service, as they only served for a few months of the year.[57] The naval manning procedures of other European nations, and how they compare to British manning success, illustrate how the British reliance on volunteer enlistment formed the backbone of Royal Navy success.

British Naval Volunteers and History

Before going into the detail of naval volunteering in Britain, the stage must first be set with discussion of what has been written thus far about volunteers by historians. Modern history has formed a general impression that most of the men of the Royal Navy were virtually kidnapped, and held in such squalid conditions that they were prepared to mutiny against their officers at any given opportunity. This mindset has proven so deep-rooted, that regardless of Britain's impressive record of naval success, both in combat and sea-keeping, the performance of seamen has been left largely unexplained or attributed to officers.[58] After 1815, and the conclusion of the wars of the eighteenth century, naval policy continued to evolve, and naval discipline, particularly flogging, became a political and social target. The spinoff is the literature produced during the 1830s. Much of this came about as a result of the market for books, pamphlets and memoirs that described the Royal Navy and discipline during the French Revolutionary and Napoleonic Wars in lurid terms.[59] The image of a warship as a floating hell, where sadistic officers kept men in appalling conditions, was created by the liberal reformers of the 1830s to support an agenda to abolish impressment and physical punishment.[60] Added to this outlook on naval life was the idea that service in the British Navy offered fewer rewards than privateering and more hardships

---

[55] Knight, *The Pursuit of Victory*, p. 22.
[56] Ibid.
[57] Harding, p. 135.
[58] Baugh, 'The Eighteenth-Century Navy as a National Institution, 1690–1815', p. 133.
[59] Rodger, *The Command of the Ocean*, p. 492.
[60] Andrew D. Lambert, *War at Sea in the Age of Sail, 1650–1850*, Smithsonian History of Warfare (Washington, DC: Smithsonian Books, 2005), p. 49.

than experienced in merchant ships.[61] In their move to abolish impressment, Whig politicians used impressment as a representation of a tyrannical arm of the Crown that encroached upon English liberties.[62] It is also important to note that it was convenient for opponents of impressment to speak of pressed men as if they were all married and had been torn from their families. This gained power for their cause, as it was easier to demand pay and liberties for men with starving families, rather than for drinking sprees ashore. The reality is that the majority of seamen were single and young.[63] The fallout from the post-1815 political and social reform of naval manning has in turn led many historians astray.[64]

John Masefield, a poet not a historian, who wrote on impressment, and described the conditions of the eighteenth-century Royal Navy as a virtual floating dungeon, with the vast majority of crews having been pressed into service completely unwillingly, revived this concept in the early twentieth century.[65] This image was further ingrained into common knowledge by the enduring image of Captain Bligh and the famous mutiny aboard the *Bounty*.[66] During the mid-twentieth century Christopher Lloyd presented the view that the Royal Navy was manned by 'brutal and arbitrary methods', though he defended these practices as the only means of dealing with such a large-scale problem.[67] His work claimed that early during the French Revolutionary and Napoleonic Wars about half of the men recruited would have been volunteers, with the remainder being pressed. He also stated that as war continued and fewer seamen were available, this ratio degraded to about a quarter of the seamen being volunteers and the remaining three-quarters being made up of pressed men.[68] He further presented evidence that contradicted his claims, and stated that at Bristol in 1805, '473 men were raised at a cost of £2,020, but only seventy-eight were pressed'.[69] This ratio is nearly the opposite of his claim that once war was underway three-quarters of recruits were pressed. He also claimed that volunteers in the seventeenth century were plentiful, as long as pay was punctual.[70] Steven Gradish further contributed to the belief that volunteers were few in number by claiming that seamen preferred to work in merchant ships where 'wages were higher, the working conditions safer, the period of employment limited to a single voyage, and they were able to change ships if they chose to do so'.[71] However, it is important to note that

---

61 Pares, 'The Manning of the Navy in the West Indies, 1702–63', p. 36.
62 Timothy Jenks, *Naval Engagements: Patriotism, Cultural Politics, and the Royal Navy, 1793–1815* (Oxford: Oxford University Press, 2006), pp. 37–38.
63 Rodger, *The Wooden World*, p. 78.
64 Rodger, *The Command of the Ocean*, p. 492.
65 J.R. Hutchinson, *The Press-Gang Afloat and Ashore* (London: Eveleigh Nash, 1913), pp. 29–30.
66 Lambert, p. 49.
67 Lloyd, *The British Seaman, 1200–1860*, p. 113.
68 Ibid., p. 196.
69 Ibid., p. 207.
70 Christopher Lloyd, *The Nation and the Navy: A History of Naval Life and Policy* (London: Cresset Press, 1954), p. 54.
71 Gradish, 'Wages and Manning', p. 46.

the claims that wages were higher in merchant ships and that working conditions were safer are both subject to argument. The naval wage was guaranteed and prize money increased the total monetary reward received by seamen in the Royal Navy to compete with merchants. Further, the lack of safe working conditions in warships in comparison to merchants is debatable.

Many other historians have taken similar views. Michael Lewis implied that poor naval conditions kept volunteers away.[72] Henry Baynham's depiction of the lower deck was one where few men were there by choice.[73] Geoffrey Jules Marcus believed that only one-fifth of seamen were volunteers, even though he also stated that in 1803 the ships at Portsmouth and Plymouth were nearly completed with volunteers.[74] Though much of his evidence pointed to a modern view of the Royal Navy, much of Marcus's work seems determined to present a view of the Navy that was popular half a century before he wrote. Jonathan Neale stated that 'no experienced seaman joined willingly' and that they despised the boredom and brutality that came with service on warships.[75] Stanley Bonnett stated that even Lord Nelson could only get 181 volunteers aboard HMS *Victory* at Trafalgar.[76] This however is incorrect and is likely an editorial mistake as there were actually 281 volunteer seamen aboard, along with 208 pressed seamen and 180 whose recruitment was unknown.[77]

Now it is important to state that this work is not suggesting that a long line of bad historians who failed to comprehend the sources has created our modern perception of social history in the Royal Navy. Several major factors have been at work in order to skew the historical view of the subject. As mentioned before, much of the primary source material originated in the years immediately following the Napoleonic Wars and was tainted by political and social influence of a movement to change naval manning policy. In fact the problem of political and social influence upon historians has been prevalent until much more recently than most have assumed. As N.A.M. Rodger stated: 'only in recent years, with the British Empire largely dismantled and the British merchant fleet greatly reduced, has it become possible to study British naval history with less distraction from current policy'.[78] Further, even the more trusted accounts produced by seamen during the eighteenth century describe bad conditions aboard Royal Navy ships. However, their descriptions of bad conditions come mainly from

---

[72] Michael Lewis, *History of the British Navy* (Harmondsworth: Penguin Books, 1957), p. 184.

[73] Baynham, p. 3.

[74] G.J. Marcus, *Heart of Oak: A Survey of British Sea Power in the Georgian Era* (London: Oxford University Press, 1975), p. 100.

[75] Jonathan Neale, *The Cutlass and the Lash: Mutiny and Discipline in Nelson's Navy* (London: Pluto Press, 1985), pp. 10–11.

[76] Stanley Bonnett, *The Price of Admiralty: An Indictment of the Royal Navy, 1805–1966* (London: Robert Hale Ltd, 1968), p. 17.

[77] Pam Ayshford and Derek Ayshford, 'The Ayshford Complete Trafalgar Roll' (Brussels: SEFF, 2004), CD-ROM.

[78] Rodger, 'Sea-Power and Empire, 1688–1793', p. 170.

the time they spent being transported from the point at which they were recruited to a receiving ship, and then the time they spent there until they were entered into a warship. William Spavens described the bad conditions he suffered for thirty-two days while being transported to a ship-of-the-line at the opening of the Seven Years' War.[79] John Stradley wrote briefly of the difficult conditions aboard a tender in the Thames near the Tower of London.[80] Joseph Bates also described similar conditions he experienced immediately after being pressed in 1810.[81] This situation was something faced by many volunteers and pressed men alike, and the only means of avoiding it was being recruited directly by a warship's officers in the close vicinity of the ship itself. Anyone recruited by the Impress Service in an area far away from the major naval bases, such as Scotland, was likely to spend several weeks in cramped dirty conditions aboard a small tender while being transported to a receiving ship and later joining a warship.[82] This experience often produced disorientation and disillusionment in the men that joined, as their first days or weeks in the Royal Navy were likely to be fraught with difficulties and unpleasant conditions.[83] These men chose to describe the conditions they experienced when first entering naval service, not because they were the ordinary conditions they experienced on a day-to-day basis throughout their service, but rather because they were extraordinary, and therefore stood out in comparison to the rest of their experience. This in turn produced a ready trap for anyone looking for firsthand accounts of naval life.

Beyond the relatively rare accounts of naval life written by seamen, there were a vast number of manning pamphlets. Few pamphleteers had a good grasp of the problems involved in naval manning, and their recommendations range 'from the helpful but marginal to the mischievous and fantastic'.[84] These pamphlets also almost always assumed that the number of seamen available for naval service was unrealistically large or virtually unlimited and that there was a shortage of volunteers. This problem was most often attributed to poor naval conditions and a lack of pay for seamen. In an 1802 example of a manning pamphlet, the author, Admiral Philip Patton, called for higher wages and prize rights, along with a pension scheme for petty officers, to get good seamen to join and remain in naval service. He further suggested a registration system or 'society of seamen' that was not unlike the French *Inscription*, where men on the register would volunteer to serve

[79] William Spavens, *Memoirs of a Seafaring Life: The Narrative of William Spavens, Pensioner on the Naval Chest at Chatham*, ed. N.A.M. Rodger (Bath: Folio Society, 2000), p. 27.

[80] Jean Choate, ed. *At Sea under Impressment: Accounts of Involuntary Service Aboard Navy and Pirate Vessels, 1700–1820* (Jefferson, NC: McFarland, 2010), p. 93.

[81] Ibid., pp. 104–105.

[82] Roy Adkins and Lesley Adkins, *Jack Tar: Life in Nelson's Navy* (London: Little, Brown, 2008), pp. 53–54.

[83] Isaac Land, *War, Nationalism, and the British Sailor, 1750–1850* (New York: Palgrave Macmillan, 2009), p. 33.

[84] Rodger, *The Command of the Ocean*, p. 209.

three years at the beginning of any armament.[85] In 1809 Patrick Holland of North Shields suggested that merchant ships should be required to produce men based upon tonnage before they could clear customs when leaving port, and that those men would be volunteers paid from a bounty provided by the merchants.[86] This system was not unlike the Port Quota Act of 1795, which was marginally successful at recruiting men, though most were not skilled seamen. Holland also estimated that at the time there were 180,000 seamen in the merchant service, which when considering that at that time the Royal Navy was almost 145,000 strong may have been a little optimistic. Further, as the Navigation Acts were relaxed during wartime, many of the men in merchant service were foreigners. Granted that, for the most part, foreigners were welcome to volunteer for naval service, they did not make up a large portion of seamen serving in the Royal Navy.

Therefore, it is easy to see why and how historians were driven to conclude that naval conditions for seamen were poor and that they would not readily wish to volunteer for service. Modern research has begun to consider that volunteers made up significant proportions of Royal Navy crews. Notably, N.A.M. Rodger examined five warships commissioned during the Seven Years' War, and concluded that just over 55 per cent of crews were volunteer men, while only 15 per cent were pressed, and 25 per cent were turned over.[87] Richard Harding also considered that as much as 60 per cent of Royal Navy crews could have been volunteers.[88] Roland Usher, in a surprising article published in 1951, implied that two-thirds of the seamen in the Royal Navy were volunteers, while the remaining third were likely pressed.[89] Further, it would seem unlikely that volunteerism in the Royal Navy was so low, when it is evident that the vast majority of British ground forces – the regular Army, the Militia, and the various 'Volunteer' units – were comprised mostly or entirely of volunteers.[90]

There are many myths of sea service that were persistent even during the eighteenth century. For example, it was commonly believed that seamen were so numerous as to be virtually infinite, and such assumptions caused most to believe that Royal Navy recruiting problems came from its unattractiveness.[91] Nearly every commentator overlooked the primary problem of naval recruitment, a shortage of skilled labour, assumed that the supply of seamen was limitless, and therefore focused on attracting men to naval

---

[85] Bromley, 'The British Navy and Its Seamen after 1688', pp. 141–150; Admiral Philip Patton was a well-informed thoughtful critic of naval manning, and subsequently much of what he proposed was implemented over the following fifteen years.

[86] Ibid., pp. 153–154.

[87] Rodger, *The Wooden World*, p. 353.

[88] Harding, p. 139.

[89] Usher Jr., 'The Civil Administration of the British Navy During the American Revolution', p. 240; Usher Jr., 'Royal Navy Impressment', pp. 678–679.

[90] Clive Emsley, 'Behind the Wooden Walls: The British Defences against Invasion, 1803–1805', in *A Great and Glorious Victory: New Perspectives on the Battle of Trafalgar*, ed. Richard Harding (Barnsley: Seaforth Publishing, 2008), pp. 81–83.

[91] Rodger, *The Wooden World*, pp. 148–149, 183.

service.[92] Such claims in source material led Hutchinson, for one, to claim that there were 'hundreds of thousands of persons using the sea'.[93] Many others had unrealistic ideas as to how many men used the sea and believed that the necessary number could be found if the Navy searched with enough enthusiasm.[94] In reality there were never enough seamen to man the Royal Navy along with the merchant and fishing fleets, as well as privateers, during wartime.[95] Records from the Sixpenny Office illustrate that prior to the Seven Years' War, there were about 34,000 seamen in foreign and coastal trade and just over 10,000 serving in the Royal Navy. However, by 1760, the Navy employed over 85,000 men and the merchant service had grown to over 36,000 men, showing a deficit of nearly 80,000 seamen, which should have explained sufficiently the Royal Navy's recruiting dilemma. Even including men in the fisheries, the demand exceeded supply by more than two to one.[96]

Nicholas Rogers stated that many magistrates were reluctant to back press warrants because they felt that the Royal Navy could get enough volunteers if they improved conditions and bounties.[97] The belief that conditions of service in British warships were so severe derives from multiple factors. First, the fact that most men who viewed the sea services did so from shore, and therefore saw seamen only out of their element, and very often either in the act of spending their hard earned money, often on alcohol and women, or after having spent their pay and looking for work.[98] In neither case were seamen observed in their vocation, exercising skills that took as many years to acquire as did those of artisans. Second, the major hardship faced by seamen in naval service was the lack of periodical leave, which, from the point of view of the lower deck, was unnecessary.[99] Some captains did allow such leave, gaining them the trust of their men; however in the big picture this may have been to the detriment of the service as a whole. As word of such deeds travelled fast in a fleet, such action may have produced resentment in ships that were not so lucky. Further exacerbating this problem was the fact that extraordinary happenings ended up being recorded and subsequently used by historians, while commonplace events generally went unrecorded.[100] Finally, it is also important to consider that in competition for funding from Parliament, it did not always benefit government officers to produce accurate figures; impressive ones stood the chance of gaining them access to more resources.

[92] Rodger, *The Command of the Ocean*, p. 209.
[93] Hutchinson, p. 20.
[94] Earle, *Sailors: English Merchant Seamen, 1650–1775*, p. 187.
[95] Peter Padfield, *Maritime Supremacy and the Opening of the Western Mind* (New York: The Overlook Press, 1999), p. 184.
[96] Starkey, 'War and the Market for Seafarers in Britain, 1736–1792', p. 40; Rodger, *The Wooden World*, p. 149.
[97] Nicholas Rogers, 'Impressment and the Law in Eighteenth-Century Britain', in *Law, Crime and English Society*, ed. Norma Laundau (Cambridge: Cambridge University Press, 2002), p. 78.
[98] Palmer and Williams, p. 111.
[99] Rodger, *The Command of the Ocean*, p. 499.
[100] Ibid., p. 212.

The contemporary and current belief that volunteers were a minority within the Royal Navy results from the aforementioned issues. The virtually universal belief that skilled seamen were a plentiful and nearly inexhaustible resource, combined with the land-based belief of poor conditions aboard warships, and the nearly constant presence of impressment during wartime, made it nearly illogical to believe that volunteers made up a large percentage of the lower deck, let alone half or more. However, the key problem was that the wartime demand for seamen greatly exceeded the supply available during peacetime, and further the skills required by seamen took years to learn and therefore such men could not be produced quickly.[101] It is important to note that during peacetime the Royal Navy had little trouble with recruiting the necessary numbers of seamen it needed through volunteering.[102] As this chapter will explain, volunteers were not the rarity that history has portrayed them to be, and in fact made up large portions of eighteenth-century naval crews.

How Many British Seamen?

It is clear from data gathered in Royal Navy muster books that the percentage of volunteers recruited into service changed from year to year throughout the war.[103] As is expected, the first year of war, 1793, had the highest percentage of volunteers recruited. Of seamen found aboard ships that commissioned in 1793, over three-quarters (77 per cent) were new volunteers. Nearly half (45 per cent) of the volunteers in the opening year of the war were able seamen or petty officers. Such a large volume of volunteers shows the patriotic zeal that drew many seamen to naval service. This is especially true, as many of the highly skilled seamen would have been away from Britain on trading voyages when war broke out, of whom many may not have returned until the following year, especially those away on the East India trade.[104] Perceived problems with the Royal Navy served to repel volunteers, and included low pay and length of service,[105] as well as the odious character that impressment placed on the Navy as a whole.[106] However, regardless of these problems, volunteers came forward in large numbers.

Throughout the eighteenth century, wartime competition for seamen was severe and the expansion of both the Royal Navy and the merchant service toward the end of the century only heightened the demand for manpower. The increased demand for seamen translated into competition for volunteers. No matter how many press gangs the Royal Navy employed to find seamen, it was clear that volunteers were the most effective way to man ships. However,

---

[101] Ibid., p. 209.
[102] Rodger, *The Wooden World*, p. 154.
[103] See Figure 3.3.
[104] Glete, p. 174.
[105] Gradish, 'Wages and Manning', p. 65.
[106] Rodger, *The Wooden World*, p. 151.

merchant ship masters, as they had no means of conscripting men, also had to rely on volunteers, and this produced ferocious competition for manpower.

The basis behind this competition was the limited number of men available to employ aboard both merchant and naval ships. In 1792, a Board of Trade report listed the total number of seamen in Britain as 118,000.[107] These numbers must be understood to be estimates, as there was no system of registration or manner of census at the time to provide any solid data.[108] However, this figure does show substantial growth over the eighteenth century, as there were approximately 50,000 seamen employed in Britain in 1700.[109] N.A.M. Rodger estimated that in 1702 there were approximately 40,000 deep-sea seamen in Britain, about 12,000 of whom sailed out of London.[110] Effectively, it appears that the number of seamen in Britain more than doubled over the course of the century. Data derived from the accounts of the Sixpenny Office, which took sixpence from each sailor's monthly pay for the Greenwich Hospital, show that incoming funding from sailors' wages tripled between 1707 and 1807.[111] However, accounts from the Sixpenny Office must be understood before they are used for estimating the number of working sailors in Britain, as they can be misleading. Such a large increase may not be solely due to more men working at sea; some of it may be due to the fact that sailors worked more often, especially during wartime; and further increases may be the result of fewer sailors being able to cheat the system as the century progressed. Tonnage estimates for the period are equally deceptive. Though tonnage went up drastically over the eighteenth century, the number of seamen needed to man ships declined. In 1680, merchant ships sailed with a manpower ratio of about one seaman for every seven tons burthen.[112] By 1773 this had changed to about one seaman per every eleven tons. This was effectively a crew reduction of one-third, so while a 200-ton ship in 1680 would have averaged about twenty-eight men, by the 1770s a ship of similar tonnage would have only needed a crew of eighteen.[113] Though it is difficult to pinpoint the exact number of seamen in Britain during the eighteenth century, it is clear that the number of seamen employed in the peacetime British merchant trade increased dramatically during the eighteenth century.

Though the data available from which to derive the number of seamen in Britain are difficult to interpret, several historians have given estimates for the number of seamen in Britain at the end of the eighteenth century. Michael

---

[107] Michael Duffy, 'The Foundations of British Naval Power', in *The Military Revolution and the State, 1500–1800*, ed. Michael Duffy (Exeter: University of Exeter Press, 1980), p. 67.

[108] Starkey, 'War and the Market for Seafarers in Britain, 1736–1792', pp. 27–28.

[109] Earle, 'English Sailors, 1570–1775', p. 92.

[110] Rodger, *The Command of the Ocean*, p. 206.

[111] Lloyd, *The British Seaman, 1200–1860*, p. 117.

[112] Note that tons burthened does not equate to the modern concept of displacement tonnage. Tons burthened is best compared to the modern tons deadweight, as it is a notional representation of the weight of cargo.

[113] Earle, 'English Sailors, 1570–1775', p. 76.

Duffy used the 1792 Board of Trade estimate of 118,000 seamen.[114] David Starkey and Christopher Lloyd both gave lower estimates of seamen in 1792. Starkey suggested that Britain had approximately 96,000 seaman employed in foreign and coastal trade as well as inland navigation and the peacetime Royal Navy.[115] Lloyd claimed 87,569 seamen in 1792 and 105,037 in 1800.[116] Peter Earl doubted that the number of seamen in Britain exceeded 70,000 at any point during the eighteenth century.[117] However, it is important to bear in mind that all of the estimates given by historians for the number of seamen in Britain during the eighteenth century are at best educated guesswork.[118]

Many problems arise when trying to assess the available data concerning British merchant seamen. In contrast to naval data, which is abundant to the point of overwhelming, figures that could be used to estimate the number of seamen in Britain during the eighteenth century are difficult to find. The records that do exist, such as figures from the payment of Seamen's Sixpences, are difficult to interpret and leave many open ends as to reliable calculations.[119] There were many men who went to sea irregularly, making occasional voyages and taking land-based jobs in the intervals, and thus Sixpence figures are not trustworthy, as using these figures directly assumes that all seamen worked all of the time.[120] Sixpence figures do suggest that at least 50,000 to 60,000 men were involved in the fisheries and coasting trade in 1790.[121] Further, fishing vessels and coasters were largely off limits to impressment,[122] meaning that the resource could only be tapped by recruiting volunteers. Estimates of ship tonnage suffer similarly, as they also assumed that all seamen worked all of the time, and further that ships were active and fully crewed all of the time.[123]

There was no doubt among contemporaries during the eighteenth century that naval power was directly connected to the size and prosperity of the merchant marine.[124] It is clear, though, that British merchant sea trade was growing throughout the eighteenth century,[125] and it was no coincidence that Britain possessed both the largest trading fleet and could put to sea the most powerful navy.[126] This was the result of a shift in the sixteenth and seventeenth centuries from continental military expeditions,

---

[114] Duffy, ed. *Parameters of British Naval Power, 1650–1850*, p. 7.

[115] Starkey, 'Quantifying British Seafarers, 1789–1828', p. 102.

[116] Lloyd, *The British Seaman, 1200–1860*, p. 285.

[117] Earle, 'English Sailors, 1570–1775', p. 78.

[118] Palmer and Williams, pp. 101–102.

[119] Ibid., p. 99.

[120] Ehrman, p. 111.

[121] Palmer and Williams, p. 100.

[122] Dwight E. Robinson, 'Secret of British Power in the Age of Sail: Admiralty Records of the Coasting Fleet', *The American Neptune* XLVIII, no. 1 (1988): pp. 5–6.

[123] Palmer and Williams, p. 99.

[124] Duffy, *Soldiers, Sugar and Seapower: The Expeditions to the West Indies and the War against Revolutionary France*, p. 20.

[125] Starkey, 'War and the Market for Seafarers in Britain, 1736–1792', p. 28.

[126] Earle, 'English Sailors, 1570–1775', p. 91.

toward a military policy based around commercial expansion and economic prosperity.[127] This was a luxury not available to the continental powers, which had to devote the bulk of their military power to defending land borders.[128] This is reflected in the rapid growth of the Royal Navy between the mid-seventeenth and the mid-eighteenth centuries.[129] However, the main difficulty lay in the fact that, though more seamen were being trained as a result of growing merchant sea trade, both the Navy and merchants drew men from a common pool.[130] The size of this pool was dictated by peacetime demands of the merchant trade, as men had no incentive to learn skills for which they could not find work.[131]

Competition for Seamen

One of the difficulties in understanding the competition for seamen, especially when it comes to the motivations for volunteering, has been the reluctance of many historians to engage the subject beyond the realms of pay. Though the monetary sum received for services rendered was then, and is today, one of the major factors in motivating an individual to take up a particular job, it did not stand alone. To properly understand the competition for seamen, as well as their motivations for volunteering for naval service, one must not think of pay as the only form of reward for service, but rather think in terms of overall compensation. With the exception of pay, the disadvantages found in the Royal Navy during wartime were largely indicative of sea service as a whole, and therefore experienced by virtually all seamen, regardless of their employer.[132]

Merchant sea trade had grown consistently throughout the eighteenth century, increasing the number of seamen in Britain, but also increasing the number required to keep merchant sea trade operating at full capacity.[133] By the end of the eighteenth century Britain had the largest trading fleet in the Atlantic.[134] From the mid-seventeenth century to the mid-eighteenth century, merchant peacetime wages remained remarkably stable, with twenty-four shillings being the average monthly pay before 1700, rising to a twenty-five-shilling average by 1750, an increase of only 4 per cent over more than half a century.[135] The lack of significant change in wages to attract seamen

---

[127] Brewer, p. 12.

[128] Black, *The British Seaborne Empire*, p. 121; Brewer, pp. 33–34.

[129] Brewer, pp. 33–34.

[130] Usher Jr., 'Royal Navy Impressment', p. 680.

[131] Harding, p. 135; Rodger, 'Mobilizing Seapower in the Eighteenth Century', p. 4.

[132] Usher Jr., 'Royal Navy Impressment', p. 687.

[133] Knight, *The Pursuit of Victory*, p. 22.

[134] Earle, 'English Sailors, 1570–1775', p. 91.

[135] Charles P. Kindleberter, *Mariners and Markets* (Hertfordshire: Harvester Wheatsheaf, 1992), p. 25; Ralph Davis, *The Rise of the English Shipping Industry in the Seventeenth and Eighteenth Centuries*, 2nd edn (Newton Abbot: David and Charles, 1972), p. 137; Earle, 'English Sailors, 1570–1775', p. 83.; Note that this is the *average* merchant pay as calculated by Ralph Davis. Pay for merchant ships varied between ports, trades, and often came in different forms, such as payment in kind, trading rights, shares and advances, and often in different currencies.

suggests that in peacetime the supply and demand for seamen was generally in equilibrium.[136] Steady pay, combined with increased shipping, implies that the number of seamen available to peacetime merchant ships rose steady alongside the trade.[137] Many coasting trades paid by the voyage, such as the coal trade on the Tyne, which in 1792 paid forty-one shillings for a voyage that generally lasted six to eight weeks depending on the weather.[138] The frequency of war and the continuous expansion of the Royal Navy along with each progressive conflict probably created a virtuous circle, where wartime demand produced seamen from unskilled landsmen, and created an excess of skilled men in the post-war market.[139] Such an increase in the supply of skilled seamen meant that many such men were forced to find work on land upon the conclusion of a conflict. This was a problem faced by Ashley Bowen, a seaman born in colonial Massachusetts, who spent long periods of time ashore for lack of employment at sea.[140] Notably, higher wages were paid in the colonies for seamen, four to five shillings more each month in the mid-eighteenth century, which points to fewer seamen being available for merchant employment.[141] However, in peacetime Britain, there were enough seamen to fulfil the labour demands for the merchant sea trade and the Royal Navy.

In wartime however this changed completely. Unlike soldiers, seamen were highly valued on both the military and civilian market.[142] Wartime wages were the main draw for men into the merchant service during the eighteenth century. Wartime merchant wages were often double or occasionally even triple peacetime merchant wages and naval wages, rising to fifty shillings or even as high as seventy shillings.[143] Though these wages were very high, they cannot be taken simply at face value. One of the disadvantages of merchant service was that damage to cargo or the ship was often deducted from the wages of the crew, regardless of the cause of damage, and this often amounted to 10 per cent or more of their wage for the entire voyage.[144] Such situations resulted in grievances between sailors and merchant ship owners. Sailors fought this process by the creation of seamen's boxes, as happened in northeast England in the 1790s.[145] These were essentially precursors to trade or labour unions. There were also many strikes by seamen in the merchant

[136] Starkey, 'War and the Market for Seafarers in Britain, 1736–1792', pp. 29–30.
[137] Harding, p. 138.
[138] Norman McCord and David E. Brewster, 'Some Labour Troubles of the 1790s in North East England', *International Review of Social History* XIII (1968): p. 367.
[139] Harding, pp. 138–139.
[140] Daniel Vickers and Vince Walsh, *Young Men and the Sea: Yankee Seafarers in the Age of Sail* (New Haven, Conn.: Yale University Press, 2005), pp. 99–103.
[141] Ibid., pp. 81–83.
[142] Glete, p. 173.
[143] Earle, 'English Sailors, 1570–1775', p. 84.
[144] Davis, *The Rise of the English Shipping Industry in the Seventeenth and Eighteenth Centuries*, pp. 145–146.
[145] Karel Davids, 'Seamen's Organizations and Social Protest in Europe, 1300–1825', in *Before the Unions: Wage Earners and Collective Action in Europe, 1300–1850*, ed. Catharina Lis, Jan Lucassen

trade throughout the eighteenth century, the frequency of which was on the rise toward the end of the eighteenth century.[146] These measures demonstrate that although merchant pay was high during wartime, employment with merchant shipping was not the pleasant experience that many historians have made it out to be. There were certainly many men who walked away from long voyages with far less than they had anticipated after having spent many hard months at work.

Privateers also competed for seamen, and while there were not nearly as many privateer berths to be had as there were in merchant or naval ships, the lure of prize money certainly captivated many men. Pay and prize distribution rates aboard privateers were much flatter than in the Royal Navy, which meant that the difference in the percentage that seamen received in comparison to the officers was not as great as in the Royal Navy.[147] However, the owners of the vessel took between a third and half of the prize value, and further deductions went to fees and the commander, leaving about 32 per cent to be divided up amongst the crew.[148] Calculations by N.A.M. Rodger for the Seven Years' War show that the average able seaman in a privateer received about 0.16 per cent of the value of the prize, while an able seaman in a twenty-eight gun frigate would have received about 0.18 per cent.[149] Though the difference between the pay received by the men was less, it did not necessarily equate to more money for the men. Further, many privateers offered no pay at all and men aboard were often entirely reliant upon capturing enemy vessels before receiving any compensation. Thus, embarking on such work was, on some level, a gamble, as an unsuccessful cruise could last for weeks with nothing to show for it at the end.

Privateering was generally most popular at the opening stages of a war, as there were fewer British warships at sea competing for prizes, as well as fewer enemy warships protecting their own merchants. Further, there were more enemy merchants available to be taken. Unlike warships, privateers were often speedily converted from merchants and could be at sea very quickly once war was declared, particularly if said declaration had been anticipated. For Britain, privateers proved an effective way to quickly wage war against enemy trade while not expending precious naval resources. However, privateer numbers tended to drop off rapidly after the first year of warfare. David Starkey demonstrated this with data from the Seven Years' War, where the number of privateers dropped sharply from 11,000 men in 1757 to 5,000 in 1758.[150] Therefore, although privateers were certainly present and competed for men, this competition declined as war progressed. For seamen,

---

and Hugo Soly, International Review of Social History (Cambridge: Cambridge University Press, 1994), p. 163.

[146] Ibid., p. 158.

[147] Daniel K. Benjamin and Christopher Thornberg, 'Organization and Incentives in the Age of Sail', *Explorations in Economic History*, no. 44 (2007): p. 339.

[148] Rodger, *The Wooden World*, pp. 128–129.

[149] Ibid., pp. 128–130.

[150] Starkey, 'War and the Market for Seafarers in Britain, 1736–1792', p. 32.

working aboard a privateer allowed for the possibility to earn a year's wage or even become wealthy in exchange for an afternoon's work. However, it was also just as or even more likely that they would return to port empty-handed, especially as a conflict continued and the number of enemy merchant ships decreased while the number of British warships competing for those prizes increased.

For the Royal Navy, competing for volunteers was very different than for merchants and privateers, for both of whom the major draw for men was monetary. The pay for seamen in the Royal Navy was fixed and unlike merchants did not rise during wartime. One disadvantage to this system was the lack of change. Pay in the Royal Navy did not change for nearly 150 years, from 1649 until 1797, while at the same time the price of living had risen nearly 30 per cent.[151] As mentioned above, merchant pay during peacetime had changed very little over the same period of time, and certainly fell below the rate of inflation. Ultimately, it was the great mutinies of 1797 that began the process of reforming pay for men in the Royal Navy; however for the first half of the French Revolutionary Wars no such pressure existed. Regardless, though naval pay was not as high as merchant pay during wartime nor as high as the possible income gained from privateering, it was certainly guaranteed. Merchant pay could be cut down due to many reasons, such as damaged cargo or medical attention for injury, and merchant masters and owners were certainly motivated to save as much as possible in labour expenses. Further, privateers offered the very realistic possibility of no pay at all.

Throughout the second half of the seventeenth and the first two decades of the eighteenth century, pay for Royal Navy seamen was often seriously in arrears, even sometimes years behind.[152] The Navy was often seriously in debt during wartime and available funds had to be prioritised. Shipbuilding and victualling were considered a higher priority than paying seamen. Over the course of the eighteenth century this improved, and the Naval Act of 1758 helped to establish a regular method of payment and bound the Navy Board to spend money intended for wages for those purposes only.[153] One clause of the Act ensured that volunteers received two months' wages in advance, upon boarding an active warship,[154] and that men were paid from the day they were recruited, rather than from when they joined an active ship for service.[155] Men were often recruited and spent several weeks aboard receiving ships

---

[151] Callender, pp. 186–187. Note that between 1700 and 1765 the price of living decreased, and it only increased marginally between 1763 and 1793, after which it rose rapidly through 1815. The value of wages against the cost of living dropped with the opening of the French Revolutionary Wars, and did not reach the 1793 level again until the 1820s. Helen MacFarlane and Paul Mortimer-Lee, 'Inflation over 300 Years', *Bank of England Quarterly Bulletin*, May (1994): pp. 157–158.

[152] Pares, 'The Manning of the Navy in the West Indies, 1702–63', p. 38. After 1715 seamen's pay was generally kept up to date; however the Royal Navy normally only paid at the end of a ship's 'voyage' or commission when a ship was 'paid off'. This should not be confused with withheld pay, in the sense that it was during the seventeenth century.

[153] Gradish, 'Wages and Manning', p. 48.

[154] Ibid., pp. 56–57; Gradish, *The Manning of the British Navy During the Seven Years' War*, p. 99.

[155] Gradish, *The Manning of the British Navy During the Seven Years' War*, pp. 99–100.

before joining an active warship in the fleet, and prior to the Naval Act of 1758 they were not paid for this time, which in turn did not help recruitment. However, seamen already serving were the major beneficiaries of the Act, and it never encouraged as many volunteers as was expected.[156] In the end, the Act fell short of its optimal capability; though Parliament enacted the Bill, they never produced enough funds to take it to its full capability, and they failed to enforce the monetary benefit so that funds allocated for wages were used solely for that purpose.[157] The main cause behind the Naval Act of 1758 was the belief that the supply of seamen was limitless and thus Royal Navy recruitment suffered due to the unattractiveness of the service, which in terms of pay, the Act aimed to improve.[158]

Pay for seamen, whether merchant or naval, was greatly affected by the hierarchy aboard ship, a system under which advancement carried greater pay. This is a concept familiar in modern times, but during the eighteenth century such advancement had few parallels on land for men of lower-class society.[159] Therefore, the quantity paid to the individual was directly linked with the quality of said individual as a seaman, and advancement to higher positions and higher pay was dependent upon performance, allowing seamen chances of advancement that were not available to most common men ashore. When naval pay did change in 1797, it was skilled seamen and petty officers who saw the largest increase in proportion to their previous pay.[160] This was again the case when pay changed in 1807, and in both cases the pay scale became steeper, meaning that promotion for seamen and petty officers came with greater increases in pay.[161] The 1808 revision of the prize system transferred one-third of prize shares (which had previously gone to captains and admirals) to the lower deck, particularly favouring petty officers and leading hands.[162] Such a pay scale served to promote retention and advancement, as advancement granted higher pay and better returns from prize money.

Throughout the seventeenth century and through the mid-eighteenth century, the reputation of a ship's officers, in particular the captain, played a vital role in volunteer recruitment.[163] During these years the Royal Navy generally depended on the officers of individual ships to fulfil the recruiting needs for those vessels. This was a time when prominent officers could obtain a near celebrity status through their exploits at sea, and such status played heavily when recruiting. Officers with a well-known track record of taking prizes and successfully engaging enemy warships drew volunteer seamen, as

---

[156] Gradish, 'Wages and Manning', p. 63; Gradish, *The Manning of the British Navy During the Seven Years' War*, pp. 106–107.

[157] Gradish, 'Wages and Manning', p. 65.

[158] Rodger, *The Wooden World*, pp. 148–149.

[159] Earle, 'English Sailors, 1570–1775', p. 84.

[160] Benjamin and Thornberg, 'Organization and Incentives', p. 331.

[161] Ibid.

[162] Ibid.

[163] Davies, *Gentlemen and Tarpaulins*, pp. 69–70.

such actions directly affected the men aboard financially. Further, ships with officers who were known for fair treatment toward their men, in respect of punishment and expectations, were also favoured by seamen.

Captains recruited volunteer landsmen to help bolster their numbers and, in doing so, often looked to their home districts.[164] This had advantages for both the men and the captain. Landsmen, who were not familiar with the ways of shipboard life, were at a disadvantage, as they did not understand exactly what they were getting into until it was too late to leave. However, if men had some loyalty to the captain, even if it was only being born in the same parish, it gave them some form of familiarity, whereas it would otherwise be completely alien. Naval discipline, as in any military force, took time to become familiar to the men, especially landsmen.[165] William Robinson described the most difficult part as being the fact that he had to take leave of the liberty to speak his mind when he so desired.[166] Such behaviour took some getting used to for the men of the lower deck, and having familiar officers over them allowed this adjustment to be less stressful. For the captains and officers, it provided a ready source of manpower, particularly if they or their family name were well known locally. The small amount of loyalty, no matter how minute, also likely made men less inclined to desert. However, by the mid-eighteenth century recruitment practices were becoming more centralised and carried out more and more by the Impress Service, and thus the reputation of the officers aboard ship began to carry less weight than in previous years. Even during the American War, key naval figures, such as Lord Sandwich, were strongly in favour of traditional recruitment methods, with captains taking the responsibility for manning.[167]

Volunteer Statistics

The importance of volunteers to the Royal Navy can be clearly seen in recruiting statistics taken from eighty-one ships commissioned between 1793 and 1801. After factoring in the recruitment of turned over men,[168] statistical data demonstrates that out of a total of 17,859 seamen and 2,354 petty officers in the survey, 73 per cent of the seamen and 78 per cent of the petty officers were recruited as volunteers.[169] These numbers, however, do not include men recruited as volunteers under the Quota Acts. Boys who joined the fleet voluntarily are not reflected in these statistics, nor does the factoring process attempt to exclude those men whose recruitment could not be determined and were entered into the database as 'unknown'. This number is very low, and makes up only 1 per cent (176 men) of seamen and 8 per cent (194 men)

---

[164] Rodger, *The Wooden World*, p. 155.

[165] Mahan, *The Influence of Sea Power Upon the French Revolution and Empire: 1793–1812*, p. 70.

[166] William Robinson, *Jack Nastyface: Memoirs of an English Seaman* (London: Chatham Publishing, 2002), p. 25.

[167] Rodger, *The Insatiable Earl: A Life of John Montagu, Fourth Earl of Sandwich, 1718–1792*, p. 201; Rodger, *The Command of the Ocean*, p. 398.

[168] See Chapter 2 for an in-depth description of the factoring process.

[169] See Figures 2.9 and 2.10.

of petty officers. The majority of seamen whose recruitment data was illegible came from the year 1801, where it appears that time and storage conditions have been particularly harsh on muster books from that year. However, for each of the other years in the survey, seamen with unknown recruitment made up 2 per cent or less of the sample.

Examining the data spread out over nine years, from 1793 to 1801, reveals how naval recruiting statistics changed as the Royal Navy went from peacetime numbers through to full mobilisation. Figure 2.6 shows recruitment trends without factoring out men turned over, and shows that during the early years of the French Revolutionary Wars volunteer naval recruitment was high. During the opening two years of the war, 1793 and 1794, volunteers accounted for 77 and 57 per cent respectively of total seamen recruitment. During the following two years, 1795 and 1796, volunteer numbers dropped, due to the enactment of the Quota Acts; however they increased again in 1797 to account for 50 per cent of total incoming manpower. It is also notable that the number of men turned over annually did not surpass volunteers aboard Royal Navy ships until 1798, a full five years into the war. When comparing this number to a flow chart of British naval strength, it becomes apparent that the shift from volunteers as the primary source of manning to turned over men coincides with the levelling off of naval growth that occurs in 1798.[170] As British naval growth slowed, turned over men naturally became the primary source of manpower for newly commissioned ships, as they served to keep the Navy at the same size. From 1798 to 1801, men turned over made up the largest portion of manpower aboard British warships and represented 49, 60, 58 and 46 per cent of seamen respectively in those four years, while volunteer numbers fell to 37, 25, 22 and 33 per cent over the same four years.

Factoring out the men turned over in the yearly returns shows a more accurate depiction of the original recruitment of ships' complements.[171] In the case of seamen this shows that ships commissioned in 1793 were manned with about 90 per cent volunteers, while in 1794 this only fell to 88 per cent. The success of the Quota Acts in 1795 caused volunteer numbers to drop to 67 per cent of seamen sampled, though it should be noted that men taken in under the Quota Acts were actually volunteers; however in this sample they have been counted separately. Though the impact of the Quota Acts was highest in 1795, the sheer size of the Royal Navy as it reached full mobilisation put a severe strain on the finite supply of skilled mariners. This meant that impressment played a more significant role, though still a minor form of recruitment in comparison to volunteers. Between 1796 and 1801 volunteers accounted for around 70 per cent of seamen aboard British warships in each year, with 1801 having the lowest ratio at 64 per cent.

Unfactored data for petty officer recruitment illustrates similar trends to those of seamen, and during the opening year of the war approximately 59

---

[170] See Figure 2.3 for naval growth.
[171] See Figure 2.11.

per cent were volunteers while 14 per cent were turned over.[172] However, unlike seamen, the ratio of petty officers who were turned over from previous warships quickly outpaced other forms of recruitment as a source of manpower aboard Royal Navy warships. During the period 1794 to 1796, there was a rise in turned over petty officers, with about half of each of these years' intake having come from other warships. At the same time, the recruitment of fresh volunteer petty officers dropped slowly, accounting for 38 per cent of petty officers in 1794 and 32 per cent in 1796. In 1797 a spike in volunteer petty officers accounted for half of the total. The most likely reason for this sudden increase, which also occurred with seamen, was the changes made to the Royal Navy as a result of the mutinies at Spithead and the Nore. However, in the last four years of the war there was a steep drop in volunteer petty officers, from 36 per cent in 1798 to 17 per cent in 1801. This corresponded with a rise in the proportion of petty officers who were turned over, from 55 per cent in 1798 to a height of 77 per cent in 1800. When compared to non-factored data of seamen recruitment, it quickly becomes apparent that a much higher proportion of petty officers arrived aboard Royal Navy warships as turned over men. However, this is a reasonable claim, as petty officers were promoted from the most experienced seamen, and seamen with previous and proven experience aboard warships were more likely to be promoted to petty officers, and therefore it would be unusual if a smaller percentage of petty officers were turned over in comparison to seamen. Just as with seamen, statistically factoring turned over petty officers to ascertain their likely original recruitment suggests that a large proportion of them were originally volunteers.[173] In fact, in every year of the survey, except 1793 and 1801, volunteers represented more than three-quarters of petty officers aboard British warships, reaching 81 per cent in both 1798 and 1800.

In 1797 there was a significant spike in the number of volunteers for both seamen and petty officers. Examination of the records used in the database shows that the majority of these men joined during the second half of 1797 and early in 1798, in the case of ships that commissioned late in 1797. Therefore, it is reasonable that this increase in volunteer numbers reflects the changes made to the Royal Navy as a result of the mutinies of 1797, at Spithead and the Nore. These changes made naval service more competitive with merchant ships when compared to earlier years. The response of the Royal Navy to the mutinies not only addressed issues raised by seamen aboard warships, but also served to make naval service a more attractive endeavour than it had been in the past. Therefore the number of men volunteering for the Navy increased for a short period of time before settling back into pre-1797 trends. The fact that this volunteer spike lasted only one year suggests that merchants raised their pay to counter the effect of increased naval wages. This lends weight to the claims made by many naval staff and

[172] See Figure 2.7.
[173] See Figure 2.12.

officials who stood against increasing naval pay as an incentive to attract volunteers, because they believed that merchants would immediately match the increase.

In total, out of the entire data sample covered by this database, 8,880 were listed as volunteers in the muster books.[174] Of these volunteers 85 per cent were seamen, 9 per cent were petty officers, 3 per cent were boys, 2 per cent were midshipmen, 1 per cent were idlers, and less than 1 per cent were warrant officers. Further, a category was created as 'Other', to include the odd professions aboard ship that are of little statistic value, as they totalled less than 1 per cent of volunteers. Only seventeen volunteers were listed as 'Other' in this database, and of these men, five had been previously listed as able seamen and two more were previously listed as landsmen before having their position changed to stewards, servants, trumpeters or similar jobs. Warrant officers, commissioned officers and marines rarely had their recruitment listed in muster books. Commissioned and warrant officers were employed full-time by the Royal Navy and thus were not recruited into individual ships as were seamen and petty officers; therefore they were 'recruited' in a different manner. There were two warrant officers listed as volunteers: one was twenty-five year old George Ross of the 74 gun *Minotaur* that commissioned in 1793; the other was twenty-three year old Thomas Wills of the sloop *Wasp* that commissioned in 1801. George Ross was simply listed as the Gunner of HMS *Minotaur*, but was given a £5.0.0 bounty, which suggests that he joined as a volunteer able seaman or petty officer and was promoted into the position immediately. Thomas Wills was promoted from a midshipman to 'Acting Master' of his sloop. Marines, on the other hand, served under a separate shore-based command and were recruited separately from seamen.[175] Marines were then attached to ships' companies, the number of marines depending on the size of the ship.

The 85 per cent of volunteers listed as seamen in this sample equates to a raw number of 7,572 men. Of these seamen just over 10 per cent, or 758 men, listed London or one of the parishes dominated by London as their place of birth. Immediately behind the greater London area, came the English county of Devon and the Irish county of Dublin, from which 487 and 430 men volunteered respectively. In both cases, the counties accounted for about 6 per cent of total volunteers. Following these were the Irish county of Cork, from which 4 per cent or 328 volunteers originated, and the English counties of Kent, with 229 volunteer seamen, and Cornwall, with 190, both accounting for 3 per cent of the total volunteer seamen covered in this sample. Clearly, the leading counties from which seamen volunteered for naval service had connections with the sea.

Of the 8,336 men listed as volunteer seamen and petty officers in this data sample, 9 per cent were rated as petty officers, 28 per cent were able seamen,

---

[174] See Figure 3.7.
[175] Britt Zerbe, *The Birth of the Royal Marines, 1664–1802* (Woodbridge: The Boydell Press, 2013), pp. 73–87.

Volunteers

Total: 8,880 men

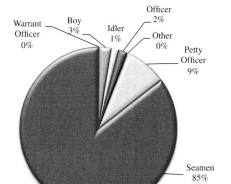

Total: 8,336 men

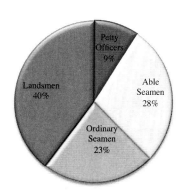

Figure 3.1 Volunteer breakdown

Figure 3.2 Volunteer seamen and petty officer skill

23 per cent were ordinary seamen, and 40 per cent were unskilled landsmen. The high percentage of landsmen volunteers demonstrates the attractiveness of the Royal Navy to unskilled men such as labourers. The ratio of skilled volunteers, petty officers, able seamen and ordinary seamen to unskilled volunteer landsmen changed as the French Revolutionary Wars advanced. The first four years of the war, 1793 to 1796, saw a relatively stable ratio of skilled to unskilled volunteer seamen. Landsmen made up 30 per cent of volunteer seamen, and this figure remained relatively stable through 1794 (36 per cent), 1795 (31 per cent) and 1796 (33 per cent). During these same four years the ratio between able seamen and ordinary seamen changed. In 1793 there was a higher percentage of volunteer able seamen (39 per cent) than ordinary seamen (25 per cent). However, by 1796 this ratio had changed and ordinary seamen made up 31 per cent of volunteers, outpacing able seamen, who made up 26 per cent of volunteers. Over the final five years of the war the number of volunteer landsmen increased dramatically. They made up well over a third of incoming seamen and petty officers in 1797 (43 per cent) and 1798 (41 per cent), increased to half in 1799 (49 per cent), and nearly two-thirds (62 per cent) in both 1800 and 1801. At the same time, the number of volunteer able and ordinary seamen dropped with each passing year. In 1797 able and ordinary seamen collectively made up 46 per cent of volunteers, while by 1801 that number had dropped to only 30 per cent.

Notably, the number of volunteer petty officers, the most highly skilled men of the lower deck, remained relatively stable throughout the war. Volunteer petty officers made up the lowest percentage in the first year of the war, only 6 per cent. This had nearly doubled by 1795 (11 per cent), and continued steadily to make up over 10 per cent of volunteers up to 1800, dropping only slightly to 8 per cent in 1801, as war began to wind down with the anticipated Peace of Amiens. The lower percentage of petty officer recruitment corresponds to a smaller overall number of petty officers in ships at the beginning of the war. This is likely to reflect the fact that as the size of the Royal Navy was inflating rapidly, officers were choosing their petty officers from men with proven naval experience, as the lower deck of a British warship was certainly a meritocracy, dependent on proven skill and ability. As the war progressed, petty officers were more and more likely to be chosen from turned over men.

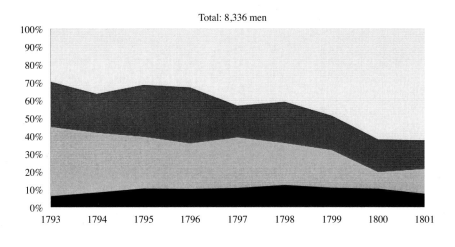

Figure 3.3 Volunteer seamen and petty officers

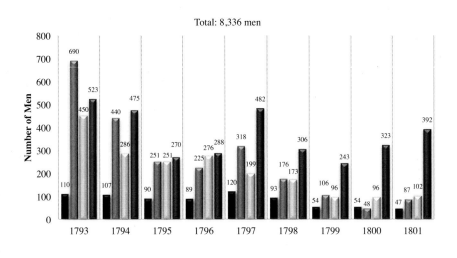

Figure 3.4 Volunteer seamen and petty officers

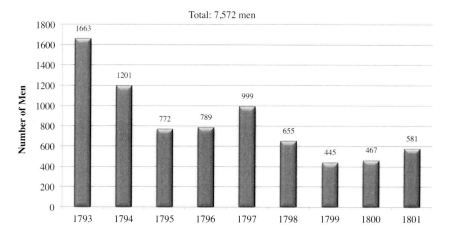

Figure 3.5 Volunteer seamen

The rapidly increasing percentage of unskilled men who volunteered for British naval service from 1793 to 1801 demonstrates two factors that governed naval recruitment throughout the age of sail. First, there were a finite number of experienced seamen in Britain. At the beginning of the war, many of these men volunteered for service; however as the conflict continued and the Royal Navy swallowed up more and more of them, there were simply fewer skilled men in a position to volunteer or be otherwise recruited. Second, this demonstrates that naval service was an attractive option for unskilled labourers, or simply men without sea skills, throughout the war. By the standards that eighteenth-century agricultural labourers were used to, the benefits of naval service, such as pay, food, and the ability to acquire skills for future use and advancement, outweighed those offered on land. However, it is important to note that these percentages come as a portion of volunteers, not of recruitment as a whole.

In examining the recruitment of volunteers from 1793 to 1801 it is apparent that volunteer numbers began enthusiastically high in the opening years of the war, but tended to drop off as the conflict advanced. The crests and troughs of incoming volunteers correspond to other recruiting efforts that took place during the war. The first low point, during 1795 and 1796, matches up with the timing of the Quota Acts. This was followed with a spike in 1797 and a drop off in overall volunteer numbers in 1798 which relates to the slowing of Royal Navy growth. Finally, overall naval numbers increased in 1800 and 1801, which coincides with a rise in the numbers of volunteers. This surge of men joining the Navy in 1800 and 1801 corresponded with an invasion scare that gripped Britain at the end of the French Revolutionary Wars.

Out of the 8,880 volunteers covered in this data sample, 53 per cent listed a location within England as their place of birth, which makes sense as the three primary naval bases, as well as most of the major commercial ports, were in England, and therefore recruiting efforts focused on these areas. Looking only at the 7,572 seamen who were listed as volunteers, we find that 51 per cent were English by birth. Correspondingly, 758 (10 per cent) seamen volunteers listed London as their place of origin. Eighteenth-century London was the largest manufacturing centre in Europe, and thus a large merchant shipping presence was only natural.[176] However, as London was such a centre of mercantile production and trade, a much higher percentage of volunteer seamen would have been recruited out of London than were actually born there, as seamen from all over Britain, and indeed the world, were drawn to the Thames.

Other areas with natural naval connections also produced high numbers of volunteers. Devon, for instance, was the second most frequently listed place of birth for volunteers, and accounted for 487 volunteers, 6 per cent of this sample. Eighteenth-century Devon had strong connections with the Royal Navy and had produced large numbers of men during the American War.[177] Further, France, Britain's major naval rival, was positioned to the south, and the southwestern end of the English Channel, with its close proximity to the French naval base at Brest, was the likely place for any French naval action against the British Isles to begin. However, after 1795 other threats began to emerge, such as the Dutch fleet to Britain's east. Correspondingly, in the seventeenth century, when England's major naval threat was the Dutch, a larger percentage of seamen were in fact from the east coast, rather than the south and west.[178] Of the 3,846 volunteer seamen who were listed as English, an impressive 20 per cent were from the greater London area. Further, 13 per cent were born in Devon; 6 per cent came from Kent, excluding London; and 5 per cent were from Cornwall. In fact, looking at the counties along the southeastern and southern coasts of Britain – those of Norfolk, Suffolk, Essex, Kent, Sussex, Hampshire, Dorset, Somerset, Devon and Cornwall – as well as the cities of London and Bristol, we find that nearly one-third (31.7 per cent) of all seamen who volunteered for Royal Navy service between 1793 and 1801 listed one of these locations as their birthplace.

Ireland accounted for 23 per cent of volunteer seamen, while the Irish counties of Dublin and Cork accounted for 25 and 19 per cent of Irish volunteer seamen respectively. Similarly, 8 per cent of volunteer seamen were Scottish, and of those 629 men covered in this data sample, the county of Fife and city of Edinburgh were listed as the origins of 12 per cent each. Glasgow and Argyll were each home to 9 per cent of Scottish volunteer seamen, while the Shetland Islands were home to 8 per cent. Welsh-born men made up the smallest group of volunteer seamen born in the British Isles. Only 3 per

---

[176] Michael Duffy, 'The Establishment of the Western Squadron as the Linchpin of British Naval Strategy', in *Parameters of British Naval Power, 1650–1850*, ed. Michael Duffy (Exeter: Exeter University Press, 1992), p. 60.

[177] Rodger, 'Devon Men and the Navy, 1689–1815', p. 212.

[178] Davies, *Gentlemen and Tarpaulins*, p. 68.

cent (236 men) of volunteer seamen in this data sample listed Wales as their birthplace, and of those men 23 per cent were born in Pembrokeshire, 17 per cent were from Glamorganshire, and 12 per cent gave Carmarthenshire as their place of birth. Examining the recruitment of volunteer seamen from Pembrokeshire, Carmarthenshire, Glamorganshire and Monmouthshire demonstrates that 61 per cent of Welsh volunteer seamen came from counties on the Bristol Channel.

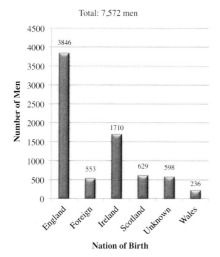

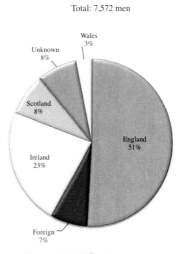

Figure 3.6 Volunteer seamen nationalities

Figure 3.7 Volunteer seamen nationalities

Separating volunteer seamen by their skill level and nationality demonstrates that a disproportionate ratio of Irish volunteers were of lower skill levels when compared to England, Scotland and Wales. Fifty-four per cent of the Irishmen on the lower deck were landsmen, while only 26 per cent were ordinary seamen, and fewer still were able seamen (16 per cent) or petty officers (4 per cent). This makes the Irish volunteer skill level low when compared to English seamen, of whom only 40 per cent were landsmen, while 20 per cent were rated ordinary seamen, 29 per cent were able seamen, and 11 per cent were rated petty officers. Scottish and Welsh volunteer seamen, though fewer in overall number, were disproportionately highly skilled. Only 26 per cent of Scottish seamen were rated as unskilled landsmen, a further 26 per cent were ordinary seamen, while 37 per cent were rated able seamen and finally 11 per cent were rated as petty officers. Welsh seamen followed a similar pattern, with 27 per cent being rated as landsmen, 25 per cent as ordinary seamen, 38 per cent as able seamen, and 10 per cent rated as petty officers. Notably, foreign volunteer seamen were the most skilled, with over half being rated as either petty officers (9 per cent) or able seamen (45 per cent).

Twenty-nine per cent of landsmen, 24 per cent of ordinary seamen, 12 per cent of able seamen, and only 10 per cent of petty officers were Irish by birth. The high ratio of Irish landsmen in the Royal Navy further demonstrates the attractiveness of naval service to agricultural labourers. Further, the high percentage of ordinary seamen when compared to able seamen and petty officers gives insight into the Irish maritime economy. Ireland did not have a large number of ports that were heavily involved in deep-sea and long-distance trade, which explains the low number of highly skilled seamen. However, the high number of ordinary seamen suggests that Ireland did have a healthy coasting trade that produced men with skill at sea, but not experience on large square rigged ocean-going vessels.

Of 764 volunteer petty officers in this data sample, 60 per cent were English, 10 per cent were Irish, 11 per cent were Scottish, 4 per cent were Welsh, and 7 per cent were foreign, while the nationality of 8 per cent remains unknown. Statistics on county of birth for volunteer petty officers show that Devon was recorded as the origin of eighty-six petty officers in this survey (11 per cent), slightly, and surprisingly, outpacing London, which only produced eighty-three (11 per cent) volunteer petty officers. This is notable, as when examining the skill levels of volunteer seamen, London was the origin of nearly double the percentage of Devon. Notably, commissioned officers were also much more likely to be English. According to Patrick Marioné's data, which records the careers of 5,537 officers who served in the Royal Navy during the eighteenth century, 74 per cent were English, while only 10 per cent were Irish, 9 per cent Scottish, and 3 per cent Welsh. A further 3 per cent came from the British Empire outside of the British Isles, and only 1 per cent were recorded as being foreign altogether.

Also, similar to petty officers, the largest proportions came from London (12 per cent) and Devon (11 per cent), further illustrating the importance of both as sources of naval skill.[179]

Volunteer seamen were also young: 55 per cent were under the age of twenty-five, and only 25 per cent were over thirty years old.[180] For volunteer landsmen, the peak ages for joining a ship were twenty and twenty-one; however the numbers dropped off quickly as age increased. Out of 3,085 landsmen volunteers covered in the database, 588 were listed as twenty years old and 555 were twenty-one. This constituted well over one-third of volunteer landsmen. However, only 380 were recorded as being twenty-two years old, and only 155 were listed as being twenty-five. Volunteer ordinary seamen followed a similar pattern; however after peaking at twenty years old, they rapidly began to drop off, even by the age of twenty-one. The ages of able seamen followed a different trend. For volunteer able seamen there

---

[179] Patrick Marioné, 'The Complete Navy List of the Napoleonic Wars' (Brussels: SEFF, 2003), CD-ROM.

[180] Daniel Vickers's research into the maritime community of Salem, Massachusetts of the eighteenth century shows a similar trend, where the majority of seamen were under the age of twenty-five. Vickers and Walsh, p. 266.

Table 3.1 Volunteer nationality

	England	Foreign	Ireland	Scotland	Unknown	Wales	Total
Petty officers	461 (60%)	55 (7%)	79 (10%)	82 (11%)	60 (8%)	27 (4%)	764
Able seamen	1,249 (54%)	274 (12%)	283 (12%)	264 (11%)	172 (7%)	99 (4%)	2,341
Ordinary seamen	882 (46%)	167 (9%)	458 (24%)	182 (9%)	173 (9%)	67 (3%)	1,929
Landsmen	1,715 (52%)	112 (3%)	969 (28%)	183 (6%)	253 (8%)	70 (2%)	3,302
Total	**4,307 (52%)**	**608 (7%)**	**1,789 (21%)**	**711 (9%)**	**658 (8%)**	**263 (3%)**	**8,336**

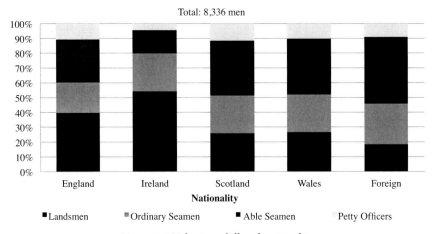

Total: 8,336 men

Landsmen   Ordinary Seamen   Able Seamen   Petty Officers

Figure 3.8 Volunteer skill and nationality

is a clear plateau from the age of twenty to twenty-three where incoming numbers were fairly stable. One reason for this would be the time and skill necessary to achieve the rating, and the fact that years' worth of experience generally came with promotion. However, after the age of twenty-three, able seamen also saw a rapid decline in numbers which mirrors landsmen and ordinary seamen. Volunteer petty officers were also noticeably young, surprisingly so when one considers the skill and experience required for their position. A full 50 per cent were under the age of thirty, and half of those were under twenty-five. Thirty per cent of volunteer petty officers were between the ages of thirty and thirty-nine, while only 13 per cent were above the age of forty. The youthfulness of seamen was not simply confined to British volunteers, as research into the waterfront society of Salem, Massachusetts demonstrates a similar pattern for American seamen.[181] Being a sailor was certainly a life for young men, and in maritime communities it seemed to be what young men did for several years before taking up lives ashore. Those who stayed until middle age generally sought their own merchant commands.[182] Logically, it seems likely that those seamen who went ashore to work in their mid- to late twenties provided the elasticity that allowed for naval expansion during wartime, and produced many of the volunteers at the onset of war.[183]

There were also boys who volunteered because they were keen on a life at sea or because they were unhappy at home.[184] Robert Hay was an example of

[181] Ibid., p. 129.
[182] Ibid.
[183] Proving this concept will require examination of the peacetime Royal Navy and comparison with age data found in this database to see if the age of volunteer able seamen rises slightly during the initial years of a conflict.
[184] Lewis, *A Social History of the Navy, 1793–1815*, p. 86.

Volunteers

Total: 7,572 men

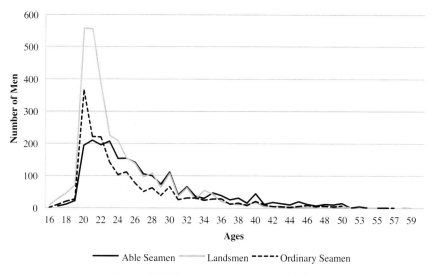

Figure 3.9 Volunteer seamen ages and rating

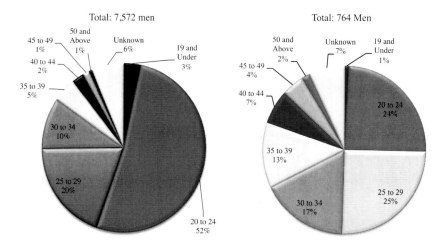

Figure 3.10 Volunteer seamen ages   **Figure 3.11** Volunteer petty officer ages

such a boy who left home as a boy wanting to go to sea and, as no merchant would have him, joined a Royal Navy ship as his only means of going to sea.[185] Between 1793 and 1801 at least 5 per cent of the average ship's crew consisted of boys.[186] For the Navy, boys proved useful on ship as they

---

[185] Robert Hay, *Landsman Hay: The Memoirs of Robert Hay, 1789–1847* (London: R. Hart-Davis, 1953), p. 33.

[186] See Figure 2.13. The actual figure is slightly higher as this data covers the years 1793 to 1801, yet

performed many tasks such as serving the officers. Some, those rated as boys first class, had the possibility of becoming midshipmen and later officers, while others grew up with the necessary skills to become first rate seamen, which in the Royal Navy were constantly in short supply.[187] The majority of boys who went to sea were between the ages of eleven and fifteen,[188] and thus were perfectly suited to thoroughly learn and master the skills of a seaman before they came into the prime of their strength. Therefore they maximised the time that they spent at sea as able seamen and possibly petty officers. For the Royal Navy this was a good investment, as boys who grew up in the service tended to stay there.[189]

Examining the volunteer recruitment statistics for each of Britain's three major naval ports produces interesting results. When considering the entire nine-year span of the French Revolutionary Wars, statistical data reveals that at both Chatham and Plymouth, turned over men did not supersede volunteers as a source of incoming manpower for newly commissioned ships. This data reveals that of men who joined ships in Plymouth, 49 per cent were new volunteers. Of men joining ships in Chatham, 43 per cent were volunteers, while in Portsmouth only 36 per cent were volunteers. Interestingly, this coincides with the fact that London and Devon were the highest listed places of birth for volunteer seamen. Closer examination of recorded birthplaces and the ports from which ships were being manned shows a trend where seamen volunteered at ports nearest their recorded place of birth. Englishmen were spread fairly evenly across the three major ports, with the majority, 40 per cent, going to Chatham, followed by Portsmouth and Plymouth, which accounted for 30 per cent each. At Plymouth, volunteer Englishmen accounted for 40 per cent of total volunteer seamen, while they accounted for more than half of the volunteers at Chatham (61 per cent) and Portsmouth (54 per cent).

Irish volunteers were not as evenly divided. The majority of volunteer Irishmen in the Royal Navy joined ships at Plymouth (56 per cent), followed by Portsmouth (26 per cent) and Chatham (18 per cent). This is geographically plausible, as Plymouth was the closest of the three naval stations to Ireland. At Plymouth, Irish volunteers made up 33 per cent of total volunteers, demonstrating the importance of Irish seamen within ships that commissioned at Plymouth. At Portsmouth, the Irish influence only made up 20 per cent of all volunteers, and at Chatham only 13 per cent. This made Irishmen a substantially smaller cultural group within ships manned at those ports.

The majority of Scottish volunteers joined ships at Plymouth (39 per cent) or Chatham (38 per cent), while only about half as many made it to

---

before 16 April 1794 boys were recorded in many years differently, often as servants. Lloyd, *The British Seaman, 1200–1860*, pp. 196–197.

[187] Lewis, *A Social History of the Navy, 1793–1815*, p. 90.
[188] Earle, 'English Sailors, 1570–1775', p. 85.
[189] Lewis, *A Social History of the Navy, 1793–1815*, p. 90.

Portsmouth (23 per cent). However, Scotsmen made up less than 10 per cent of the total number of volunteers in each port. Men who volunteered in Scotland were likely sent down the east or west coast in tenders which deposited them in the first naval base they came to, which in neither case was Portsmouth. Similarly, and for the same geographic reasons, 57 per cent of volunteer Welshmen entered warships at Plymouth. Only 23 per cent of volunteer Welshmen ended up in ships that commissioned at Portsmouth, and only 20 per cent went to Chatham. As discussed earlier, the majority of Welsh volunteers came from counties bordering the Bristol Channel. Thus these men were very close to Plymouth, and undoubtedly ships commissioning at Plymouth would have sent recruiting parties up the Bristol Channel. Overall, volunteer Welshmen made up the smallest proportion of any volunteer group, and accounted for only 5 per cent of volunteer seamen in Plymouth, and only 2 per cent in both Chatham and Portsmouth.

Notably, 43 per cent of foreigners volunteered at Plymouth, while only 34 per cent volunteered at Chatham, and only 26 per cent at Portsmouth. This is surprising, as London was the centre of British foreign trade, and logic would expect that the highest number of volunteer foreigners would have been recruited there, rather than Plymouth, which was not the commercial powerhouse that London was. However, most foreign shipping did transit the English Channel, and thus would have passed Plymouth well before reaching the Thames, and many such ships would have been boarded by press gangs that supplied ships fitting out in Plymouth. Though these foreign seamen were not pressed, nor were they legally able to be pressed, it is almost certain that recruiting parties would not turn down volunteers as they searched for men.

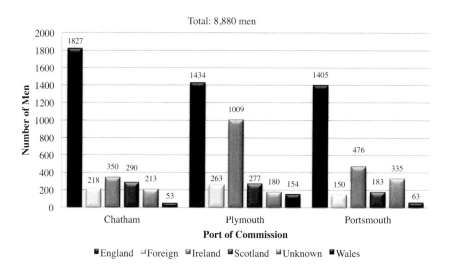

Figure 3.12 Volunteer seamen and petty officer nationality by port

Total: 7,572 men

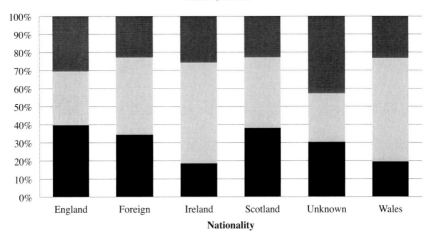

Figure 3.13 Volunteer seamen nationality by port, 1793–1801

Motivations for Volunteering

The motivation behind why men joined is greatly open to discussion,[190] especially as it is apparent that most of the firsthand accounts of seamen's lives were written by pressed men. Further, the possible motivations for volunteering for naval service were as broad as can be imagined. Even historians who have claimed that volunteers made up a small minority of crews in eighteenth-century British warships readily admit that patriotism, bounties, advertisements, and the hope of prize money encouraged many men into naval service.[191] There were certainly men who joined because they were attracted by posters and proclamations that were posted in public places by recruiting parties.[192] However, although posters and flyers certainly led those who wished to volunteer to the right place, advertisement alone was not a motivating factor. Even though the possible motivating factors for volunteering for naval service were virtually limitless, there were several that need discussion.

Patriotism, especially during the early stages of a conflict, was likely one of the most powerful motivators for men who joined any form of military service.[193] The threat of foreign attack, and the fact that the threat came

---

[190] Harding, p. 139.
[191] John Masefield, *Sea Life in Nelson's Time* (London: Methuen & Co., 1905), p. 55.
[192] Brian Lavery, *Royal Tars: The Lower Deck of the Royal Navy, 875–1850* (London: Conway, 2010), p. 206; Lloyd, *The British Seaman, 1200–1860*, p. 197.
[193] Masefield, p. 55.

from Revolutionary France, at least in the early phases of the war, produced a sudden growth of counter-revolutionary loyalism in Britain, and this produced patriotically motivated volunteers for the Royal Navy.[194] Just as the French Revolution sparked a fire of liberal nationalism across Europe, it also clearly helped to strengthen conservative nationalism in response, and this was encouraged as much as possible by the British government. Such encouragement can be seen in the figure of Britannia, which had often been considered a libertarian symbol, but after 1793 became increasingly identified as 'royal' and property of the state.[195]

Patriotic response to military success also played heavily on the public, and news of the victory of the Glorious First of June spawned three nights of 'celebrations' in London. These demonstrations went on to the point of illuminating the windows of houses at the insistence of the 'mob' and the breaking of windows of known opponents of the war.[196] Such a post-victory atmosphere certainly made for a favourable recruiting environment throughout Britain, especially in places with strong naval ties. There was also a perceived possibility for the opportunity to acquire honour and distinction in battle, even though such opportunities were far fewer in number than was realised by young men wishing to embark on military service. Even today young men leave home for military service in hopes of gaining honour and distinction that would otherwise prove unobtainable.[197] The British government and Admiralty also saw the value of glorifying battle-proven heroes, as it not only bolstered public support for the war but also produced volunteers for naval service.

The Royal Navy of the eighteenth century was far more popular in public perception than the Army, in great part due to the fact that the political function of the Army was always a matter of contention, even when the strategic necessity was obvious. However, as there was little fear of naval forces marching on Parliament or holding a locality under martial law, the Royal Navy nearly always received public and political support that British land forces did not.[198] The public saw Britain's 'wooden walls' as a necessary line of defence, as well as an offensive force that could do great damage to its enemies. The Army was best used offensively, removing the burden of feeding and housing such a force from the British public and placing it on a given enemy. Ultimately, this worked in favour of naval recruiting, as for many unskilled men seeking such glory, the Royal Navy proved the viable option. Granted, the men that naval lieutenants actively sought were skilled seamen, who if inclined toward military service would have likely chosen the Navy anyway. Unskilled landsmen were also necessary to achieve the large-

[194] Cookson, 'The English Volunteer Movement of the French Wars, 1793–1815', p. 867.
[195] Linda Colley, 'The Apotheosis of George III: Loyalty, Royalty and the British Nation, 1760–1820', *Past and Present*, no. 102 (1984): p. 106.
[196] Michael Duffy and Roger Morriss, eds *The Glorious First of June 1794* (Exeter: Exeter University Press, 2001), p. 2.
[197] Smith, p. 53.
[198] Brewer, pp. 55–59.

scale naval expansion that occurred during the 1790s without destroying merchant trade and the economy that revolved around it. Undoubtedly, the threat of French invasion late in the war helped to kindle the patriotic fire that produced volunteers in the opening years of the conflict.

Closely related to, if not intertwined with, the ideas of patriotism and glory was the sense of adventure. For young men and boys in ports frequented by naval ships, there was surely a lure to seeing the largest and most technologically advanced creations of their day on a regular basis anchored just off shore. This combined with hearing seamen's stories and seeing naval officers in uniform certainly attracted young men, especially those whose futures as common labourers looked bleak.[199] It is certain that working as a merchant seaman at the end of the eighteenth century was more profitable than being a craftsman or labourer on shore.[200] Naval service, though not as financially rewarding during wartime, had many other benefits that appealed to men inclined to leave behind a shore-based livelihood. For landsmen who did not go to sea at an early age, it may have proved the only means by which to escape a life as a common labourer. For many, the simple lure of being fed, along with receiving alcohol, tobacco, medical attention, and guaranteed pay, was more than enough to move them into naval service, not to mention the cash bounty they received for volunteering.[201]

Though eighteenth-century naval pay was always lower than merchant pay during wartime, it still had the ability to attract men into service. British naval pay was certainly steady in contrast to that of the French Navy, which due to financial collapse was often unable to retain men because it could not consistently pay them.[202] The security of naval pay had an attraction of its own, especially when that was paired with the benefits of food, shelter and medical care.[203] Memoirs of seamen, having served both in merchant and naval ships, suggest that less work, better food, and more certain wages made up for the lower naval pay rate during wartime.[204] As merchant pay was based on supply and demand, higher naval pay would not have overcome recruiting problems, which were largely due to the finite number of trained seamen available.[205] A significant increase in naval pay would have likely driven up merchant pay in response, as merchants needed to offer high pay to obtain men, demonstrated by the fact that naval and merchant pay in peacetime were roughly equal. Advantages of the naval over the merchant service were evident in peacetime when the Royal Navy virtually had the pick of skilled

---

[199] Smith, p. 54.
[200] Vickers and Walsh, p. 268.
[201] Adkins and Adkins, pp. 60–61.
[202] Lambert, p. 51.
[203] Rodger, *The Wooden World*, p. 137.
[204] Rodger, *The Command of the Ocean*, p. 397.
[205] Rodger, "'A Little Navy of Your Own Making': Admiral Boscawen and the Cornish Connection in the Royal Navy', pp. 83–84.

seamen.[206] One of the major advantages of naval pay was its steep structure.[207] Merchant pay, when compared to naval, was much flatter, and offered far less compensation for advancement, whereas naval pay offered higher compensation to seamen who remained in service and were promoted with time and experience. Such a system had obvious appeal to anyone who had any inclination to plan in a long-term fashion. At the beginning of the French Revolutionary Wars, naval pay had not changed for nearly a century and a half, and it was not until after the mutinies of 1797 that any serious changes were made. Seamen viewed low wages as detrimental to naval service and many, such as seamen in Newcastle,[208] petitioned Parliament to increase pay for Royal Navy seamen – a plea which fell on deaf ears. However, such protests must not be seen as problematic for all volunteers. Though naval wages may not have been attractive to skilled seamen who could earn more on merchant ships, for unskilled landsmen they certainly had an appeal, especially when considering that they came with a hammock, food, medical attention, a bounty, and the chance for prize money.[209]

The naval pay structure did have other advantages over merchant pay, a major advantage being a fixed deduction of 1s 6d per lunar month. Merchant pay had a fixed deduction of sixpence that went to the Greenwich Hospital, for which merchant seamen received very little benefit. However, merchant seamen ran the risk of encountering large deductions for damaged cargo or damage to the vessel itself, especially from an unscrupulous master.[210] Robert Hay described a very unsatisfactory time he spent on a West Indiaman in 1811, where after months of time at sea, making the round trip from England to the West Indies and back, he received only a very meagre sum once deductions had been taken out by the ship's master.[211] Such experiences must have affected many seamen, and though wages paid by the Navy were certainly lower, the fact that pay was guaranteed must have attracted men who either had similar experiences to Robert Hay, or had heard of it happening to others.

Men serving in the Royal Navy also had the advantage of the Navy Act of 1758, which merchant seamen did not. This allowed serving seamen to forward portions of their pay to relatives through government channels. Initially at least, this was not heavily used, and in 1759 only 655 men (3 per cent) out of the ships paid in Plymouth elected to use this function to remit funds to family.[212] From a sample of nineteen pay books, examined by N.A.M.

---

[206] Rodger, *The Command of the Ocean*, pp. 397–398.

[207] Benjamin and Thornberg, 'Organization and Incentives', p. 318. The 'steep structure' of pay here refers to the differences in pay between ratings. A steeper pay structure offered more incentive to remain in naval service in hopes of promotion. Naval pay for the lower deck became even steeper in 1807 when it was again restructured.

[208] Emsley, *British Society and the French Wars, 1793–1815*, p. 34.

[209] Rodger, '"A Little Navy of Your Own Making": Admiral Boscawen and the Cornish Connection in the Royal Navy', p. 85.

[210] Rodger, *The Wooden World*, p. 127.

[211] Hay, pp. 196–214.

[212] Rodger, *The Wooden World*, p. 134.

Rodger, only 4.6 per cent of men made remittances; however the sum of these was 5.6 per cent of the net pay of the ships. Just over half of these payments went to wives, or at least women of the same surname as the men.[213] The fact that the percentage of net pay was higher than the percentage of men paying suggests that it was senior men, who were higher paid, who forwarded pay to relatives. Also, these same men would have been more likely to have been married, as they were naturally a bit older than less experienced men.

The Royal Navy only paid recruiting bounties to volunteers. Like naval pay, the bounty for men differed by experience. For highly skilled able seamen, with the onset of war in 1793, the King's bounty was £5.0.0, and had been during wartime since 1759. Prior to that, from 1739, the bounty had been two guineas for an able seaman.[214] From 1759 volunteer ordinary seamen received a bounty of £2.10.0, and volunteer landsmen received 1.10.0. This certainly attracted many seamen, as it represented nearly half a year's pay for an able seaman. On top of the bounty, volunteers could expect two months' wages in advance, thus an able seaman could expect around £7.0.0 in cash upon joining a seagoing warship.[215] This policy helped recruit many volunteers, both skilled and unskilled, into naval service, and its longevity of use, from well before the navies of the Restoration monarchy in the 1660s, demonstrates its perceived effectiveness to the administrators who guided naval policy. The combination of pay and bounty proved enough motivation for Jacob Nagle, an American-born seaman, to join Royal Navy service in August of 1783, only weeks before the Treaty of Paris was signed, officially ending the war. From his account, he and a friend had been some time in England and had spent all of their money; looking for a ship, they volunteered to HMS *Scipio*, and were later transferred to HMS *Ganges*.[216] In the end, Nagle must have had some motivation for staying in naval service, as he spent the following nineteen years in British naval service, followed by a further twenty-two years of service in merchant vessels, finally retiring from the sea when he was in his sixties.

In addition to the King's bounty, many cities, towns and corporations throughout Britain offered supplements to increase the value of the bounty received by seamen. In early 1793, before war had even been declared, the City of London supplemented the royal bounty by an additional forty shillings for able seamen and twenty shillings for ordinary seamen who volunteered, bringing the total bounty for able seamen to £7.0.0 and £3.10.0 for ordinary seamen.[217] By the end of 1794 this had been increased by a subscription opened by the Lord Mayor, which brought the bounty to £10.10.0 for able

---

[213] Ibid.

[214] Lloyd, *The British Seaman, 1200–1860*, p. 132.

[215] Rodger, *The Wooden World*, p. 127.

[216] John C. Dann, ed. *The Nagle Journal: A Diary of the Life of Jacob Nagle, Sailor, from the Year 1775 to 1841* (New York: Weidenfeld and Nicolson, 1988), pp. 72–73.

[217] Peter Kemp, *The British Sailor: A Social History of the Lower Deck* (London: J.M. Dent & Sons Ltd, 1970), p. 161; Rodger, *The Command of the Ocean*, p. 442.

seamen, £8.8.0 for ordinary seamen, and £6.6.0 for landsmen.[218] Further, boys were provided with a bounty of £2.2.0 or £1.1.0 according to their height.[219] Many other towns did likewise. Wrexham provided an additional two guineas and one guinea for 'those Ancient Britons, natives of this country, who are ready to come forward and defend the wooden walls of Old England, against her natural and inveterate enemy'.[220] This process was not without precedent, as such offers for volunteers had been made throughout the eighteenth century. Even amongst the turmoil and political unrest associated with the American War, supplements to the royal volunteer bounty came from Southampton, Montrose, Glasgow, Liverpool, Beverly and Hull.[221] During the opening year of the Seven Years' War, the Corporation of Lynn offered twenty shillings to any volunteer, as did Liverpool, Whitehaven, Newcastle and Stockton. In 1756 the East Riding of Yorkshire offered £3.0.0 and £2.0.0 to able and ordinary seamen volunteers, and in 1759 Aberdeen offered £2.2.0 and £1.1.0, while Glasgow offered £1.10.0 to all volunteers, regardless of skill.[222] Such additions to the King's bounty made for a very potent form of compensation for prospective volunteers, and undoubtedly provided the necessary motivation for many of the vast number of men who volunteered. For others it proved to be the icing on the cake of what they already perceived to be a good deal.

Though not an official form of salary, and certainly not guaranteed, prize money allowed seamen to supplement their naval income, and in some cases provided a sum worth several years' pay in an afternoon. During the War of Austrian Succession, the Whig Member of Parliament and former Lord Mayor of London, Sir John Bernard, stated that 'war is the harvest of a sailor, in which he is to store provisions for the winter of old age'.[223] This statement referred to prize money and illustrated the view of naval prize taking from a person without any sea experience. For men ashore, the large number of prizes taken during wartime must have seemed an economic boon for seamen aboard warships, and such assumptions may have played a major role in the fact that naval pay rates did not rise for nearly a century and a half. For seamen aboard ships, prizes that would make a ship's company wealthy were few and far between, and the income from such prizes did not make many seamen wealthy. Although prize money was never guaranteed, it presented the opportunity for seamen to substantially raise their earnings.[224] Prizes had great potential to provide a significant reward for a ship's crew. Between 1793 and 1815 the average prize return for a captured privateer was £1,000; for a merchant including cargo it was £2,000; for a small enemy frigate it was

---

[218] W. Laird Clowes, *The Royal Navy: A History from the Earliest Times to the Present*, vol. IV (London: Chatham Publishing, 1997), pp. 155–156; Kemp, p. 161.

[219] Kemp, p. 161.

[220] Quoted in Rodger, *The Command of the Ocean*, p. 442.

[221] Conway, 'The Politics of British Military and Naval Mobilization, 1775–83', p. 1198.

[222] Gradish, *The Manning of the British Navy During the Seven Years' War*, p. 73.

[223] Brewer, p. 199.

[224] Starkey, 'War and the Market for Seafarers in Britain, 1736–1792', pp. 33–34.

£10,000; and ships-of-the-line could easily exceed £40,000.[225] Sailors had, or at least were believed to have, good opportunities for prize money, and the allure of fortune, though much like playing the lottery, encouraged many volunteers.[226]

The government also recognised the attraction of advertising prize money, and its ability to attract volunteers. During the mid-seventeenth century changes were made to prize money terms, in 1649 and again in 1652, in order to attract volunteers.[227] The division scale for prize money, much like the naval pay scale, was steep, especially in comparison to the privateers, and advancement in 'rank' offered significantly higher payouts from captured prizes.[228] A further revision of the prize system in 1808 markedly increased the steepness in regard to promotion and payouts on the lower deck. It also reallocated one-eighth of the money received for a prize vessel, which had been a portion of what was awarded to captains and admirals, and paid it to the men of the lower deck.[229] Though the 1808 revision was revoked in 1816, once peace arrived, it was in effect at the time when the size of the Royal Navy peaked at well over 140,000 men.[230]

Prize money certainly motivated recruitment of volunteers. Robert Hay, who as a boy was searching for a ship to go to sea, was enticed to join the Royal Navy over a merchant ship, as there was a promise of less work and an opportunity to gain prize money.[231] On occasion, some men even became wealthy by common standards. In 1801, James Lowery received £100 in prize money for three ships taken over the course of two days.[232] Although Lowery was a ship's surgeon rather than a seaman, the sum still represented nearly two years' worth of naval pay for him. For seamen, prize money was certainly an attraction to naval service, as it promised at least a supplement to their income, and offered a 'thread of hope' of becoming wealthy in an afternoon.[233]

General living conditions aboard British warships exceeded expectations of seamen aboard merchant ships, as well as those of a common labourer on land. In the Royal Navy, a sailor could expect better victuals, their pay was guaranteed, though not necessarily timely, there was medical attention for injuries, and a pension system for severe or permanent injuries, and their work was not as hard as in merchant ships.[234] Even in the seventeenth

---

[225] Daniel K. Benjamin and Christopher Thornberg, 'Comment: Rules, Monitoring, and Incentives in the Age of Sail', *Explorations in Economic History*, no. 40 (2003): p. 198.

[226] Smith, p. 53.

[227] Capp, p. 260.

[228] Benjamin and Thornberg, 'Organization and Incentives', p. 318.

[229] Ibid., p. 331.

[230] Ibid., p. 332.

[231] Hay, p. 33.

[232] James Lowry, *Fiddlers and Whores: The Candid Memoirs of a Surgeon in Nelson's Fleet*, ed. John Millyard (London: Chatham, 2006), pp. 49–51.

[233] David Davies, *A Brief History of Fighting Ships* (New York: Carroll & Graf Publishers, 2002), pp. 47–48.

[234] Earle, *Sailors: English Merchant Seamen, 1650–1775*, pp. 186–187.

century, the Royal Navy was a better option than labour ashore.[235] The backbone of good naval conditions was food, and as the Admiralty understood that ships ran on the labour of seamen, and consequently calories, the quantity of victualling was generous.[236] The naval diet consisted of over 4,000 calories a day, which was more than could be expected ashore or in merchant ships. Although a diet of salt meat, dried peas and hard bread was not ideal, it certainly proved adequate food for hard work. In contrast to Britain, the French Navy consistently failed to meet such standards, and poor supply and quality met with disastrous results.[237]

By the standards of merchantmen, British warships were lavishly manned.[238] This comes from the different philosophies behind manning in each case. Merchant ships were manned based on their tonnage, and only the number of men necessary to sail the vessel would be hired, especially as merchant masters were motivated to save as much money as possible. However, warships were manned based on the number of guns they carried. The reason for this was that in battle a warship needed to be able to operate at least a broadside of cannon, while still having enough men to tend the sails and rigging, the wheel, and various other duties, such as damage control. Therefore, with the relatively rare exception of the work produced during battle, the day-to-day workload placed on the individual in a warship was light in comparison to their merchant counterparts.

Further motivation for seamen to volunteer came from the medical attention and pension system provided by the Royal Navy. Unlike the French fleets, Britain considered the health of seamen as a vital component of success and invested heavily in medical attention.[239] The medical attention available was of prime importance to all seamen, not just men in warships. Contrary to popular belief, the vast majority of men killed or injured during the age of sail were victims of accidents and disease rather than combat. Thus, men aboard any ship, not just warships, were liable to encounter the same danger to life and limb.[240]

Few merchants employed anyone with medical training, while virtually all Royal Navy ships had a surgeon. Although most of the surgeons were not of the high quality of the medical practitioners who would have cared for the wealthy and important in society, they were at least of a better quality than common men would have been used to on shore. Further, any medical attention given would have been paid for out of the pocket of the sick or injured man on merchant ships or on shore, whereas the Royal Navy provided these services free of charge to the men. Beyond the availability of medical attention, British captains were directed to be attentive to the

---

[235] Davies, *Gentlemen and Tarpaulins*, p. 80.
[236] Kemp, p. 166.
[237] Lambert, pp. 51–52.
[238] Rodger, '"A Little Navy of Your Own Making": Admiral Boscawen and the Cornish Connection in the Royal Navy', p. 83.
[239] Lambert, p. 52.
[240] Benjamin and Thornberg, 'Comment: Rules, Monitoring, and Incentives in the Age of Sail', p. 200.

cleanliness of men aboard their respective ships, and to have them bathe frequently and change their linen twice each week. They were also to ensure, when possible, that men did not sleep in wet clothes.[241] Thus, not only was medical attention provided, but preventative measures were put in place to try to avoid sickness and injury. It is important to note that not only did these measures help attract volunteers, they also reduced the wastage of manpower due to sickness. This in turn aided the overall manning situation for the Navy.

However, regardless of preventative measures, sea service entailed some level of danger, especially to those who were less experienced. Injuries and deaths did occur on ship, both from daily work and from battle, even though combat casualties made up the minority of men killed or injured at sea. Pensions were available to Navy men who were injured, and the widows of seamen could also apply for pensions when their husbands died in service.[242] This system was not perfect and the pensions offered made no one rich, but it did represent a form of security for a naval man that was unavailable to his counterpart in a merchant ship, or any other working man before the twentieth century.

Conditions aboard Royal Navy ships were the major advantage that naval recruitment offered over merchant shipping, and life aboard a British warship was certainly an improvement over what a common labourer could expect on land. History has often portrayed life aboard eighteenth-century warships as a type of floating dungeon; however this was simply not true. Warships could not be run effectively as floating concentration camps.[243] Success in the Royal Navy was based on a system with a well-rounded structure in which the officers on the quarter deck and the men of the lower deck worked together through consent.[244] Tyrannical officers did not rule sailors of the Royal Navy, and those that did exist in naval service were often not promoted to command. The men of the lower deck certainly disliked officers who treated them poorly, and the fact that well-known and successful officers were highly respected by their men goes to show the difference in efficiency between a happy and a miserable crew. British warships were filled with many respectable officers who, like Vice Admiral Cuthbert Collingwood, showed firm discipline aboard ship, yet condemned excessive flogging for the effect it had on morale. It is noteworthy that Collingwood was greatly admired by the seamen he commanded.[245] However, even though discipline in the Royal Navy could be considered harsh at times, it probably was not as severe as commoners could expect ashore, where stealing a piece of cloth could result in hanging.[246] Further, men were subjected to similar conditions aboard merchant ships, where unscrupulous masters could easily become tyrants.

[241] Brian Lavery, ed. *Shipboard Life and Organisation, 1731–1815*, Publications of the Navy Records Society (Aldershot: Ashgate, 1998), p. 54.

[242] Davies, *Gentlemen and Tarpaulins*, p. 81.

[243] Cormack, pp. 28–29.

[244] Lambert, pp. 49–50.

[245] Rodger, 'Shipboard Life in the Georgian Navy, 1750–1800: The Decline of the Old Order?', p. 35.

[246] Rogers, *The Press Gang: Naval Impressment and Its Opponents in Georgian Britain*, pp. 1–2.

Perhaps men did not go to sea at all because of the stories of harsh conditions, but the conditions aboard naval ships were not worse than aboard merchant ships. The fact of the matter was that conditions within the Royal Navy far exceeded those experienced in merchant ships, with the exception of pay.

Another point on which the Royal Navy far exceeded its merchant counterpart was the opportunity for advancement. The prospect of promotion to higher ranks, and the benefits that accompanied it, was essential to the incentive structure that encouraged volunteer recruitment.[247] The opportunities that came with advancement within the Navy outweighed the likely prospects available on land and in the merchant service, especially when considering that the prospect for promotion was far higher in a King's ship than in any merchant ship.[248] The key benefits of promotion were earning higher pay, along with an increased percentage of prize money.[249] Promotion aboard British warships was based on performance.[250] Men were rated once a ship's company had been received and usually when the ship first put to sea, where men could be observed while working. The task of rating the men was usually carried out by the captain on smaller ships or a senior lieutenant on larger warships. Generally speaking, to be considered as an ordinary seaman, an individual needed at least twelve months at sea and further had to be able to perform some of the duties of a seaman. Able seamen needed to have at least three years at sea and had to be capable of doing all of the duties of a seaman, including going aloft to handle sails, manning the helm, and heaving the lead.[251]

Only commissioned and warrant officers had terminal career positions in the eighteenth- century Royal Navy. Petty officers and seamen served for the term of a given ship's commission, at which time they were either released from naval service or turned over to another ship. When turned over to a different ship, petty officers and seamen had no guarantee of keeping the position they had earned previously, as they were re-rated by the officers of their new ship.[252] Generally, it could be expected that seamen would retain their ratings. However, petty officers were rated as they were needed aboard a warship and thus if a man was formerly a quarter gunner in one ship and was turned over to a ship that had no need of further quarter gunners, then it would be logical to assume that he would be rated in another capacity, whether as a different petty officer or an able seaman. Nevertheless, the fact that the lower deck of a Royal Navy ship was a meritocracy meant that hard work and skill progression were rewarded with advancement and thus lost ratings could be regained. Notably, it seems that the best opportunity for advancement was statistically in smaller ships due to the fact that larger ships

[247] Benjamin and Thornberg, 'Organization and Incentives', p. 318.
[248] Earle, *Sailors: English Merchant Seamen, 1650–1775*, p. 186.
[249] Benjamin and Thornberg, 'Organization and Incentives', p. 323.
[250] Ibid., p. 321.
[251] Lavery, *Shipboard Life and Organisation, 1731–1815*, pp. 54–55.
[252] Benjamin and Thornberg, 'Organization and Incentives', p. 320.

had a higher ratio of seamen to petty officers and of petty officers to warrant and commissioned officers.[253]

One advantage of volunteering, which was disappearing by the end of the eighteenth century, was the choice of ship on which to serve. Before the mid-eighteenth century, men who volunteered for naval service were allowed to choose the ship on which they would serve. As most recruiting at the time was done by the officers of individual ships, this did not pose any great difficulty, as men approached the officers of the desired ship when they were ashore looking for men. This was also a time in which officers, particularly captains and commanders, sent recruiting parties to their home towns and traded on the weight and popularity of their name in areas where they were well known. However, this was a time when the Royal Navy was much smaller and therefore required less manpower. As the size of the Navy increased, the necessity for larger numbers of men meant recruiting respon- sibilities were partially taken out of the hands of ships' officers and placed under the direct control of the Admiralty. This brought about the birth of the Impress Service during the Seven Years' War. It also made the choice of ship for volunteers more difficult, as men were less likely to volunteer directly to a given ship's officers, but rather to a lieutenant working with the Impress Service. Getting men to the ship that they wished to go to, while still fulfilling the needs of the Navy, would have proved an administrative nightmare. Evidence of this is found when future Admiral Keith, during the American War, experienced great difficulty in collecting a group of volunteers who had signed for his ship in London, while he was anchored at Portsmouth.[254] It also afforded the real possibility of leaving less known or unpopular captains with crews made up solely of pressed men. The slow disappearance of this system stands nearly alone as an advantage that was taken away from volunteers; however statistics show that it clearly did not dissuade men from volunteering.

Even at the end of the eighteenth century, when ships' officers were less involved in recruiting their crews, captains and lieutenants used local connections to recruit men who knew them or knew of them. Seamen also recognised the advantage in this, as they could reasonably expect future favour if they performed well, and the reality and comfort of this was greater with officers they knew.[255] Seamen also certainly sought to volunteer to ships commanded by well-known men, highly skilled and accomplished with a track record of success. Not only did this translate to the safety of the crew, but increased success also translated to returns in prize money for seamen. Further, captains' reputations were intricately tied to how they treated their men. History has often treated eighteenth-century seamen as men with little or no ability to think for themselves, but the reality was that seamen were as

[253] Ibid., pp. 327, 338–339.
[254] Peter Hore, *The Habit of Victory: The Story of the Royal Navy, 1545 to 1945* (London: Pan Books, 2006), p. 85.
[255] Rodger, *The Command of the Ocean*, p. 398.

capable of judging when they were treated well and judging the competence of their officers as was any other person, then or today.[256] Well respected captains and commanders with good reputations for fair treatment of men would undoubtedly have had better access to volunteers.

Men were clearly willing to volunteer to popular officers, an example being Sir Sidney Smith, who in the summer of 1795 was able to man his ship from several homebound Indiamen, solely with volunteers:

> I am glad to have it in my power so soon after my lamentations of yesterday to acquaint you that I am not longer in the distressed stated I was in for want of seamen. I am not a man to call out to Hercules while there is a possibility of getting out of the mire by putting my own shoulders to the wheel. I accordingly, on the wind coming fresh to the westward, placed myself in the track of the homeward bound trade which I had reason to suppose must have accumulated during the easterly wind. This morning I fell in with several homeward bound Indiamen and have manned myself completely out of them by taking volunteers only.[257]

Similarly, in July of 1797 Edward Pellew received about thirty men that he needed to complete his complement out of a French cartel returning about 200 prisoners of war from France.[258] Though Pellew did not mention explicitly that the men were volunteers, the nature of the situation, combined with the fact that he later mentions that the remaining men were sent to Portsmouth to be discharged, suggests that the men he took were on a voluntary basis. Further, such men, after spending time being held as prisoners, had the necessary motivation to take up arms against their former captors.

In addition to the motivation provided by well-known officers, seamen often joined ships where they had friends or family aboard. George Watson volunteered for service in the *Flame* in 1808 at the age of sixteen because he had a close friend serving in the ship.[259] After spending an evening aboard the ship visiting with his friend and messmates and enjoying the experience, Watson decided to volunteer for service rather than return ashore when morning came. Clearly the effect of a good friend and friendly messmates was enough to persuade him not to return ashore and to work in merchantmen. The *Belleisle* in 1777 had a varied crew in which above half of the petty officers, idlers and able seamen came from nine counties: in descending order, Devon, London, Cork, Cornwall, Lancashire, Kent, Dublin, Northumberland and Dorset. This is distinctive because, although spread out amongst maritime counties, none came from Hampshire or Sussex, both of which were heavily maritime. The ship only sent one recruiting party to London, and nowhere

---

[256] Lavery, *Shipboard Life and Organisation, 1731–1815*, p. 355.

[257] Sidney Smith to Spenser, Diamond, off Beachy Head, 22 July 1795, in *The Channel Fleet and the Blockade of Brest, 1793–1801*, ed. Roger Morriss, Publications of the Navy Record Society (Aldershot: Ashgate, 2001), p. 97.

[258] Pellew to Admiralty, HMS *Indefatigable*, 30 July 1797, in ibid., p. 261.

[259] Lewis, *A Social History of the Navy, 1793–1815*, pp. 90–91.

else. Significantly, when the ordinary seamen and landsmen are examined it becomes clear that they came from the same areas in nearly the same proportions. It seems unlikely that men would make their way to Plymouth to join a ship which they had likely not heard much of, let alone seen. Thus it is plausible that men already on board and in contact with home districts were attracting volunteers, possibly with letters telling of good conditions aboard and good officers.[260] Further, for men both with and without sea experience, the transition into a new environment would have been much easier if an individual already knew men in the ship.

Motives for volunteering for service in the Royal Navy at the end of the eighteenth century were certainly present, and both seamen and landsmen alike took advantage of them. Some men were simply adventurous by nature and liked the life, or at least liked the idea of the life they had at the point they joined, while others found refuge in the Navy from troubles on land.[261] Life at sea was certainly challenging and filled with hard work; however life on land was just as unpleasant for common men, possibly worse, depending on the situation. Further, civil law in the eighteenth century was certainly as harsh as naval discipline, and punishment was often worse, as a death penalty could be handed out for far more minor offences than in the Royal Navy.[262] Naval officers also had to consider that they needed the men to be able to work when they decided on punishments, an advantage to men that was not afforded on land. Landsmen volunteers would not have likely understood the advantages of naval service as well as experienced seamen; however they joined anyway, demonstrating that they at least recognised the advantage of food and shelter. Seamen may have seen naval service and a bounty as advantageous in comparison to trying to find work ashore or a berth in a merchant ship and risking impressment.[263]

Volunteer men may have also come from the volunteer militia forces or the sea fencibles. These forces existed to give able-bodied civilians rudimentary military training, and functioned as an ultimate reserve force in the event of a French invasion.[264] It is important to note that the records do not show any significant number of men arriving in naval service from these units; however this does not mean that men did not volunteer after serving in such units, as they were free to volunteer for military service at any time. It is reasonable to assume that the training and involvement in national defence experienced by men in the militia units instilled patriotism, and as such men were exempt from impressment, their only means of entering naval service was volunteering. For landsmen especially, this may have been a way of getting their foot in the door and experiencing a small facet of military life, which they may have later decided to choose over life ashore. Determining

[260] Rodger, *The Wooden World*, p. 157.
[261] Davies, *Gentlemen and Tarpaulins*, p. 47.
[262] Ibid., pp. 48–49.
[263] Lewis, *A Social History of the Navy, 1793–1815*, p. 92.
[264] J.R. Western, 'The Volunteer Movement as an Anti-Revolutionary Force, 1793–1801', *English Historical Review* LXXI, no. 281 (1956): p. 605.

the number of seamen in militia units is difficult, if not impossible. However, it seems unlikely that many seamen would have joined, as doing so would deny them the ability to work on a merchant ship, due to the necessity of remaining near their unit. This would in turn deny them the ability to work in the occupation for which they had skills and the best opportunity for earning at or above subsistence levels. These units were most likely made up of landsmen, of whom a few may have found the experience enough to persuade them into volunteering for naval service.

Another small group that may have been persuaded to volunteer for naval service were older seamen who had years of experience at sea and had chosen jobs ashore. Such a 'retirement' ashore may have been the result of the plentiful number of young seamen during peacetime available to merchants and the small peacetime Royal Navy, evidenced, as described above, by the very steady peacetime merchant wages that lasted for nearly a century and a half. However, with war came a shortage of skilled seamen and men who had been forced ashore may have taken the opportunity to once again find their sea legs.[265] This is especially true as such men may have had the skill necessary to become petty officers. Vast naval expansion made such a possibility a serious reality for experienced men, especially during the opening years of war when the Navy grew very rapidly. It is clear that there were few jobs ashore available to seamen past their prime labour years that offered the compensation that naval service offered a petty officer. Such men were also a key component in the elastic nature of the British maritime labour market, and allowed for naval wartime expansion without sacrificing merchant trade. It is likely that older seamen, perhaps past the age of speed and agility sought by the Navy, may have been tempted into merchantmen by high wages, and therefore indirectly eased the Navy's shortage without leaving evidence in naval records.

There were drawbacks to being a seaman, and to a great extent volunteers, especially experienced seamen, understood these disadvantages before they joined a warship. By far the greatest hardship faced on board a warship was the inescapable psychological pressure caused by overcrowding.[266] This heavily crowded environment was further exacerbated by the lack of shore leave and the resulting debauchery that this brought on board when warships, particularly large ships-of-the-line, lay at anchor just off shore.[267] Over the course of the eighteenth century, leave for seamen had become less and less frequent, and by the onset of the French Revolutionary Wars, it had become almost non-existent. The lack of leave was largely due to the coppering of ships' bottoms that occurred during the 1770s and 1780s.[268] Prior to this,

---

[265] Charles R. Foy, 'Hidden Lives: Elderly Cooks, Powder Boys, and Fugitive Slaves among Eighteenth-Century Anglo-American Naval Crews', in *New Interpretations in Naval History: Selected Papers from the Fifteenth Naval History Symposium*, ed. Maochun Miles Yu (United States Naval Academy: Naval Institute Press, 2007), pp. 270–271.

[266] Rodger, *The Command of the Ocean*, p. 400.

[267] Lambert, pp. 52–53.

[268] Rodger, 'Shipboard Life in the Georgian Navy, 1750–1800: The Decline of the Old Order?',

ships had to go into dock several times a year to have their bottoms cleaned, which provided opportunities for seamen to take leave. However, on copper-bottom ships this was no longer necessary, and consequently any convenient 'shore leave' opportunities disappeared. Officers also understood that men who were relative newcomers were the most likely to run, so they were often not permitted ashore until they had settled into the ship's company.[269] Had leave been made a standard practice during the wars of the eighteenth century, especially at the end of the century when naval numbers were so high, it might have alleviated some of the manning problems for the Royal Navy and reduced desertion.[270] However, at this time all that can be offered on this point is conjecture.

The most important factor in denying leave, which has often been overlooked, is that these men were aboard warships in a time of war. Such ships had to be expected to leave port at very short notice, which did not allow time to gather men if they were ashore, especially when considering communications at the time. The requirements of the service took precedence above leave to go ashore, as is still the case today. This was especially true for ships at Portsmouth and Plymouth, as they were often involved in the blockade of Brest, even when in port. At any time a signal from an approaching frigate could bring news of the French fleet leaving port, which necessitated that they get to sea with all due haste. Though seemingly unfair to the men, the requirements of the Royal Navy at war exceeded those of comfort and welfare.

Further Evidence for Volunteers

Clearly the evidence presented demonstrates the importance of the volunteer to British naval manpower. However, one of the problems encountered when researching naval manpower is trying to decide who were the 'spontaneous' volunteers, those that volunteered due to a combination of some or all of the above-discussed motivations. One such example is John Nicol, who volunteered during the American War simply because he had 'read Robinson Crusoe many times over and longed for the sea'.[271] The other form of volunteer might be considered the 'coerced' volunteer. Data found within muster books leave little or no clue as to which volunteers may have volunteered under more or less forced conditions. There is also a vast grey area between a 'spontaneous' and a 'coerced' volunteer, where men cannot be clearly assigned to one category or the other. It is true that some seamen were certainly motivated to volunteer by the fact that the presence of press gangs ashore made their lives miserable;[272] however this is still not the same as a man volunteering when in the hands of a press gang.

---

pp. 30–31.

[269] Rodger, *The Wooden World*, p. 196.

[270] Rodger, *The Command of the Ocean*, p. 500.

[271] Lewis, *A Social History of the Navy, 1793–1815*, p. 90.

[272] Earle, *Sailors: English Merchant Seamen, 1650–1775*, p. 193.

Throughout most of the eighteenth century the Admiralty admonished officers who allowed men taken by a press gang to accept the bounty, because it cost the Crown money.[273] However, this changed near the end of the century and by 1793 it is clear that the Admiralty was encouraging regulating officers to allow men to volunteer if they so desired after being cornered by press gangs.[274] These men were the true 'coerced' volunteers, as they volunteered when the only other option was impressment, and the act of volunteering at least afforded them the bounty. The difficulty encountered in the historiography is the tendency to dismiss the implications of large numbers of volunteers, and justifying the action with the assumption that most of these men only volunteered because they had no other choice but impressment.

One key piece of evidence to dispel this claim can be found in recruiting statistics for the years 1793 to 1801.[275] Careful observation shows a relatively steady rate of impressment during each year of the war, while over the same period of time the number of men volunteering for naval service fell dramatically. As the Admiralty had anticipated war, the Impress Service was set up and ready to press men and take in volunteers before war was officially declared, and thus the steady number of pressed men from the very onset of the war suggests that the Impress Service was working at or near its capacity throughout the war.[276] However, if a large number of volunteers were simply pressed men making the best out of the situation, there were also a number of pressed men who refused to volunteer. Therefore, if a large number of volunteers were actually pressed men who volunteered at the eleventh hour, then as the number of volunteers in this data sample rose and fell, the number of pressed men should have fluctuated similarly in proportion. The data, however, shows otherwise, and impressment remained relatively steady, while volunteers were exceptionally high at the beginning of the war, then fell to much lower numbers as the conflict continued.

Examples of seamen who refused the bounty and were pressed include Robert Hay who, though he had volunteered in 1803, refused to do so in 1811, because he wanted to return home to Scotland after having been away for eight years.[277] Hay attempted to escape impressment by pretending to be a landsman with no experience at sea, and even continued the ruse until he reached a warship, where he finally purchased second-hand sailor's attire, so that he would be treated with the respect deserved of a seaman. Joshua Penny refused to volunteer during the French Revolutionary Wars, even though he had been treated well by the captain and officers of the ship. He was pressed despite the fact that he was an American, or at least claimed to be one.[278]

[273] Rodger, *The Wooden World*, p. 163.
[274] Rodger, *The Command of the Ocean*, p. 442.
[275] See Figure 3.3.
[276] Note that the drop in pressed men in 1795 is a reaction to the Quota Acts and does not apply to this argument.
[277] Hay, pp. 217–223.
[278] Choate, p. 57.

James Durand also refused a bounty in 1809 under similar circumstances, claiming to be an American.[279]

The majority of men recruited during the French Revolutionary and Napoleonic Wars were volunteers, especially during the initial years of the war.[280] The evidence for this goes beyond muster books, and can be seen in the records of officers responsible for naval recruiting. During the first twelve months of the war, Captain Smith Child, who ran the regulating office in Liverpool, recruited 976 volunteer landsmen, 688 volunteer seamen, 136 pressed men, and received 18 men that were sent to him by magistrates.[281] The large numbers of landsmen were actually useful aboard British warships, as a large amount of unskilled labour was necessary on deck to heave the ropes that controlled a ship's rigging.[282] Further such men could, over time, obtain some or even all of the skills necessary to be rated an able seaman. The dilution of skills proved to be the key component to the simultaneous success of Royal Navy and British seaborne trade during the eighteenth century.[283] However, for skilled men, the presence of unskilled landsmen made for more work until they picked up some of the necessary skills of a sailor. Many captains desired taking willing landsmen over a knowingly dissatisfied seaman, as an eager landsman could be taught the skills of a seaman in time.[284] Further, captains and officers were encouraged by the Admiralty to take pains to teach unskilled men the skills of seamen. To be considered useful on deck and able to go aloft, an unskilled landsman needed to know the names of all of the ropes, the exercise of cannon and small arms, and to be able to row, among other small tasks. The perfecting of these skills and many others was necessary to be rated as an ordinary and later an able seaman.[285]

Another prominent problem within the historiography has been a general assumption that volunteers liked naval service while pressed men did not. Notably, this comes from an antiquated view of naval history, and over the last thirty years several historians have worked to dispel this myth; however it still persists in a surprisingly large amount of work published in the last decade. It certainly was not true that all men pressed hated the Royal Navy and all who volunteered loved it. Records exist of pressed men who petitioned for their release and then changed their minds and decided to stay in naval service. Further, there are large amounts of evidence for volunteers who deserted.[286] Research by John Byrn, about Royal Navy discipline in the West Indies,

---

[279] Ibid., pp. 152–153.
[280] Knight, *The Pursuit of Victory*, pp. 142–143.
[281] Emsley, *British Society and the French Wars, 1793–1815*, p. 35.
[282] N.A.M. Rodger, 'Officers and Men', in *Maritime History: The Eighteenth Century and the Classic Age of Sail*, ed. John B. Hattendorf (Malabar: Krieger Publishing Company, 1997), p. 138; Rodger, '"A Little Navy of Your Own Making": Admiral Boscawen and the Cornish Connection in the Royal Navy', p. 83.
[283] Rodger, 'Shipboard Life in the Georgian Navy, 1750–1800: The Decline of the Old Order?', p. 29.
[284] Rodger, *The Wooden World*, p. 163.
[285] Lavery, *Shipboard Life and Organisation, 1731–1815*, p. 266.
[286] Rodger, *The Wooden World*, p. 163.

shows that 55 per cent of those who received corporal punishment were volunteers.[287] Moreover, 85 per cent of men who were entered in the books for intoxication were volunteers,[288] and 48 per cent of the men who were deserters were volunteers.[289] Some consideration needs to be taken with these statistics, as they do not attempt to factor for men turned over. Therefore, when considering Byrn's numbers, and that, without factoring, 42 per cent of seamen and 33 per cent of petty officers were volunteers,[290] it would seem that volunteers were slightly more likely to receive punishment aboard ship, were more likely to be intoxicated, and just as likely to become deserters. These facts may have been related to the presence of landsmen among volunteers, who likely had no experience of the sea or the Royal Navy, and naturally made mistakes that experienced seamen did not. Thus arguments that pressed men were unhappy and more likely to run or face punishment have no statistical base to back them up. In fact, they were quite the opposite.

The Value of Volunteers

For the Royal Navy recruiting effort, a volunteer was more valuable than a pressed man. As far as a ship's officers were concerned, one able seaman was generally as good as the next, at least in theory, though in reality some men had better qualities than others. The difference in value between a volunteer and a pressed man for the recruiting effort was that volunteers came willingly and sought out employment with the Navy, whereas pressed men required a costly and time-consuming process to recruit, which caused social friction that the Royal Navy wished to avoid. Therefore, the Royal Navy did all it could to modify the seafaring labour market to meet its immense and critical demands.[291]

One of the major steps taken to facilitate the intake of more volunteers was the streamlining of recruitment operations. Essentially this consisted of taking the responsibility for ship manning out of the hands of officers and creating an administrative unit to handle a large portion of naval recruitment. The roots of centralisation date from the War of Austrian Succession in the 1740s, with the introduction of two Regulating Captains in London who inspected men taken by press gangs. This was small in the overall scheme of naval recruiting, compared with the first major step in centralising naval recruitment, which was the introduction of the Impress Service during the Seven Years' War. The Impress Service began the process of taking the primary responsibility of manning out of the hands of ships' captains. However, it was not until the opening of the French Revolutionary Wars that the Impress Service really began to take on the majority of the responsibility

---

[287] John D. Byrn, *Crime and Punishment in the Royal Navy: Discipline on the Leeward Islands Station, 1784–1812* (Aldershot: Scolar Press, 1989), p. 76.

[288] Ibid., p. 126.

[289] Ibid., pp. 156–157.

[290] See Figures 2.4 and 2.5.

[291] Starkey, 'War and the Market for Seafarers in Britain, 1736–1792', p. 25.

of recruiting. Captains were previously responsible for recruiting men for their own ships, each going about the task in different ways, which not only proved inefficient and distracted officers from readying their ships for sea, but also ensured that recruiting parties could only operate in areas within a reasonable distance from their ship.[292] This did not just apply to pressed men, but to volunteers as well.

With the Impress Service taking over a large amount of recruitment responsibilities, officers no longer recruited volunteers as before.[293] Naval officers aboard ships were still allowed to recruit men, both accepting volunteers and pressing seamen, but by 1793 the majority of the responsibility lay upon the administrative shoulders of the Impress Service. The Impress Service, despite its name, carried the responsibility of the organised entry of volunteers.[294] Apart from the streamlining effect this had on volunteer recruitment, the other major advantage was that the Impress Service stretched into every maritime district and to many inland towns as well.[295] Lieutenants of the Impress Service were well supplied with proclamations of the bounty, as well as other patriotic flyers to post up in public places to entice volunteers.[296] The result of this process was that prospective volunteers no longer had to travel as far to find a ship to enter; rather, naval recruiting came to them. For the Royal Navy, this made recruiting far more efficient, especially when considering prospective volunteers who did not live close to ports that were frequented by ships of the Royal Navy. The success of centralised recruitment in respect to entering volunteers can be seen in the records of the Impress Service between 1776 and 1783, where out of the 116,537 men recruited by the service, 72,658 received bounties as volunteers.[297]

Recruiting Volunteers 'Outside of the Box'

There were certainly captains who proved exceptions to the trend of centralised naval manning. Edward Pellew was such a captain. He was based at Falmouth at the opening of the war and used his Cornish family connections to man his ship, to a great extent with followers who sought both fortune, based upon his reputation, and patronage, from his being a highly respected naval officer. However, Pellew was likely one of the last officers to have such a following of men, and owed much of the success of the quick and nearly effortless manning of his ship to the fact that war had only just been declared.[298] Captains manning their own ships increased their independent authority, as they were personally linked to their men, and the Admiralty

---

[292] Lewis, *A Social History of the Navy, 1793–1815*, pp. 92–93.
[293] Rodger, 'Shipboard Life in the Georgian Navy, 1750–1800: The Decline of the Old Order?', pp. 34–35.
[294] Lloyd, *The British Seaman, 1200–1860*, p. 130; Usher Jr., 'Royal Navy Impressment', p. 675.
[295] Starkey, 'War and the Market for Seafarers in Britain, 1736–1792', p. 34.
[296] Lavery, *Royal Tars: The Lower Deck of the Royal Navy, 875–1850*, p. 206.
[297] Usher Jr., 'Royal Navy Impressment', p. 677.
[298] Rodger, '"A Little Navy of Your Own Making": Admiral Boscawen and the Cornish Connection in the Royal Navy', p. 89.

was beholden to them for these efforts. However, the Admiralty saw these manning efforts as a threat to its control and by the 1790s, the increasing size and capability of the Impress Service ensured that the majority of men came from the centralised control of the Admiralty.[299]

Though not an official part of the Royal Navy, the Marine Society was likely the most original contributor, and certainly the most successful of manning schemes of the eighteenth century.[300] Jonas Hanway started the Marine Society in June of 1756. It took poor, but not criminal, boys from the streets of London, clothed them, gave them elementary training, and sent them to serve in the Royal Navy. Between 1756 and 1762 the Marine Society sent over 4,500 boys into the Royal Navy, accounting for nearly 5 per cent of total recruitment.[301] In laying out the rules and forms of the Marine Society, the passion and patriotism of Hanway can be seen in a quote directed to the boys his organisation intended to take in: 'You are sons of freemen. Though poor, you are the sons of Britons, who are born to liberty; but remember that true liberty consists in doing well; in defending each other, in obeying your superiors and in fighting for your King and Country to the last drop of your blood.'[302] The value of these boys can be seen in a 1793 letter from Nelson asking to be sent 'Twenty Lads from your Society', claiming that 'the greatest care shall be taken of them on board the *Agamemnon*.'[303]

Beyond procuring boys for the Royal Navy, the Marine Society also provided clothing for volunteer landsmen who entered through the Society. For poor labourers ill-equipped for shipboard service, the addition of new clothes to take to sea along with a landsman's bounty provided further incentive for prospective volunteers. The rapid and continuing naval expansion required such landsmen, regardless of their lack of skill. Over the twenty-two-year course of the French Revolutionary and Napoleonic Wars the Marine Society sent 22,973 landsmen into naval service.[304] Though this averages just over 1,000 men a year, the reality was that early years of the war produced far more men, with 2,293 landsmen entering naval service via the Marine Society in 1793, and the figure dropping to 766 by 1799.[305] The yearly intake statistics for landsmen volunteers entering the Royal Navy through the Marine Society closely resemble the overall volunteer statistics, with the highest numbers occurring in the opening year of the war and quickly dropping off. Regardless of the decreasing numbers as the war continued, the

[299] Rodger, 'Shipboard Life in the Georgian Navy, 1750–1800: The Decline of the Old Order?', p. 34; Rodger, '"A Little Navy of Your Own Making": Admiral Boscawen and the Cornish Connection in the Royal Navy', p. 90.
[300] Rodger, *The Command of the Ocean*, p. 313.
[301] Roland Peitsch, 'Ships' Boys and Youth Culture in Eighteenth-Century Britain: The Navy Recruits of the London Marine Society', *The Northern Mariner* XIV, no. 4 (2004): p. 13.
[302] Colley, *Britons: Forging the Nation, 1707–1837*, p. 97.
[303] 'Nelson to the Governors of the Marine Society', 6 February 1793, in *Nelson: The New Letters*, ed. Colin White (Woodbridge: The Boydell Press, 2005), p. 157.
[304] Lewis, *A Social History of the Navy, 1793–1815*, p. 94.
[305] Ibid.

influx of nearly 23,000 men was substantial for the Royal Navy. Depending on the method used to attempt to find out how many men actually served in the Navy between 1793 and 1815, the landsmen alone generated by the Marine Society came to between 5 and 10 per cent of the total number of men who served in the Royal Navy.

The Royal Navy did not simply rely upon various bounties, the hope of prize money, patriotism and charitable organisations to provide volunteers. The Admiralty, as well as most naval officers, understood the manning problem. This was especially applicable to the Regulating Captains stationed around Britain whose primary concern was recruitment. They proved to be exceptional opportunists as they took advantage of situations that proved beneficial to naval recruitment. Their skill and ability to negotiate with local interest groups allowed the Royal Navy to recruit many volunteers and avoid the social friction caused by impressment. An example being in October of 1793 when the Regulating Captain for Liverpool, Captain Smith Child, who had successfully recruited in the city since the opening year of the war and had a good standing with the local populace, suffered two recruiting houses destroyed. Then a seven-hour riot broke out, all due to a frigate captain who ignored his counsel and turned a press gang loose on the port. The chaos resulted in the press gang killing the master of a merchant ship, as well as several injuries. The Regulating Captain suffered the fallout of the riot even though he had nothing to do with the events that provoked it.[306]

The Admiralty was also happy to have local interest groups recruit men for the Royal Navy, often in exchange for protection from impressment. During the Seven Years' War, the Bristol Society of Merchant Venturers had an agreement to provide men for the Royal Navy in exchange for protection from the press and the further condition that two warships were to be kept in the Bristol Channel for protection. In that year the agreement raised 200 volunteers.[307] During the same war, the Watermen's and Lightermen's Company provided 500 men in exchange for protections against impressment, and further provided an additional 240 men to assist with impressment in London.[308] At the same time Aberdeen and Edinburgh fishermen provided one man out of every fishing boat belonging to those cities in exchange for protection.[309] This process also worked overseas, and in the West Indies, where manpower was exceptionally short, Commodore James Douglas sought a deal with the Lieutenant-Governor of Guadeloupe to produce enough men to man a sloop that would be used specifically to protect that port.[310]

---

[306] Emsley, *British Society and the French Wars, 1793–1815*, p. 35.

[307] Bromley, 'The British Navy and Its Seamen after 1688', pp. 150–151; Rodger, *The Wooden World*, p. 162.

[308] Gradish, *The Manning of the British Navy During the Seven Years' War*, p. 67.

[309] Ibid.

[310] Commodore James Douglas to Lieutenant-Colonel Robert Melville, 3 May 1760, quoted in *The Naval Miscellany, Volume V*, ed. N.A.M. Rodger, Publications of the Navy Records Society (London: The Navy Records Society, 1984), pp. 251–252.

The tradition of brokering deals that favoured Royal Navy recruitment efforts was not exclusive to the Seven Years' War. With the rapid naval expansion of the French Revolutionary and later the Napoleonic Wars, such deals proved exceptionally profitable in terms of naval manning, as the Royal Navy had to invest very little in manpower or resources to procure men from areas or interest groups willing to negotiate such deals. The winter of 1792 and 1793 was witness to an illegal strike on the Tyne and Wear, as the seamen who sailed the colliers to and from London sought to increase the wage of £2.10.0 for winter voyages by an additional £0.10.0.[311] With war inevitable, Captain Peter Rothe, a local hero, was ordered by the Admiralty to open the Impress Service on the Tyne and Wear. Once established he used the united nature of the seamen to pressure local merchant interests into providing an increased bounty and amplify the number of volunteers from the area. The outcome was less of a need to press, which avoided the friction caused by press gangs, and able seamen received, in addition to the King's bounty, £4.4.0 from the fund raised by the Newcastle Corporation, Newcastle Trinity House, and an unofficial fund collected specifically for the purpose.[312]

In 1795 the East India Company raised 3,000 men for the purpose of manning ships it had lent to the Navy, in exchange for protection from impressment.[313] Another strike on the Tyne and Wear in 1803 brought the coal trade to a standstill. After pressing fifty-three men, the Royal Navy came to an agreement with local merchant interests to provide a fixed quota of volunteer men, which was based on the number of keelmen employed.[314] In 1803 and 1804 merchant interests on the Tyne and Wear negotiated to provide one seaman or two landsmen for every ten adult keelmen protected from the press.[315] In 1810 the Admiralty came to an agreement with the East India Company to offer protection from impressment for a fixed number of men for each ship based on tonnage.[316] Throughout the war the Admiralty negotiated for quotas of men in return for exemption from the press with corporations like the London Watermen and local authorities like those of the Orkneys.[317]

The attraction of such deals appealed to both the Royal Navy and local authorities.[318] For the Admiralty, these types of arrangements were ideal, as they avoided all of the difficulties and expense that came with impressment. It also proved cost-efficient, as not only was there no need to provide funds for the operation of press gangs, but there was further a lesser need to spend time and effort seeking volunteers, allowing for those resources to be allocated to areas where they would be better used. These arrangements were also ideal

---

[311] McCord and Brewster, 'Some Labour Troubles', p. 367.
[312] Ibid., pp. 377–378; Rodger, *The Command of the Ocean*, p. 443.
[313] Bromley, 'The British Navy and Its Seamen after 1688', pp. 150–151.
[314] Emsley, *British Society and the French Wars, 1793–1815*, p. 100.
[315] Bromley, 'The British Navy and Its Seamen after 1688', pp. 150–151.
[316] Rodger, *The Command of the Ocean*, p. 497.
[317] Ibid., pp. 442–443.
[318] Ibid., p. 443.

for local authorities and interest groups as it allowed them to recruit for the Royal Navy with minimal interruption to trade. It further increased naval and merchant relations by giving more 'power' to local authorities, increasing their standing within their own communities. The success of these arrangements also likely fathered the ideas that led to the Quota Acts of 1795 and 1796, as well as a manning scheme proposed by Melville in 1805.[319]

Negotiation for volunteers also occurred between individual captains and the men they wished to recruit. Many skilled seamen were offered advancement if they volunteered. This, combined with the royal and possibly a local bounty, proved a very attractive offer, as a prime able seaman could obtain a substantial sum of money and rating as a petty officer, with the entitlements that accompanied such a position aboard a warship.[320] In 1802 Commander William Cathcart commissioned HM Sloop *Renard*, and used an unorthodox but successful scheme to recruit. He gave volunteer men advanced wages and allowed them leave to go ashore, keeping their clothes as collateral, but without entering them on the ship's books until they returned. Though risky this proved effective, as men going ashore spread the news of Cathcart's generosity by word of mouth. This method soon produced many more volunteers from which he had his pick of the best men. Moreover, Cathcart underestimated the readiness of his ship in his weekly returns to the Port Admiral, which gained him the necessary time to pull off the scheme.[321]

Such actions by serving officers were certainly bold. However, commanding officers, and prospective commanders, were expected to be bold and creative in battle, and it therefore stands to reason that many would translate such behaviour to recruiting practices. Further, captains and commanders were not simply motivated to man their ships for the sake of having a stated number of men, but rather the quality of their crew directly affected the performance of the ship. Therefore, commanding officers had all of the motivation necessary to adopt any scheme they deemed capable of gaining them an advantage in the quality and quantity of manpower aboard their ships.

One of the claims that has been made almost throughout the historiography is that magistrates used naval recruitment as a means to empty their jails and jurisdictions of undesirable people. This simply was not true; however the Admiralty was willing to accept men from debtors' prisons, as long as their debt was less than £20, a position made official within the provisions of an Act in 1706.[322] By the middle of the eighteenth century there were about 2,000 people in debtors' prisons in England and Wales, some of whom would undoubtedly have had skills that were of interest to the Royal

---

[319] Ibid., pp. 443, 497.
[320] Ibid., p. 497.
[321] Ibid., pp. 497–498.
[322] Rodger, *The Wooden World*, pp. 158–159.

Navy.[323] Rather than giving the men a bounty, the Royal Navy often chose to pay their debts in lieu of the bounty, as long as they had skills needed by the Navy.[324] The Navy was not interested in taking men from debtors' prisons if they had no sea skills, as landsmen volunteers were not in short supply. Though such men were occasionally sought as volunteers, it must be emphasised how small the number actually was. Out of the sample of 27,164 men in this database only nineteen were recorded as having come from civil prison. Such a small number had virtually no effect on naval manning numbers, and would also have had little chance to affect the morale or morals of the lower deck as a whole.

The Royal Navy did accept volunteers from the vast number of prisoners of war kept within Britain, as long as they were not French. As the maritime community was distinctly international, and France managed much of its eighteenth-century overseas trade in foreign vessels, many non-French sailors were taken from captured French merchant ships. During the French Revolutionary Wars alone, 42,000 prisoners were taken, and in 1814 there were 27,000 French seamen being held in Britain, many, possibly even most, of whom had sailing skills that the Royal Navy could use.[325] In 1756 Admiral Boscawen suggested employing non-French prisoners, as many had enquired about serving in the Royal Navy in exchange for release from prison. A year later the Admiralty began canvassing the nine prisoner-of-war camps in England for volunteers, paying them the same bounty as regular volunteers. Rather than being paid to the men, the sum was applied to essentials such as clothes and supplies needed by the men.[326] However, after an attempt to mutiny on the frigate *Raven*, this policy was placed on hold from 1759 to 1761. When it was reinstated, far more attention was paid to ensuring the men were spread out amongst the fleet, rather than placing them in large groups on a relatively small number of ships.[327] As with men from civil prison, the number of prisoners of war who entered the Royal Navy as volunteers was relatively low. Within this data set of 27,164 men, only fifty were recorded as having volunteered as prisoners of war. Even when considering that the data covers only 17,859 seamen, these men still account for less than one-fifth of 1 per cent of seamen recruited. Although prisoner-of-war camps and civil prisons produced a few men here and there, it was by no means a way of increasing naval manpower in any substantial way, and could not be relied upon as a dependable source of manpower.

There were also a few men and boys who voluntarily entered the Royal Navy under special circumstances. These included young boys, often orphans or sons of widows, who were sent away to sea as a way of both increasing their chances in life, as well as lessening the burden upon their caretakers.[328] These

[323] Ibid., p. 158.
[324] Gradish, *The Manning of the British Navy During the Seven Years' War*, p. 84.
[325] Rodger, *The Command of the Ocean*, pp. 501–560.
[326] Gradish, *The Manning of the British Navy During the Seven Years' War*, p. 80.
[327] Ibid., p. 81.
[328] Foy, pp. 271–272.

boys, much like the London boys taken in by the Marine Society, were placed aboard ships and with time became well-trained prime seamen, well suited to the task, as they essentially grew up within the Navy. Many of the cooks aboard British warships joined because injury had left them with little chance to find work ashore, and life at sea had been all that they had really known.[329] Out of the sample covered in this database, 108 men were listed as 'Cook', 'Cook's Servant', 'Cook's Mate', or 'Captain's Cook', and of these only seventeen had more than their name and position recorded in the muster books. Of those seventeen men, the youngest was twenty-five and the oldest was fifty, with the average age being thirty-one. Only twelve of them had their manner of recruitment listed, and five were turned over from other ships, while seven were volunteers. Nine of these twelve were listed as 'Captain's Cook' and four of those received bounties as volunteers, two received £5.0.0 as able seamen and two received £1.10.0 as landsmen. However, such a small sample does not work well for statistics, and the data do not describe any disabilities they may have had. All that can be said is that of the few that do have age data, the average age was nine to ten years older than most prime seamen, and ships' officers would have had little motivation to put able bodied seamen to work as cooks, as such skilled men were always in short supply.

There were also fugitive slaves from the United States or West Indies who entered the Royal Navy as a means of refuge, many of whom may have had ample maritime experience.[330] Additionally, free black men may have found the Royal Navy one of the few places where they could exist at any position other than the very bottom levels of society. As the Royal Navy was a meritocracy, the colour of a man's skin played very little part in his position within the lower deck, and naval ships were likely one of the more cosmopolitan forms of eighteenth-century society in Europe. Such men are very hard to track as far as recruitment is concerned. Out of this entire data sample only twenty-four men were recorded as being born in Africa, mostly with Christian names; however further assumptions as to their identity are difficult to make without risking substantial error. Further, many black men, slaves or not, would have been born in the United States or West Indies and would have been recorded as such when recruited, and therefore tracking them within this database is nearly impossible. However, as the colour of an individual's skin has no effect upon their ability to learn, given time these men made skilled seamen just the same as their white shipmates.

Volunteer recruitment certainly did have a drawback for the Royal Navy during the French Revolutionary and Napoleonic Wars. One particular problem was the Peace of Amiens, which forced the Royal Navy to demobilise and mobilise again in a very short period of time, and after nearly ten years of war already, volunteers were less forthcoming in 1803 than they had been a decade earlier.[331] Though evidence does exist that at the very beginning of the

---

[329] Ibid., p. 270.
[330] Ibid., pp. 268–270.
[331] Emsley, *British Society and the French Wars, 1793–1815*, pp. 99–100.

renewed war there was a good number of volunteers, they did not equal the vigour of 1793.[332] One downside to naval service, experienced by volunteers and pressed men alike, was that seamen, as they belonged to a highly mobile professional group, were used to coming and going as they pleased, serving aboard ships for voyages that were as long or short as they pleased, and this was obviously impinged upon by naval service.[333]

Summation

The eighteenth-century British Navy was undoubtedly the dominant sea power of the Atlantic, if not the world, and by the French Revolutionary and Napoleonic Wars this domination was taken to an entirely new level as the size of the Royal Navy grew without precedent to face the rest of the Atlantic World. Britain's ability to put a naval force to sea, capable of facing down the combined navies of all of Europe and the United States, was a direct result of the strength of British merchant sea trade, which effectively trained the men necessary to field the wartime Royal Navy as well as keeping merchant sea trade functioning.[334] Further, the fact that Britain was able to meet its naval and manpower needs without recourse to major financial or administrative upheaval was a critical factor in its dominance at sea.[335] This research shows that the numbers of volunteers entering into the Royal Navy were dramatically higher than had been previously considered, and must have played a significant part in the lack of turmoil faced by the Navy when manning its fleets. With the data presented in this chapter, there can be no denying that volunteers played the leading role in manning Britain's wooden walls.

Skilled seamen were a precious commodity to both the Royal Navy and merchant ship owners. They knew their value and expected naval officers to treat them with fairness and respect.[336] Warship crews had self-respect and pride, both in themselves and their ship, and under high-quality leadership they were not unhappy.[337] There was certainly a very strong satisfaction and pleasure in being part of a well-led ship's company with *esprit de corps*, which cannot be underrated. It certainly compensated for much of the hardship experienced aboard warships, and can still be witnessed today when elderly veterans speak about the companionship they once enjoyed.[338] The experience, which is difficult to understand for those who have not undergone it, has transcended generations, and many historians have been oblivious to it when they have written the history of men of the lower deck.

---

[332] Lloyd, *The British Seaman, 1200–1860*, p. 204. The fact that volunteers were less forthcoming in 1803 must take into account that when war renewed in 1803, the Navy had only about half demobilised.

[333] Rodger, *The Wooden World*, pp. 200–201.

[334] Starkey, 'War and the Market for Seafarers in Britain, 1736–1792', p. 25.

[335] Harding, p. 140.

[336] Rodger, *The Command of the Ocean*, p. 489.

[337] Davies, *Gentlemen and Tarpaulins*, p. 55.

[338] Ibid., p. 56.

The motivation for volunteers was certainly apparent. Beyond pay, the major shortcoming for seamen, the bounties available offered a significant sum of money upon first joining a ship's company. Though pay in the Royal Navy did not change with the onset of war as it did for merchant shipping, the prize system sharply increased the overall compensation provided for naval service.[339] Further, life afloat offered the hope of advancement for many, where life ashore did not.[340] The Royal Navy offered a system of hierarchical structure that offered pay rises and increased prize money based on promotion, as an incentive for both recruitment and retention.[341] For unskilled labourers who entered as landsmen, this offered an opportunity of advancement well beyond the opportunities available to them ashore. For semi-skilled and seasoned seamen it offered the prospect of promotion to petty officer positions that commanded better pay and higher returns in prize money. The result of these motivations is clear, with the increased number of volunteers throughout the century, in each successive conflict.[342]

However, it is certainly true that the Royal Navy could not recruit enough skilled volunteers to entirely man the fleet in the labour-intensive era of sail.[343] Therefore, press gangs were necessary, though rather than functioning as the primary system of increasing the quantity of men in the Navy they served to bolster the quality of naval manpower as a whole. Further, press gangs could never cover the entire country in the search for seamen, as they worked predominantly in and around major naval and merchant centres. Even with the Impress Service, naval recruitment was restricted to spheres of operation that centred on areas where seamen could reliably be found,[344] and the areas adjacent to the Royal Dockyards at Chatham, Portsmouth and Plymouth tended to be the focus of heavy naval recruitment.[345] Volunteers, however, came from many places, both inside and outside of the areas where the Impress Service operated, driven by their motivations, patriotic or otherwise, to serve King and country at sea. The recruitment of volunteers also did not produce the social friction that impressment served to exacerbate.

Amazingly, Britain's total mobilisation, when considering the manpower serving actively and in the auxiliaries, both on land and at sea, during the French Revolutionary and Napoleonic Wars far exceeded the efforts made by France in terms of population.[346] To a great extent, this was due to the volunteerism of the British people, and is one reason that, unlike France, Britain did not have to find a more systematic means to exploit the national consciousness.[347] Britain's ability to raise men, especially naval manpower,

[339] Benjamin and Thornberg, 'Organization and Incentives', p. 338.
[340] Lambert, p. 55.
[341] Benjamin and Thornberg, 'Organization and Incentives', p. 338.
[342] Gradish, *The Manning of the British Navy During the Seven Years' War*, p. 71.
[343] Rogers, *The Press Gang: Naval Impressment and Its Opponents in Georgian Britain*, p. 4.
[344] Lavery, *Royal Tars: The Lower Deck of the Royal Navy, 875–1850*, pp. 205–206.
[345] Starkey, 'War and the Market for Seafarers in Britain, 1736–1792', p. 32.
[346] Cookson, 'The English Volunteer Movement of the French Wars, 1793–1815', p. 890.
[347] Colley, 'Whose Nation? Class and National Consciousness in Britain, 1750–1830', p. 106.

was unparalleled and ensured that the nation maintained an unmatched strength at sea.

Ultimately, merchant ship owners were forced to offer extraordinarily high pay to seamen, not because press gangs drained the maritime labour market dry, but because vast numbers of seamen volunteered for naval service during wartime. The only way that merchant shipping could compete was with drastically increased pay that exceeded peacetime levels by double or even triple. The Royal Navy of the French Revolutionary and Napoleonic Wars was a force where four out of five seamen were there as volunteers, and like all servicemen before or since, they were 'very ordinary, most of the time cheerful, or at least resigned, and some of the time heroic'.[348]

---

[348] Davies, *Gentlemen and Tarpaulins*, p. 56.

4

Impressment

Few topics of eighteenth-century history have engaged both historians and the general public with such fervour yet have been depicted with less accuracy than impressment.[1] Today, press gangs are probably the first thing most people think of when confronted with naval recruiting in the age of sail. Fiction and history alike have filled the popular mindset with images of press gangs dragging husbands from weddings and people who have no experience of the sea off to serve in what amounted to a seaborne dungeon. The images that have filtered down through the historiography have been of groups of oversized brutal men wielding clubs and walking the streets under the direction of a sadistic lieutenant, looking for any man unfortunate enough to stumble across their path, regardless of their skills as a seafarer. This view fits very well with the traditional view of navies in the age of sail; that is, the popular image of 'rum, sodomy, and the lash'.

Manning the Royal Navy was a problem of immense proportions, and the problem had been growing increasingly throughout the eighteenth century,[2] as the Navy, along with British sea trade, expanded.[3] This resulted in ever-larger struggles for the scarce resource of skilled manpower, which made itself most evident during the initial mobilisation from peacetime to wartime footing.[4] In the French Revolutionary Wars the problem was greater than ever before, as the Royal Navy had expanded from 17,000 in 1792 to over 130,000 men in 1801.[5] Recruiting seamen in the eighteenth century was essentially a problem of mathematics, pitting the requirements of the Navy against the population of mariners available to draw upon.[6] In the end there simply were not enough seamen to fully man the Royal Navy and the

---

[1]   Rodger, *The Wooden World*, p. 164.
[2]   Talbott, p. 22.
[3]   See Figure 2.2.
[4]   Oppenheim, p. 115.
[5]   See Figure 2.3.
[6]   Lloyd, *The British Seaman, 1200–1860*, p. 112; Morriss, *Naval Power and British Culture, 1760–1850: Public Trust and Government Ideology*, p. 18.

merchant fleets at the same time.[7] By 1810 the Royal Navy had reached a size of over 145,000 men, which was 2.7 per cent of Britain's male population.[8]

Addressing the topic of impressment is difficult at best. Impressment consisted of more than press gangs, and press gangs themselves were occupied with more than simply conscripting men for naval service, a fact that has clearly led many historians astray. The records and expenses of the Impress Service consist of data for men who were volunteers as well as those that were pressed. Failing to take this into account inflates the estimated number of pressed men, which has filtered down through the historiography. Beyond this, most pressing took place at sea; however not all impressment at sea was under the control of the Impress Service. Most captains were obliged to send press gangs ashore and on board merchant ships at sea to find recruits, both volunteer and conscript, and these returns are not found with the records of the Impress Service.[9] Thus the data available creates a trail ready to mislead the unwary scholar. Beyond these hazards, in its day, impressment was easy and popular to condemn, and often attacked in print.[10] This is evident within the large number of eighteenth- and nineteenth-century pamphlets that addressed the manning problem,[11] most of which attempt to resolve the issue by making naval service more attractive to seamen.[12] Crowning all of these hazards lies the fact that 'supplying men for the British Navy during the eighteenth century and the early part of the nineteenth was so different from present-day recruitment that there are few points where analogy will suffice'.[13]

Impressment, embodied in the 'disreputable' press gang, was very much in the public eye. One way to view the high-profile nature of impressment is by comparing it to the Army, which was also suspiciously watched by the public. The public feared that an army on home territory would become an instrument of autocratic control.[14] In the same light they saw the press gang as the symbol of the Navy on land, which during war took men away from their chosen livelihoods to serve the Crown. Moreover, naval impressment, unlike army conscription, usually lasted throughout a given war, which in the eighteenth century lasted for many years. In the public eye the organisation of naval impressment appeared capricious in comparison to army conscription, as there was no requirement for pressed men to be brought before a civilian

---

[7] Rodger, *The Wooden World*, p. 153.

[8] Blake and Lawrence, p. 64.

[9] Rodger, *The Wooden World*, pp. 146–147. For more information on officers manning their own ships in the eighteenth century see Rodger, '"A Little Navy of Your Own Making": Admiral Boscawen and the Cornish Connection in the Royal Navy'.

[10] Rodger, *The Wooden World*, p. 164.

[11] For a selection of these pamphlets see Bromley, 'The British Navy and Its Seamen after 1688'.

[12] Rodger, *The Wooden World*, pp. 148–149.

[13] Usher Jr., 'Royal Navy Impressment', p. 674.

[14] Note that by the end of the eighteenth century the Army was becoming more accepted by the public. J.E. Cookson, *The British Armed Nation, 1793–1815* (Oxford: Oxford University Press, 1997), p. 22.

body to ascertain fitness or eligibility for service.[15] Many heated debates sprang from these issues and produced publications and records from both sides of the argument, as press gang activities served to raise public tempers just as much as the fear of military autocracy.[16]

From these debates and the sources they have produced, many misconceptions have arisen, both in the eighteenth and nineteenth centuries and in modern scholarship. One key false impression from the eighteenth century that has filtered through to modern-day research is the idea that seamen were plentiful and, in some minds, nearly unlimited in Britain. This has led many writers, both contemporary and modern, to the belief that the Royal Navy's problems in manning did not spring from competition between naval and merchant sectors for seamen, but were rather the fault of the Navy, as it had made service conditions so intolerable that few skilled sailors volunteered for naval service. The core of the argument was that impressment would not be needed if naval service were made more attractive.[17] The actual heart of the matter was a critical shortage of skilled seamen, especially topmen, for service both in the Royal Navy and in the merchant fleets of Britain during war, and chiefly during the mobilisation that occurred during the early stages of conflict in the eighteenth century.[18]

The Royal Navy drew its manpower from a world-leading mercantile and fishing fleet,[19] which had increased in size, power and prosperity throughout the eighteenth century.[20] This chapter will examine how impressment was used to acquire skilled seamen, who proved invaluable in sail-driven warships, each of which needed a minimum of skilled men in order to operate and manoeuvre safely.[21] This chapter will also demonstrate that impressment was vital as a means of increasing the skill level of crews aboard warships, which translated to a victorious naval campaign, as Britain's position as the dominant naval power was made possible in part by the Royal Navy's ability to employ more skilled seafarers than its rivals.[22]

Impressment was one of the key tools available to the Admiralty in procuring the necessary men for naval service to ensure that the Navy stood

---

[15]   Brewer, pp. 46–51.

[16]   Lloyd, *The British Seaman, 1200–1860*, p. 113.

[17]   Hutchinson, pp. 17–20; J.G. Bullocke, *Sailors' Rebellion: A Century of Naval Mutinies* (London: Eyre and Spottiswoode, 1938), p. 191.

[18]   Rodger, "'A Little Navy of Your Own Making": Admiral Boscawen and the Cornish Connection in the Royal Navy', p. 83.

[19]   Black, *Naval Power: A History of Warfare and the Sea from 1500*, p. 104; Earle, 'English Sailors, 1570–1775', p. 91; Glete, pp. 173–174; Rodger, 'Mobilizing Seapower in the Eighteenth Century', pp. 5–6; Mahan, *The Influence of Sea Power upon the French Revolution and Empire: 1793–1812*, p. 70; Lincoln, p. 78.

[20]   Brewer, p. 12; Palmer and Williams, p. 97; Starkey, 'War and the Market for Seafarers in Britain, 1736–1792', p. 28.

[21]   Sam Willis, *Fighting at Sea in the Eighteenth Century: The Art of Sailing Warfare* (Woodbridge: The Boydell Press, 2008), pp. 28–31. For the vast list of skills needed by topmen see Sam Willis, 'The High Life: Topmen in the Eighteenth-Century Navy', *The Mariner's Mirror* XC, no. 2 (2004).

[22]   Starkey, 'War and the Market for Seafarers in Britain, 1736–1792', p. 28.

ready to defend its island realm. However, the topic of impressment itself has seen relatively little scholarly work, and the research that has been done generally suffers from a mistaken approach to the subject. To quote one historian who has worked to amend the historiography, impressment and the press gang are 'so encrusted with myth and emotion that some effort is required to address it rationally'.[23] Thus, the value of a statistical study of naval manning and its implications in relation to impressment can clearly be seen, as a foundation of statistical data provides a good basis from which to approach the matter rationally.[24]

The core of this chapter is the examination of impressment as a tool of naval manning during the French Revolutionary Wars. In doing so, it will look at what has been written thus far on the topic, as well as how this has affected modern perceptions. It will engage the question of what impressment and press gangs actually did, whom they sought to find for naval service, and why they were needed. Further it will explore the administrative structure of the Impress Service and how the press operated both on land and at sea. However, the primary asset this chapter brings to the study of naval conscription is statistical data, as the historiography has yet to produce any reliable statistics that determine what proportion of the Royal Navy was recruited via impressment.[25] Through the use of statistics, a basis can be built for a new understanding of naval impressment during the eighteenth century.

The subject of naval conscription in Britain, which has been entrenched with so much emotional and political sentiment, tends to draw historians into two camps, one which supports the Royal Navy's search for men by impressment, and the other that condemns the British government and the Navy for tyrannically forcing men into the service of the Crown. Granted these are the two extremes, but most historians who have addressed the topic have ended up on one side or the other of this argument, though some have taken a position closer to the centre than others. This work, on the other hand, aims not to end up in the quagmire of 'A' versus 'B'. This chapter uses statistics as a foundation to build arguments from new and steady ground, rather than from generations of work that have suffered from a problematic historiography. Therefore, rather than defending impressment, or even attacking it, this chapter looks to explore it as a topic well worth scholarly attention, and in need of a baseline from which further research can be done.

In comparison to other topics that fall within the bounds of naval history, surprisingly little has been written about manning and the historical understanding of the subject remains limited.[26] However, most of what has been written has addressed the topic of impressment. In the decades following the end of the Napoleonic Wars there was a market for books and pamphlets

---

[23] Rodger, 'Officers and Men', p. 140.
[24] For more information on the shortcomings of research on maritime manpower see Bromley, 'The British Navy and Its Seamen after 1688'.
[25] Rodger, 'Officers and Men', p. 140.
[26] Rodger, *The Command of the Ocean*, p. 148; Rodger, *The Wooden World*, pp. 145–204; Palmer and Williams, p. 105.

that described naval service, especially impressment, as dreadful.[27] William Robinson's memoir of his service during the Napoleonic Wars provides a good example. Originally published in 1836, it gives such an account.[28] These types of diaries and pamphlets have filtered down through the historiography of the issue and cast a shadow over research on the subject. As a result, most research has looked at the restrictions and arbitrary injustice of the press, as seen through the pamphlets, diaries, and memoirs such as Robinson's.[29] However, many naval historians have also defended impressment as the only option available to man the Royal Navy;[30] although without complementary quantitative research, most work on the subject ends up being based on the observations of individuals who either served in the Royal Navy, or wrote about naval manning from a landsman's prospective.

Overall, it is fair to say that impressment has generally been viewed negatively by naval historians. Common themes have emerged in modern research, such as the popular idea that press gangs conscripted anyone they could find,[31] and that deficiencies in skilled mariners were made up by pressing landsmen.[32] The popular image of British naval manning from the eighteenth century is the view that the majority of men serving in the Royal Navy were in fact impressed and therefore forced to serve.[33] Beyond this, many historians have also blamed the need for naval conscription on problems within the structure and conditions of service of the Royal Navy.

Impressment in Britain

In eighteenth-century Britain, the press gang may have indeed been the fear of many sailors and even the bane of numerous maritime communities. However, before any serious argument concerning the two can unfold, it is important to understand the differences between the abstract principle of procuring men and the concrete entity that actually preformed the task.[34] Impressment was a right that had long been claimed by the Crown.[35] The problems of manning a wartime navy were not new in the eighteenth

---

[27] Rodger, *The Command of the Ocean*, p. 492.

[28] Robinson, *Jack Nastyface: Memoirs of an English Seaman*.

[29] Earle, *Sailors: English Merchant Seamen, 1650–1775*, p. 190.

[30] Ibid., p. 189.

[31] One of many examples of modern research claiming that press gangs took in anyone they could come to grips with: Duncan Crewe, *Yellow Jack and the Worm: British Naval Administration in the West Indies, 1739–1748* (Liverpool: Liverpool University Press, 1993), p. 99.

[32] G.V. Scammell, 'War at Sea under the Early Tudors: Some Newcastle-Upon-Tyne Evidence', in *Seafaring, Sailors and Trade, 1450–1750: Studies in British and European Maritime and Imperial History*, ed. G.V. Scammell (Aldershot: Ashgate Publishing, 2003), Section I, p. 196.

[33] Lincoln, p. 5. See also: Gradish, *The Manning of the British Navy During the Seven Years' War*; Lewis, *A Social History of the Navy, 1793–1815*; Rogers, *The Press Gang: Naval Impressment and Its Opponents in Georgian Britain*.

[34] Lewis, *A Social History of the Navy, 1793–1815*, p. 96.

[35] Davies, *Gentlemen and Tarpaulins*, pp. 71–72; Hutchinson, pp. 15–16; Rogers, 'Impressment and the Law in Eighteenth-Century Britain', p. 75; Spavens, p. 12; Usher Jr., 'Royal Navy Impressment', p. 679.

century, as it had probably been the most difficult administrative task undertaken by the various governments of seventeenth-century England.[36] Even then impressment had been around for a long time, and was accepted as a necessary evil; a requirement if a naval force capable of protecting the southern and eastern coasts of England was to be raised with enough speed to prove effective in war. However, naval impressment during the seventeenth century faced different problems than it did a century later. Notably, pressing seamen was more tolerable because seventeenth-century naval operations were largely seasonal and wars themselves only lasted a few years. Therefore, the requirement of seamen who were pressed into the Navy was temporary and usually ended with the completion of the summer campaigning season, thus relieving many of the tensions that accompanied conscription.[37]

Impressment was a necessity if the Royal Navy was to fight wars at sea.[38] This fact became painfully clear as the eighteenth century Navy grew ever larger and moved from seasonal to year-round operations in wars that lasted far longer. To comprehend the dilemma of naval manning and the methods adopted to combat the problem, the magnitude of eighteenth-century naval manning must be understood.[39] As has already been explained, the demand for seamen far exceeded the available supply. This was not simply a naval problem, as merchant ships were equally impacted by the scarcity of skilled manpower, evidenced by the high wages they were forced to offer during wartime. A further problem experienced by the Royal Navy was that the market for seafarers was local and highly variable, depending greatly on trade of a given locality as well as the season. However, this system did not function effectively to meet the Navy's national need for seamen, as attempting to compete with merchant shipping in each individual location would have produced an administrative nightmare in which naval recruiting would have taken on a different form in every port across Britain. Though the Navy offered better incentives than merchant shipping in nearly every aspect except pay, and drew in large numbers of volunteers, impressment was necessary as a means of ensuring that the Royal Navy had access to men from all areas of maritime Britain. Local maritime labour markets simply did not function efficiently to satisfy the Navy's national demand without government intervention.

The number of men that Parliament voted for the Navy functioned as a means of funding, as the naval budget was based on funds per man. To a great extent this number was based on the quantity of ships available to be fitted out for sea, which in turn was a reflection of the threat perceived and the necessity to protect Britain's ever-growing trade empire. The size of the Royal

---

[36] Davies, *Gentlemen and Tarpaulins*, p. 67.
[37] Michael Duffy, 'The Foundations of British Naval Power', in *The Military Revolution and the State, 1500–1800*, ed. Michael Duffy (Exeter: Exeter University Press, 1980), p. 69.
[38] Earle, *Sailors: English Merchant Seamen, 1650–1775*, p. 190.
[39] Lloyd, *The British Seaman, 1200–1860*, p. 113.

Navy grew drastically across the eighteenth century, and by the end of the Napoleonic Wars it required about four times as many men as did the Navy of William III.[40] However, peacetime naval forces were small and therefore the initial mobilisation from peace to war proved a tremendous stress on the maritime manpower resources of Britain.[41] Further to this problem was the fact that many of Britain's skilled deep-sea mariners were overseas when war broke out, due to the nature of their occupation, and therefore not available to the Royal Navy in any capacity.[42] Though volunteers made up the primary method of naval manning, there simply were not enough volunteers to fill the Navy's vast need for manpower, and there were not enough skilled seamen among them.[43] The supply of professional deep-sea sailors, most importantly highly skilled topmen who could work aloft, was critically short, and impressment was the only politically acceptable way for the Navy to acquire enough of these men to make up the difference between volunteers and the minimum needed for naval wartime operations.[44]

Impressment can therefore be seen as a reaction to the complex nature of manning the Royal Navy during wartime. It was a necessary response to the growth of the Navy over the eighteenth century,[45] as well as being a response to competition from merchant sea trade,[46] which competed with the Royal Navy for men, and it was one of the limited options available to perform the given task.[47] Wartime fleets could have been manned more easily by conscripting every man available; however the dangers to merchant trade were well recognised in government circles.[48] Occasionally, embargoes had been attempted in order to free up seamen, but this came with devastating effects for merchants, a problem which quickly made its way into the political arena and the pressure from such measures ensured that they were not acceptable as a manner of naval manning, illustrating that there were limits to what was considered tolerable.[49]

Just as impressment was a reaction to the problems of finding men for the Royal Navy, reactions to impressment included attempts to find alternative means of procuring skilled seamen. One of the major obstacles to changing impressment was that it only existed in periods of war. Therefore, peacetime bureaucracy did not do much to fix the problem, which to an extent was

40 See Figure 2.2.
41 Clowes, p. 155; Rodger, 'Mobilizing Seapower in the Eighteenth Century', p. 1.
42 Glete, p. 174; Mahan, *The Influence of Sea Power upon the French Revolution and Empire: 1793–1812*, p. 70.
43 Earle, *Sailors: English Merchant Seamen, 1650–1775*, p. 189; Palmer and Williams, pp. 104–105; Rodger, *The Wooden World*, p. 153; Clowes, pp. 155–156.
44 Harding, p. 138; Rodger, 'Officers and Men', p. 141; Spavens, p. 11; Rodger, 'Mobilizing Seapower in the Eighteenth Century', p. 4.
45 Brewer, pp. 32–33; Lloyd, *The Nation and the Navy: A History of Naval Life and Policy*, p. 157.
46 Rodger, *The Wooden World*, pp. 149–150.
47 Crewe, p. 63.
48 Duffy, *Parameters of British Naval Power, 1650–1850*, p. 7.
49 Gradish, *The Manning of the British Navy During the Seven Years' War*, pp. 64–65.

seen as the best solution for Britain's style of mobilisation.[50] However, this lack of action by the British government did not stop people from offering what they saw as better solutions to the problem. Literally hundreds of pamphlets that addressed the manning problem appeared across the eighteenth and nineteenth centuries, of which a great number have survived. They originate both from the naval community and from landsmen who often misunderstood the nature of life at sea. Nearly all claim to have the answer to the problem that had confounded a nation for generations, and some even describe themselves as infallible.[51] The Navy Records Society has devoted a volume to manning pamphlets of the eighteenth and nineteenth centuries, which examines twenty-five pamphlets carefully selected from the multitude that were written.[52] Though it barely scratches the surface of what exists, it provides a good survey of how people, both with and without knowledge of the sea, viewed the problems of naval manning, even though most of their suggested solutions were unlikely to produce positive results.

The papers of Pitt the Younger, housed at the National Archives in London, contain dozens of pamphlets sent to him during his tenure as Prime Minister.[53] The majority of these pamphlets illustrate the limited knowledge of most people when it came to sea service and maritime communities. Generally speaking, they all pin their arguments around three assumptions: that the maritime population of Britain was virtually limitless; that sailors would volunteer in droves if naval service were made more attractive; and that a system similar to the French *Inscription Maritime* would solve the manning problem. In reality, the maritime population of Britain was far from limitless, and further seamen took years to train and their numbers were directly related to peacetime maritime trade and fishing in Britain.[54] It is important to note that most of Britain's seamen were not employed year-round, and many men likely took up shore jobs as they aged out of their early to mid-twenties, the prime effective age of able seamen. Thus, in peacetime seamen spent more time ashore. During wartime, impressment was used to increase the effective supply of seamen by ensuring they worked twelve months out of the year.[55] Equally problematic was the idea that seamen would volunteer if the naval environment were improved, which assumes that naval service was harsh in comparison to that of merchant ships. In

---

[50] Richard Harding, *The Evolution of the Sailing Navy, 1509–1815* (London: St. Martin's Press, 1995), p. 141.

[51] For example see: NMM: E/4559, 'Infallible Project for the Speedy Manning of the Royal Navy, 1745'.

[52] Bromley, *The Manning of the Royal Navy.*

[53] A few examples are: TNA: PRO 30/8/248, Navy Office papers relating to seamen and mariners; TNA: PRO 30/8/249, Letters on Manning the Navy; and TNA: PRO 30/8/250/1, Essays, propositions &c on Manning the Navy. Each of these are made up to a large extent of pamphlets and essays for manning the Royal Navy along with supporting evidence.

[54] Rodger, '"A Little Navy of Your Own Making": Admiral Boscawen and the Cornish Connection in the Royal Navy', p. 83; Rodger, 'Mobilizing Seapower in the Eighteenth Century', p. 4; Spavens, p. 11.

[55] Rodger, 'Officers and Men', p. 141.

fact naval service, generally speaking, was certainly no harsher than that in merchant ships and in most cases conditions were better. Although some individual officers were obviously harsher than others, looking at the whole it is clear that officers of the Royal Navy respected the skills and abilities of their seamen, understanding that they could not operate a warship without them and further that harsh treatment would not aid morale or help the problems associated with manning.

European Comparisons

Finally, there was the idea that impressment could be done away with if a system similar to the French *Inscription Maritime*, a register for seamen, was adopted in Britain. In comparison to the French *Inscription*, impressment was clearly a superior method of getting the necessary skilled labour required for Britain's naval forces to work effectively.[56] The idea of a similar system to that of France was briefly adopted by Britain in 1696, and Bills were passed to try to continue it in 1706, 1720, 1740 and 1758.[57] The British system was based on a volunteer register that offered sailors benefits for registration. However, seamen viewed the system as an attempt at entrapment, considered the inducements insufficient, and therefore did not register. The only thing that could have made the system successful at getting seamen to register would have been compulsion; however, any such ideas reeked of French absolutism and were not adopted.[58]

The reality of the French *Inscription Maritime* was that it only worked in a governmental system based on the traditions and resources of absolute monarchy.[59] Unlike the British, the French maritime population stayed relatively stable throughout the eighteenth century, only increasing from about 50,000 to 70,000 between 1660 and 1789, while at the same time tonnage quadrupled, and of these men, one-third only had experience in the Mediterranean.[60] The system was put into place as a means for the French Crown to have more access to the pool of seamen,[61] but it did nothing to increase the actual number of seamen; rather its major advantage was making

---

[56] Jeremy Black and Philip Woodfine, eds, *The British Navy and the Use of Naval Power in the Eighteenth Century* (Leicester: Leicester University Press, 1988), p. 18; Denver Alexander Brunsman, 'The Evil Necessity: British Naval Impressment in the Eighteenth-Century Atlantic World' (unpublished PhD thesis, Princeton University, 2004), pp. 111–112; Knight, *The Pursuit of Victory*, p. 22.

[57] Bromley, 'The British Navy and Its Seamen after 1688', p. 150; Duffy, 'The Foundations of British Naval Power', p. 70; Earle, *Sailors: English Merchant Seamen, 1650–1775*, p. 190; Richard Harding, *The Emergence of Britain's Global Naval Supremacy: The War of 1739–1748* (Woodbridge: The Boydell Press, 2010).

[58] Duffy, 'The Foundations of British Naval Power', p. 70.

[59] Rodger, *The Insatiable Earl: A Life of John Montagu, Fourth Earl of Sandwich, 1718–1792*, p. 52; Rodger, 'Officers and Men', pp. 141–142; Spavens, p. 12.

[60] Harding, *Seapower and Naval Warfare, 1650–1830*, p. 136; Rodger, 'Mobilizing Seapower in the Eighteenth Century', p. 5.

[61] Harding, *Seapower and Naval Warfare, 1650–1830*, p. 136; Knight, *The Pursuit of Victory*, p. 22.

the initial mobilisation for war smoother.[62] Though the French *systéme des classes*, renamed the *Inscription Maritime* in 1792, had 60,000 registered under Louis XIV, the lack of growth of the French marine population meant that it never proved an effective manning tool.[63] By the Seven Years' War the number of mariners registered had declined, meaning that the French Navy could not fully mobilise even by taking in all of its registered mariners.[64] These problems continued in France, resulting in the Navy not being able to fully mobilise in 1779 when French naval opportunity was at its greatest.[65] On the eve of 1793, France had still not solved its longstanding problem of naval manning.[66] Further, French manning problems were exacerbated again at the onset of war by the loss of men killed in action or taken prisoner by the British. Four decades earlier, in 1756 alone the British took between 6,500 and 7,500 French sailors prisoner, crippling the French ability to mobilise ships.[67] Similarly, in the summer of 1794, Howe's action of the Glorious First of June resulted in the loss of over 5,000 French sailors killed or captured.[68] This problem was made increasingly worse for France by Britain's realisation that it could starve the French Navy of men by only giving back landsmen and officers in prisoner exchanges, while keeping valuable French seamen as prisoners in England.[69] Even further restraints resulted from the fact that one-third of French seamen resided in France's Caribbean colonies, making their inclusion in the French Navy even more difficult and less likely as war progressed and French contact with its colonies became more and more difficult due to British naval efforts.[70]

Though the French *Inscription Maritime* did offer its registered sailors many theoretical advantages, such as medical services, certain tax exemptions, and freedom from impressment, it ended as a failure.[71] It failed in great part due to financial problems that resulted in the Crown's inability to follow through on its promises, combined with shipboard conditions that were considered harsh and prison-like when compared to the British

---

[62] Rodger, *The Insatiable Earl: A Life of John Montagu, Fourth Earl of Sandwich, 1718–1792*, p. 63; Rodger, 'Officers and Men', p. 141.

[63] Aldridge, pp. 56–57. Note, it is possible that seamen of the big commercial ports of France may have been badly undercounted by the *systéme des classes*, because ship owners wanted to keep their men out of the Navy's hands. If so, the French were not as badly off as has been suggested, rather the system was not as efficient at finding seamen. However, currently this theory is only conjecture.

[64] Jonathan R. Dull, *The French Navy and the Seven Years' War* (Lincoln, Neb.: University of Nebraska Press, 2005), p. 47.

[65] Lloyd, *The British Seaman, 1200–1860*, p. 175; Starkey, 'War and the Market for Seafarers in Britain, 1736–1792', p. 30.

[66] Cormack, p. 18.

[67] Dull, p. 62.

[68] Black, *The British Seaborne Empire*, p. 150.

[69] Richard Harding, *Seapower and Naval Warfare, 1650–1830* (London: Routledge, 2003), p. 137; Rodger, 'Officers and Men', p. 142.

[70] Duffy, 'World-Wide War and British Empire, 1793–1815', p. 187.

[71] Harding, *Seapower and Naval Warfare, 1650–1830*, p. 136.

Navy.[72] The French *Inscription* devolved into a form of compulsion that relied on violence more than the British press,[73] which is ironic as it was initially put forward as a fair means of recruiting men that would avoid the problems of conscription.[74] This resulted in the *Inscription* being resented in the maritime provinces, and French mariners dodged naval service just as much or more than their British counterparts.[75] In the end, France could not produce enough men to man its fleets, demonstrated in 1809 when the French Toulon fleet was nearly as large as the British blockaders, but could never put to sea due to a shortage of experienced seamen.[76]

France was not alone in employing this type of system. Spain created the *matrícula del mar*, a civil administration intended to provide the Spanish Navy with access to its maritime population in times of war. However, in comparison to Britain and France, Spain had a small deep-sea merchant fleet and a smaller number of mariners to draw from in times of war. Though the Spanish register contained about 47,000 men in the 1760s and about 65,000 by 1793, evidence suggests that many of these men were not actually the deep-sea sailors needed to man warships or in some cases not familiar with the sea at all.[77] The reality was that to man its 200 warships in 1793, Spain needed nearly 60,000 men, or 90 per cent of the men on the register, and further, to man the 311 ships desired by Charles IV, Spain needed 111,000 men.[78] By 1800, the strains on the system had brought it to near collapse, not helped in the least by the fact that the trickle of men deserting from warships had become a flood.[79] By 1802, the system had come under full military control and registration requirements changed, allowing men to leave the register only by leaving any occupation that was associated with the sea, as Charles IV did not want to 'compel' anyone to sign up for the register.[80] Simply put, the only way for a Spanish mariner to avoid registering was by choosing another occupation. The final result was that Spain's *matrícula del mar* could not stand the weight and continued strain of the Napoleonic Wars; without the administrative power or the necessary skilled seamen to support the system, it simply crumbled, as did the Spanish Navy.[81]

Overall, the compulsory registration systems of France and Spain functioned in a more tyrannical manner than did the British system of impressment.[82] The fact that they required mariners to register made them a

[72] Cormack, pp. 26–29.

[73] Rodger, 'Officers and Men', p. 142.

[74] Cormack, pp. 46–47.

[75] Ibid., p. 26; Mahan, *The Influence of Sea Power upon the French Revolution and Empire: 1793–1812*, p. 64.

[76] Black, *The British Seaborne Empire*, p. 155.

[77] Knight, *The Pursuit of Victory*, p. 22; Palmer and Williams, pp. 436–437; Rodger, 'Officers and Men', p. 142; Rodger, 'Mobilizing Seapower in the Eighteenth Century', p. 5.

[78] Phillips, 'The Life Blood of the Navy', p. 439.

[79] Ibid.

[80] Ibid., p. 440.

[81] Ibid.

[82] Baugh, *British Naval Administration in the Age of Walpole*, p. 238; Lloyd, *The British Seaman*,

pseudo press, which was more oppressive than pressing, as it gave the mariners no real opportunity to avoid naval service or find a berth in a merchant ship during war. Neither system provided any increase to the number of men with the necessary skill to work aloft in square rigged warships; thus when war ensued, there were never enough men to perform the rotation they suggested. One third of the mariners in either country could never have provided the manpower necessary to fight the naval wars of the eighteenth century. The only opportunity it really afforded was a way to quickly mobilise men in the opening year of war. Both systems quickly broke down and basically turned into conscription during wartime.[83] Britain tried a similar scheme in 1696 based on a volunteer registry, along with further attempts to provide a register that continued throughout the first half of the eighteenth century. Only the 1696 scheme successfully made it through Parliament, and it was a clear failure.[84] Even British naval officers agreed that a registration system was of no use, an example being Captain Augustus Harvey, who returned to London in January 1759 to sit in Parliament and help quash a Bill that would have used registration accompanied by a lottery.[85] Impressment, though universally admitted to be an evil, was a lesser evil than registration, especially as it allowed opportunities of evasion to seamen that would have been less likely in France and Spain.[86]

The Search for Skilled Seamen

The system of impressment was designed to function as both a method of manning the Royal Navy and a means of restraint. Though few historians have looked at impressment and press gangs in this light, current research confirms that impressment targeted specific men, as well as ensuring that certain men were not taken for naval service. The Admiralty understood the dangers that manning could inflict on trade and therefore, along with the government, placed restrictions regarding who could be pressed and when it was legal to do so – an example being press warrants that were issued during the French Revolutionary Wars. British press warrants of the 1790s were largely generic, printed forms with instructions and blank lines for filling in names and dates. Examining press warrants reveals the restrictions placed upon officers involved in pressing men. The warrant provided a definition of the man the Royal Navy wished to impress: 'Seamen, Seafaring Men, and Persons whose Occupation and Callings are to work in Vessels and Boats upon Rivers'[87] – a statement that agrees with instructions found in an 1807

1200–1860, p. 182; Rodger, *The Wooden World*, p. 151.

[83] Rodger, *The Wooden World*, p. 151.

[84] Rodger, *The Command of the Ocean*, pp. 210, 312.

[85] Tim Clayton, *Tars: The Men Who Made Britain Rule the Waves* (London: Hodder & Stoughton, 2007), p. 91.

[86] Rodger, 'Officers and Men', p. 141.

[87] NMM: PLT/56, Press Warrant issued to William Affleck of HMS *Alligator*, 20 December 1794; TNA: HO 44/42, Press Warrant issued to Philip D'Auvergne, Prince of Bouillon of HM Floating

manual for officers in the Impress Service,[88] as well as what most present-day historians have written on the subject.[89]

Essentially, impressment sought deep-sea sailors for Royal Navy service.[90] Deep-sea sailors were young men who had usually begun working at sea in their early teenage years, likely in coasting or fishing vessels which used light sailing rigs capable of being handled by boys.[91] The key factor was acquiring able seamen, who by definition were capable of working aloft in a ship's rigging. Three skills were necessary for impressment. First, the men had to have the necessary skill to work aloft, which took years of experience; secondly, they required the agility of youth to work in the rigging; and finally, they needed the strength of a full-grown man to be able to handle the large and heavy sails involved in sailing warships. Therefore, the age window at which men could fill this vital position aboard a naval ship was relatively narrow, reflected by the majority of able seamen taken into the Royal Navy between 1793 and 1801.[92] Further, due to the years it took to acquire the necessary skill to become an able seaman, these valuable assets could not simply be trained once war had begun and thus they had to come from the existing supply produced by peacetime merchant demands.[93] The Navy experienced a flood of volunteer landsmen; thus impressment specifically sought experienced seamen to increase the ratio between skilled and non-skilled men aboard warships. This is demonstrated by comparing the skill levels of volunteer and pressed seamen. These statistics show that 9 per cent of volunteers were rated as petty officers, 28 per cent were rated as able seamen, 23 per cent were rated as ordinary seamen, and 40 per cent were rated as landsmen.[94] Essentially, 60 per cent of volunteer seamen were skilled, being rated ordinary seamen, able seamen or petty officers. An analysis of men pressed into service shows that 7 per cent were rated as petty officers, 42 per cent were able seamen, 35 per cent were ordinary seamen, and 16 per cent were landsmen. This means that 84 per cent of pressed men were skilled, of whom three-fifths were rated able seamen or petty officers. Of the 16 per cent of pressed men who were entered into the books as landsmen, a sizable proportion of them were seafaring men who possessed skills crucial to the upkeep and maintenance of warships, such as skills in shipbuilding or

Battery the *Nonsuch*, 1 July 1794, ff. 314–317; TNA: HO 69/6, Press Warrant issued to Philip D'Auvergne, Prince of Bouillon, of HMS *Bravo*, 14 December 1795.
88 TNA: ADM 7-967, 'Instructions to Officers Raising Men, 1807', pp. 3–4.
89 For a few examples see: Earle, *Sailors: English Merchant Seamen, 1650–1775*, p. 190; Starkey, 'War and the Market for Seafarers in Britain, 1736–1792', p. 37; Usher Jr., 'Royal Navy Impressment', pp. 679–680.
90 Duffy, *Soldiers, Sugar and Seapower: The Expeditions to the West Indies and the War against Revolutionary France*, pp. 20–21; Rodger, '"A Little Navy of Your Own Making": Admiral Boscawen and the Cornish Connection in the Royal Navy', p. 83; Starkey, 'War and the Market for Seafarers in Britain, 1736–1792', p. 37.
91 Rediker, pp. 12–13.
92 See Figure 2.19 for ages of seamen and petty officers.
93 Rodger, *The Insatiable Earl: A Life of John Montagu, Fourth Earl of Sandwich, 1718–1792*, p. 62.
94 See Figure 3.2 for the skill of volunteer men.

sail-making. One of the major problems in the historiography thus far has been the view that press gangs took up anyone they could find; however this research contradicts that strongly. Further, the Royal Navy was not interested in employing malcontents or vagrants, much less going to the trouble of impressing them. Undoubtedly, magistrates viewed naval recruiting drives as a way to rid their jurisdiction of such unwanted persons;[95] however the statistics do not reflect any significant quantity of these men having made it as far as a ship at sea. Thus, with naval impressment concentrating on men with valuable skill and experience at sea, naturally press gangs working on land were concentrated around the naval and maritime centres of Britain.[96]

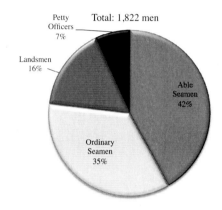

Figure 4.1 Pressed seamen and petty officer skill

Notably, impressment was not only a system to target specific men for naval service, but also a system for preserving specific men from naval service. Many men with seafaring skills were essential to the infrastructure of wartime Britain, and their loss to naval service would have proved catastrophic to the Royal Navy's ability to build, supply and service warships, and would have further been problematic for Britain's economy as a whole. Men were either protected by their position, such as masters of merchant ships, or they were given protections, such as men working in naval dockyards. These last mentioned protections took the form of a piece of paper signed by various naval or civilian officials either locally or at the Admiralty.[97] In 1757, during the heat of the Seven Years' War, an estimated 50,000 protections from impressment existed, while at the same time Parliament had voted funds for 55,000 men to serve in the Navy.[98] Thirty-nine years later, in 1796, double

---

[95] Brewer, p. 51.

[96] Starkey, 'War and the Market for Seafarers in Britain, 1736–1792', pp. 32, 34.

[97] An example of an Admiralty protection is one given to John Chew, a labourer at Deptford Dockyard, in November of 1805. Though not protected by Parliamentary Statute, such labourers were important to the smooth and efficient running of the dockyards, as well as other vital facilities. Hattendorf *et al.*, p. 552.

[98] Earle, *Sailors: English Merchant Seamen, 1650–1775*, p. 190; Rogers, 'Impressment and the Law in

that number were voted for naval service, 110,000 men.[99] Therefore, with a naval growth of this magnitude it is safe to figure that greater numbers of protections were needed to keep the British economy and infrastructure running. Statutory protections covered merchant officers, such as masters, chief mates, boatswains and carpenters, who could not be taken when their ship was at sea, provided it was greater than fifty tons.[100] Other seamen were also protected; these included fishermen, men serving on coasters, colliers and whalers, apprentice boys, and foreigners, as long as they had served less than two years in a British ship.[101] Press gangs did not simply sweep up everyone who fell into the category of seaman or 'person who used the sea'. Many of these individuals were vital to Britain's infrastructure and consequently the ability to wage war. Many men who lived in port towns, especially naval ports, performed vital tasks for the Navy and therefore required protections from impressment, which were issued by the Admiralty.

Impressment, however, was liked by few and hated by most, especially those whom it targeted. To a great extent, impressment was an absolutist solution to a manpower problem faced in a non-absolutist state.[102] Therefore, the act met with lots of resistance from the public, as well as from civilian law. In the eyes of the law, impressment existed in the 'grey area', as there were no specific laws that allowed it;[103] rather it was considered a right of the Crown, and had been in place since time immemorial. Officials from all levels had come down on both sides of the issue. In 1743, a murder case was tried against a seaman named Broadfoot for shooting a member of a press gang, and the judge recognised impressment as legal, though the particular act was illegal, as the gang's lieutenant was absent.[104] On the other side, magistrates ensured that press gangs faced prosecution, fines and imprisonment, sometimes regardless of whether or not they had exceeded the bounds of the law.[105] There were also often problems with local magistrates or other office holders refusing to back press warrants.[106] The fact that impressment existed in such controversial territory meant that it had to follow strict rules to ensure that men were pressed legally. Press officers had to have properly dated warrants and had to be physically present before entering any establishment or vessel in search of men. Further, upon finding the proper men they had to be careful not to use undue force.[107] Although this was not always the case, generally speaking impress officers followed the guidelines. Cases of

Eighteenth-Century Britain', p. 88.
[99] TNA: PRO 30/8/248, 'Account of Seamen ...', f. 29.
[100] Lewis, *A Social History of the Navy, 1793–1815*, p. 106.
[101] Robinson, 'Secret of British Power', p. 6; Clayton, p. 170; Brunsman, p. 11.
[102] Glete, p. 174.
[103] Brian Lavery, *Nelson's Navy: The Ships, Men and Organisation, 1793–1815* (Annapolis: Naval Institute Press, 2005), p. 118.
[104] Rodger, *The Command of the Ocean*, p. 314.
[105] Ibid.
[106] Rogers, 'Impressment and the Law in Eighteenth-Century Britain', p. 78.
[107] Ibid., pp. 80–81.

gangs pressing without warrants or even the required officers do exist, as well as cases of overbearing force being used to subdue men, though they were rare when compared to the number of men pressed.[108] When cases did arise, the Admiralty by and large supported the officers whom they employed to find mariners, so long as they had not been overtly in the wrong. Obviously, experience, money and influence were almost always on the Admiralty's side during legal battles, though seamen not wishing to serve in the Navy undoubtedly took every opportunity afforded to work the system to their advantage.[109]

One reason that naval impressment faced such resistance derives from its location and the manner in which it was carried out, as opposed to conscription for the British Army. Unlike Army conscription, which sought men from most walks of common life and from nearly all parts of Britain, naval impressment was concentrated in areas of marine activity, and therefore focused on a narrow band of the population. Further, Army conscription was subject to a civilian body to review and determine that those who had been seized were eligible for service. The fact that naval impressment had to go through no such civilian review made it seem arbitrary from the point of view of civilians; though in fact by the second half of the eighteenth century, men taken by the Impress Service did have to pass under the inspection of a Regulating Captain.[110] At this stage, men who were picked up by the gangs and tenders of the Impress Service would have been evaluated. Men that the Navy did not need or desire would have been sent away, as well as those with protections and foreigners with less than two years of employment in British merchant ships.

Impressment also encountered friction due to the fact that it served as a policy of the Crown, which took precedence over local government jurisdiction and power. The system of British liberty in the eighteenth century rotated around a weak central government, and a strong local government. Impressment, however, undermined the strength of local government by forcing Crown policy upon them, and it further endangered the liberty of the magistrate, which naturally produced resentment and antagonism.[111] To a great extent, the problem developed from national government, in this case the Crown, overriding the magistrate's power in his own jurisdiction.[112] From the point of view of local authority, this sounded like the tyrannical system of absolutism that Britons observed across the Channel in France. Naturally, such a hot topic found its way through politics on all levels, and is one reason behind the attention impressment has received in historical writing. However, both civil and military powers preferred that liberties of seamen be encroached upon rather than sacrificing the liberties of Englishmen

---

[108] Rogers, *The Press Gang: Naval Impressment and Its Opponents in Georgian Britain*, pp. 25–27.
[109] Rogers, 'Impressment and the Law in Eighteenth-Century Britain', p. 94.
[110] Brewer, pp. 47–48, 50–51.
[111] Rodger, 'Officers and Men', p. 140; Rodger, *The Command of the Ocean*, p. 315.
[112] Capp, pp. 265–267.

everywhere, as would be the case had an invasion or overwhelming defeat of Britain taken place.[113] The friction between national and local government over impressment reached its height during the American Revolutionary War. Naval conscription was met with opposition at all levels of government, where it was often claimed that impressment formed an infringement on the rights of British subjects.[114] In Plymouth in 1780, local garrisons were openly fighting press gangs.[115] Much of this came from the fact that the war itself contained elements of internal civil war, and therefore made the already high-profile topic of impressment doubly divisive.[116]

Naturally, such a controversial topic as impressment was also occasionally accompanied by violence. One firsthand example from 1799 involved the Duke of Cumberland who, upon hearing that impressment was a violent ordeal, dressed himself and a naval officer as common seamen and staggered around a port town until they were impressed. They were dragged off to a tender where they were roughed up and nearly flogged before he revealed himself and had the commander of the tender arrested.[117] It should be noted that this particular event was likely written about for the specific purpose of attacking the practice of impressment, and some of the details could have been embellished; however it nevertheless provides an example of the fact that impressment was not a simple process and not particularly kind to the men who were pressed, especially if they resisted.

However, press gangs themselves also experienced various acts of violence against them. In the seventeenth century press officers were attacked by mobs, often with the collusion of local officials.[118] As the numbers of pressed men increased during the eighteenth century, violence against impressment also increased. The Seven Years' War also saw an influx of violence against impressment in Liverpool, which, to a great extent, was the result of weak local government.[119] This aggressive behaviour made pressing difficult within Liverpool, and denied press gangs access to seamen there.[120] The Admiralty was aware of the regulations relating to impressment and was strict in their application. As a result, many seafaring towns took up violent means to resist impressment.[121] Even rare occurrences of murder over resistance to impressment were documented, as was the case in the summer of 1759, when a lieutenant boarding a Greenland

[113] Rodger, 'Officers and Men', p. 141.
[114] Conway, 'The Politics of British Military and Naval Mobilization, 1775–83', pp. 1191–1192.
[115] Oppenheim, p. 108.
[116] Rodger, *The Command of the Ocean*, p. 395.
[117] *The Naval Chronicle for 1799* (London: Joyce Gold, 1799), p. 307. Note that this is the only record of this incident that I have been able to find, which may suggest that it either did not happen, or that the truth of the matter was greatly embellished.
[118] Davies, *Gentlemen and Tarpaulins*, p. 74.
[119] Rodger, *The Command of the Ocean*, p. 315.
[120] Clayton, p. 171.
[121] Morriss, *Naval Power and British Culture, 1760–1850: Public Trust and Government Ideology*, p. 42.

whaling ship was wounded by the crew and later died in hospital.[122] Violence against press gangs probably reached its zenith at the 'Battle of Portland' in 1803, an episode that left sixteen gangsmen wounded and four civilians dead. The gang's officers were eventually acquitted after a plea of self-defence, but this demonstrates the volatile nature of impressment even after nearly ten years of warfare.[123] However, though examples do exist of violence associated with impressment, there were relatively few occurrences when compared to the number of men pressed across the eighteenth century.

Contrary to much of the historiography, impressment was not cheap.[124] Figures for the American Revolutionary War demonstrate that impressment did not come at low cost. Research has shown that pressed men from this conflict cost the Crown about £10 each to recruit, when considering the expenses of the Impress Service, while volunteers simply received the King's bounty, which for able seamen was half that sum and required substantially less work from the press gangs.[125] Expense reports state that the total cost of the Impress Service during the American Revolutionary War was £1,603,438.[126] This averages at about £13.15.0 per man recruited by the Impress Service at a time when a year's wage for an able seaman was £15.12.0. However, this document does not separate the difference in cost for men pressed and volunteers; rather it is just a total expense account. Some research suggests that in 1803 each pressed man cost the Admiralty around £20 to recruit.[127] Though difficult to calculate accurately, it is clearly obvious that impressment was not cheap; however the expense was on the quality of the men pressed, not the quantity.

The Impress Service and Press Gangs

Impressment ashore, and to a great extent at sea in coastal waters, was controlled and directed by the Impress Service. This service was an administrative branch of the Royal Navy and was designed to better organise and expedite the recruitment of men into the Royal Navy, which took a large portion of the burden away from ships' officers. By doing this, one administrative branch could manage the largest portion of the manning problem, while the officers of warships concentrated on readying their ships for sea. The Admiralty handled command and control of the Impress Service, as all officers took their orders from the Admiralty either directly or indirectly. However, by the American War, the Navy Board administered the Impress Service and controlled its financial management throughout the British

---

[122] Clayton, p. 170.

[123] Duffy, 'The Foundations of British Naval Power', p. 70.

[124] For figures dealing with the Seven Years' War, see Neal, 'The Cost of Impressment During the Seven Years' War'.

[125] Lloyd, *The British Seaman, 1200–1860*, pp. 126–130.

[126] NMM: MID 7/3/2, 'Expense of the Impress Service in the American War of Year 1775 to 1783'.

[127] Baynham, p. 6.

Isles. Further the Navy Board was responsible for the tenders of the Impress Service and their crews.[128]

The concept of centralised manning originated from problems faced by an ever-growing naval force and the necessity to make wartime mobilisation as fast and efficient as possible. By the War of Austrian Succession the wartime Navy had grown by nearly 50 per cent over that of the War of Spanish Succession, to over 58,000 in 1747.[129] Throughout the eighteenth century, British merchant trade was growing, which provided more mariners for the Royal Navy to draw from, but the wartime Navy grew faster than its civilian counterpart and required more men to man its ships. By 1745, the crisis had risen to the point that the Admiralty revoked its protections to the trading companies and claimed one in six of their sailors to man warships.[130] During the War of Austrian Succession, the Royal Navy also introduced two Regulating Captains in London, who inspected men taken by press gangs before sending them to ships. This streamlined the process of impressment on land and ensured that the men being pressed were actually mariners and not simply vagrants or criminals. This was also the first step in the development of the Impress Service.[131]

The first introduction of the Impress Service as a wartime establishment was during the Seven Years' War. Regulating Captains employed for the Impress Service were posted in several coastal cities including Bristol, Liverpool, Whitehaven, Newcastle, Yarmouth and Edinburgh. With further expansion in 1756, 1759 and 1762, many other cities received Regulating Captains to supervise press gangs; these included Gloucester, Winchester, Reading, Southampton, Aberdeen, Exeter and Cork.[132] Making press gangs a permanent fixture, with Regulating Captains to manage them, made impressment more effective.

Regulating Captains, as their title implies, regulated the practice of impressment by inspecting men taken up by press gangs, imposed common standards, and ensured that those taken were men of seafaring skill, releasing those who were not. Regulating Captains also released men with protections, those that belonged to other ships, or those suspected of being criminals or vagrants, who had been pressed by local magistrates to rid their jurisdictions of the burden.[133] Further to this responsibility, they directed the operations of press gangs that functioned in the region under their control.[134] Each Regulating Captain, depending on the size and location of their region, would have had several press gangs or tenders working under them.

---

[128] Usher Jr., 'The Civil Administration of the British Navy During the American Revolution', p. 229.

[129] See Figure 2.2.

[130] 'Admiralty Memorial to the Lords Justices, 1 August 1745', in Baugh, *Naval Administration, 1715–1750*, pp. 137–138.

[131] Lloyd, *The British Seaman, 1200–1860*, p. 128.

[132] Gradish, *The Manning of the British Navy During the Seven Years' War*, p. 57.

[133] Lloyd, *The British Seaman, 1200–1860*, pp. 128–129; Rodger, *The Command of the Ocean*, pp. 313–314.

[134] Usher Jr., 'Royal Navy Impressment', p. 675.

As the eighteenth century progressed, Regulating Captains became more numerous and thus the Impress Service was able to recruit from more and more of Britain's coastline. Under Regulating Captains were the press gangs. Press gangs sent out from ships, under the orders of an individual captain, were likely to be composed of trusted seamen, which proved a waste of maritime skill. The Impress Service, however, generally manned its gangs with local 'tough men' who likely needed employment, and assigned naval lieutenants to command them. As working in a press gang required little or none of the skills of a seaman, it was more efficient and cost-effective to fill the position with people whose skills were not needed at sea. The gang would comprise one lieutenant and about ten men, depending on the area, and would set up a base of operations, referred to as a rendezvous, usually in a local inn.[135] The rendezvous and the gang itself acted not only as a means of conscripting men, but also as a point where volunteers could join the service. Thus the rendezvous was highly visible and marked with flags and was sometimes advertised by drummers and men marching up and down the streets.[136] It was important that these places did not look ominous, as such places had little chance of attracting volunteers.

The lieutenants of the gangs were issued with press warrants that gave them the right to legally take men for service in the Navy. By 1793, these gangs were actively working in and around fifty-one ports.[137] As the conflict had been well anticipated, before war was even declared the Impress Service was operating at full capacity, armed with signed warrants that only required a date to make them official.[138] As soon as war was declared, the Navy began to ingest as many men as it could find in order to get ships mobilised, and press gangs swung into action on land and sea. On land, press gangs began collecting mariners as quickly as they could, both impressing them as well as accepting volunteers. Press tenders at sea were also armed with undated warrants and ready to collect men from incoming merchant ships once war broke out.

The process of creating a dedicated administrative branch of the Navy, specifically for the purpose of recruitment, had greatly streamlined the process of naval manning and mobilisation.[139] In the American Revolutionary War, the Impress Service accounted for about half of the men recruited, of whom around two-thirds were paid bounties and were volunteers.[140] Though statistical data for the Impress Service during the French Revolutionary Wars is difficult to obtain, logic suggests that with the added administrative power

---

[135] Blake and Lawrence, p. 64; Usher Jr., 'Royal Navy Impressment', pp. 675–677.

[136] Note that small parties of men recruiting volunteers by beat of drum was the same means used by the British Army for most of their recruiting. Guy, pp. 123–128.

[137] Blake and Lawrence, p. 64.

[138] NMM: KEI/45/2, 'Signed but undated order to press men from Merchant Ships'; see also Lewis, *A Social History of the Navy, 1793–1815*, pp. 102–105.

[139] Ibid., p. 103.

[140] Rodger, *The Command of the Ocean*, p. 396; Usher Jr., 'Royal Navy Impressment', p. 678; Usher Jr., 'The Civil Administration of the British Navy During the American Revolution', p. 240.

and men dedicated to recruiting, combined with preparations for manning before war broke out, the Impress Service during the opening phases of the French Revolutionary Wars was more successful than it had been previously.

Impressment operated in two main ways, on shore and at sea. By far the best known of these methods are the shore-based operations, in which the infamous press gang played a prevalent role.[141] By the 1790s, most of the press gangs operating on shore fell under the direction of the Impress Service; however, individual ships also sent gangs ashore to press men, particularly if they were not near one of the major naval centres where the Impress Service concentrated its efforts. The richest hunting grounds for the press gangs were the major merchant and naval centres of the south and southeast coasts, of which Sheerness, Gravesend, Wapping, Portsmouth and Plymouth all saw heavy naval recruitment. The popular image of the press gang, an image of men wielding wooden clubs or cudgels who brutally and violently took men for naval service, derives from such places.[142] It was these areas where men of the sea interacted with those who rarely, if ever, left dry land, and much of what has been passed down has been the product of the latter rather than the former.

Press gangs were not the brutal force that has generally been written about. Press gangs did function as a means of conscripting men, and occasionally this did result in violence. Research by Nicholas Rogers has revealed 602 affrays that were reported and recorded over sixty-seven years, between 1738 and 1805. Though this number sounds high, in the scale of events it is rather low. His research estimates that 450,000 men were pressed into naval service in those years, making the frequency of incidence around one affray for every 750 men pressed.[143] This appears to be exceptionally low for a practice with as violent a received reputation as impressment. This may derive from the fact that Rogers's estimate of 450,000 pressed men is likely too high, combined with the fact that he could only work with reported cases of violence. However, even if his ratio was halved, and it stood at one affray in every 375 men pressed, it would still be exceptionally low. Therefore, it is unlikely that press gangs were actually as brutal as they have been built up to be. Rather, they functioned to select skilled men for naval service, and occasionally problems occurred that resulted in some form of violence. Violence was not, however, the primary tool of press gangs, and much of the violence reported was directed at press gangs, generally by groups of mariners or members of a local community.

Conscripting men was not the sole occupation of press gangs. Rendezvous were one of the critical points at which men volunteered for naval service. Volunteers made up over 70 per cent of the total seamen found on board warships during the French Revolutionary Wars and, to a great extent, these men volunteered on land via press officers. In fact, processing volunteer

---

141 Earle, *Sailors: English Merchant Seamen, 1650–1775*, p. 191.
142 Bonnett, p.17.
143 Rogers, *The Press Gang: Naval Impressment and Its Opponents in Georgian Britain*, pp. 39–40.

men was the average press gang's primary occupation.[144] They were further often charged with monitoring and controlling the movement of men on leave, to ensure they did not desert, though this aspect was diminishing by the 1790s.[145] Officers were well motivated to receive volunteers, as their pay depended upon the number of men they raised. Volunteers were more valuable to the Royal Navy, in part because they did not require nearly as much effort or expense as pressed men, a factor which the Admiralty was keen on taking advantage of.[146] From the beginning of the French Revolutionary Wars, Regulating Captains were instructed to encourage men to volunteer even when the only alternative they faced was impressment.[147] Press gang officers also went to lengths to encourage men into naval service by recruiting drives. These would take place in areas where seamen congregated and involved posters, improvised bands playing patriotic tunes, speeches, and talk of the excitements of naval life, such as glory and prize money.[148] One example of a recruiting poster is that for the frigate *Pallas* under the command of Lord Cochrane in 1804.[149] This poster is filled with references to prize money, and played on the slim but very real possibility of men making substantial amounts of money. The poster states, 'none need apply but Seamen or Stout Hands', giving the clear impression that landsmen were not wanted, and further emphasised financial reward, with the idea of special men for a special task. The poster focuses around Lord Cochrane, who was already famous as a daring and lucky officer when it came to prize money. Though this poster is exceptional, similar documents were used to lure seamen to volunteer.

To be successful and remain within the bounds of law, press gang officers had to be clever.[150] Seamen and sympathisers alike worked to help sailors avoid impressment, and often went to great lengths in doing so. Maritime centres were a hive of information and alert sailors who did not wish to serve in the Royal Navy used this to ascertain the intentions and focus of the local press gang. Officers recognised that leaking information about forthcoming impressment activities could destroy any chance of success for a press gang. In his plans to send a large number of press gangs from his squadron to press men from merchant ships in Carlisle Bay, Barbados, in June of 1780, Admiral Rodney expressed that the information in his orders 'be kept a profound secret', so as to ensure that seamen were unaware of his intentions.[151] Pubs,

---

[144] Lloyd, *The British Seaman, 1200–1860*, p. 130; Rodger, 'Officers and Men', p. 141; Usher Jr., 'Royal Navy Impressment', p. 675.

[145] Rodger, 'Officers and Men', p. 141.

[146] Rodger, *The Command of the Ocean*, p. 396.

[147] Ibid., p. 442.

[148] Lewis, *A Social History of the Navy, 1793–1815*, p. 93; Lloyd, *The British Seaman, 1200–1860*, p. 130.

[149] NMM: PBH3190, 'Recruitment Poster for the *Pallas*'.

[150] Lewis, *A Social History of the Navy, 1793–1815*, pp. 107–109.

[151] 'Rodney to all the Captains of the Squadron, 3 June 1780', in David Syrett, *The Rodney Papers: Selections from the Correspondence of Admiral Lord Rodney, Volume II, 1763–1780*, Publications of the Navy Records Society (Aldershot: Ashgate, 2007), p. 540.

gin shops and taverns proved to be double-edged swords, as they provided great places for information on impressment activities; however as public houses they were also open for press gangs to enter and seize men.[152] Merchants often sent their men into the country to protect them from the press.[153] In March of 1803, William Dillon was posted as lieutenant in the Impress Service in the port of Hull.[154] While there he experienced many attempts to elude the press, one of which was the organisation of a 'Grand Ball' designed to keep Dillon occupied and allow seamen to move in the port unnoticed by the local press gang. Becoming aware of the situation, Dillon attended the Ball and had a member of his gang call upon him to leave early, after which the gang found several unwary seamen attempting to move about Hull. Dillon's time with the Impress Service was successful and during his six weeks in Hull his efforts helped to secure 150 men for naval service.[155]

Officers of the Impress Service also had to be intuitive, not only to avoid ruses such as Dillon's 'Grand Ball' experience, but simply identifying seamen often presented difficulties. Generally speaking, sailors with years of experience were easily identifiable when on land, as they dressed, acted and spoke distinctively compared with common landsmen.[156] However, during times of war, when press gangs worked waterfront communities where seamen frequented and kept attentive eyes open for prospective recruits, sailors did what they could to blend into the population when they moved about at all. Therefore, to a great extent, impress officers worked on instinct and experience. As they themselves had ample experience at sea, they were in a better position than most to spot the type of men the Navy sought. Mistakes were bound to happen and they did. Simply put, a common labourer trying to find work in a port could have been mistaken for a mariner trying not to draw the attention of a press gang. However, these mistakes were almost always corrected when the local Regulating Captain inspected the men before they were sent off to a ship. The press officers were concerned with quality as well as the number of men they could acquire.[157] Lieutenants of both the Impress Service and those sent ashore with press gangs from warships were under unequivocal instructions from the Admiralty:

> not to impress any Landmen, but only such as are Seafaring Men, or such others as are described in the Press-Warrant, and those only as are able and fit for His Majesty's Service, and not to take up Boys or infirm Persons, in order to magnify the Numbers upon your Accounts, and to bring an unnecessary charge upon His Majesty.[158]

---

[152] Rediker, p. 27.
[153] Lincoln, p. 84.
[154] Lewis, *A Social History of the Navy, 1793–1815*, pp. 105–111.
[155] Ibid., pp. 110–111.
[156] Lloyd, *The British Seaman, 1200–1860*, pp. 161–162; Rediker, p. 11.
[157] Starkey, 'War and the Market for Seafarers in Britain, 1736–1792', p. 37.
[158] TNA: ADM 7-967, 'Instructions to Officers Raising Men, 1807'.

Clearly, the Admiralty was not desirous of press gangs bringing in more unskilled landsmen, as they were already volunteering in droves; however, in such a large operation some mistakes were unavoidable, especially as sailors not wanting to be conscripted commonly claimed not to be seamen.[159]

Press gang operations on land came with the inherent risk of altercation and possible violence.[160] As previously stated, Nicholas Rogers's book documents 602 altercations involving press gangs between 1738 and 1805, and suggests about one affray in every 750 men pressed.[161] The number of such events that escalated to the point of being documented was low, especially considering the duty press gangs were tasked with carrying out. However, some minor violence did occur, especially when press gangs were outnumbered. Such a case can be seen again with William Dillon in Hull. After impressing a carpenter and while returning to the local rendezvous, Dillon and his gang were confronted by a small crowd that had been incited by the carpenter's wife. Though the press gang thwarted the rescue attempt, Dillon did suffer bricks being thrown through his window.[162]

Shore-based press gangs have generally been viewed as a large group of men, bent on violence. It seems that the necessity for gangs to consist of ten or more men likely came more from the fact that to perform their set task they needed the safety of numbers. However, though some large press gangs did exist, Roland Usher has demonstrated, through the examination of expense reports for the Impress Service during the American War, that most press gangs actually only consisted of a lieutenant and between two and six men.[163] One of the quickest ways for violence to break out during impressment operations was for a gang to find itself outnumbered. During the Seven Years' War, William Spavens spent time as part of an eighty-man press gang in Liverpool, which says something both about the problematic nature of pressing in Liverpool as well as the lengths officers would go to to find the necessary men.[164] Though violently controversial and occasionally violently opposed, a great deal of impressment on land was actually a matter of negotiation.[165] Impress officers negotiated with local authorities to smooth their work. Cases in which press gangs did not get the cooperation of the local government reveal high levels of friction. This caused press gangs' expenses to increase and the resulting number of men they recruited to decrease. Such friction became even more intense during a 'Hot Press', which occurred only at times when the Navy was in dire need of men. When this happened, only men with protections sanctioned by Parliament were granted protection, meaning that maritime communities were swept of virtually everyone who

---

[159] Lloyd, *The British Seaman, 1200–1860*, pp. 161–162.
[160] Scammell, 'Mutiny in British Ships, c. 1500–1750', p. 350.
[161] Rogers, *The Press Gang: Naval Impressment and Its Opponents in Georgian Britain*, pp. 39–40.
[162] Lewis, *A Social History of the Navy, 1793–1815*, p. 108.
[163] Usher Jr., 'The Civil Administration of the British Navy During the American Revolution', pp. 224–225.
[164] Spavens, p. 48.
[165] Rodger, *The Command of the Ocean*, p. 396.

exhibited some knowledge of the sea that a given press gang could get hold of.[166] Naturally, conscripting men who normally had protections did not bode well for the reception of a press gang in a given location.

Compared to the press on shore, pressing men at sea was much tidier and more cost-effective, and acquired more skilled seamen.[167] However, researching impressment at sea as opposed to its shore-based counterpart proves difficult. Essentially, a substantial portion of the pressing at sea operated by warships and tenders did not fall under the control of the Impress Service, and therefore the Impress Service's records do not reflect any figures in their statistics.[168] Often this was done to complete a ship's company, and commonly by frigates or smaller warships sailing in protection of convoys as they entered the English Channel on their return to Britain.[169] Press tenders, often working under the Impress Service, would also lie in wait for homebound merchant ships, just outside of British ports or even well out within the Channel.[170] The success of impressment at sea can be accounted to the fact that boarding a merchant ship almost certainly guaranteed an officer the opportunity to find skilled men, and further those men had little or no chance to evade impressment as there was simply nowhere to run.[171] Such officers, however, were not totally free to take any man from any ship. Restrictions were put into place to protect merchant shipping and chief among these was the fact that officers could not press men from outward-bound shipping. Only returning ships, once they had reached the relative safety of the Channel, could be boarded in search of men. Further, men had to be provided to ensure the merchant ship's safe return. Referred to as 'men in lieu', these were generally trusted men who could be depended upon to return to their ship once the merchant had made its port.[172] Occasionally, these men may have been men of little value to the pressing warship, such as older less agile seamen; however this did not necessarily mean they did not have skill or were of no value in sailing a merchant vessel into port. The occasional case of officers bending these rules also occurred, such as the case of Nelson, when pressing men from the merchant ship *Amity Hall* in 1779 as she had only just left the West Indies bound for the British Isles, although the two men pressed by Nelson were eventually released.[173]

Pressing men from convoys was not necessarily easy and straightforward. Merchant ships within a convoy would often disperse without notice in order

---

[166] Clayton, p. 170; Earle, *Sailors: English Merchant Seamen, 1650–1775*, p. 192.

[167] Earle, *Sailors: English Merchant Seamen, 1650–1775*, p. 191; Starkey, 'War and the Market for Seafarers in Britain, 1736–1792', p. 38.

[168] Rodger, *The Wooden World*, p. 146; Usher Jr., 'Royal Navy Impressment', p. 678.

[169] Lewis, *A Social History of the Navy, 1793–1815*, p. 112.

[170] Masefield, p. 55.

[171] Rodger, *The Command of the Ocean*, p. 315.

[172] Lewis, *A Social History of the Navy, 1793–1815*, pp. 102–103; Masefield, p. 55.

[173] Knight, *The Pursuit of Victory*, pp. 61–62.

to avoid the press.[174] Many merchants would run the risk of being captured when close to home waters rather than allow their ships to be boarded by naval officers in search of men. As captain of HMS *Albemarle* during the American Revolutionary War, Nelson was ordered to intercept a group of East Indiamen bound for the Thames. They were located at night trying to slip past the naval ships engaged with pressing men. Upon contact the merchant ships would not drop anchor until compelled to by the firing of twenty-six nine-pound cannon shot into their rigging. Even at that they resisted Nelson's crew boarding until the following morning.[175]

Pressing at sea could be dangerous, as the merchant's crew usually outnumbered the crew of any boat that approached a ship with the intent to press.[176] William Spavens, while serving in a merchant ship, witnessed the extent to which the master of his vessel went to avoid being boarded by officers with press warrants. Eventually, though, his ship was boarded and a portion of the ship's crew were taken, and a few days later he was himself pressed into naval service.[177] With what seems to be not so uncommon irony, Spavens later worked as part of a press gang on a tender in the area of Dublin.[178] Undoubtedly for the seamen being pressed, to be taken near or even within the sight of land after having already spent a long time at sea was a difficult hardship.[179] Just like impressment on land, impressment at sea proved to be loathed by merchants.[180]

The Statistics of Impressment

Analysing eighteenth-century naval manning, and in particular impressment, has always proved to be challenging. The main problem is a lack of statistical data on the subject, without which the actual impact of impressment is difficult to determine. Without solid numbers, obtaining an accurate picture of how impressment fitted into the overall picture of naval manning is nearly impossible. Examining primary source material, such as letters or Admiralty instructions, goes a long way toward understanding impressment and its reception; however it does little to show how many men impressment accounted for in comparison to other forms of recruitment such as volunteers. Further, without statistical evidence, there is little that can be said about the skill levels of men that were impressed, their ages, their nationalities, and so on. As mentioned earlier, speculation simply on what proportion of the Royal Navy's seamen were pressed varies widely. Michael Lewis stated that somewhere between 50 and 75 per cent of men serving between 1793 and

---

[174] Earle, *Sailors: English Merchant Seamen, 1650–1775*, p. 192; Knight, *The Pursuit of Victory*, p. 67; David Syrett, 'The Organization of British Trade Convoys During the American War, 1775–83', *The Mariner's Mirror* LXII (1976): pp. 174–178.

[175] Knight, *The Pursuit of Victory*, pp. 65–66.

[176] Rediker, p. 238.

[177] Spavens, p. 27.

[178] Ibid., p. 45.

[179] Earle, *Sailors: English Merchant Seamen, 1650–1775*, p. 192.

[180] Bonnett, p. 18.

1815 were conscripted into the service.[181] Stephen Gradish agreed with these figures when he wrote that most of the seamen serving in the Royal Navy 'had been recruited under duress'.[182] Most recently, Nicholas Rogers, writing out of York University in Toronto, suggested that half or more seamen in the eighteenth century were pressed.[183] None of these numbers are based on any statistical data, but rather on estimates that have filtered through two hundred or more years of historiography that has never addressed the problem with statistical analysis. The only glimpse of statistical data available is that of N.A.M. Rodger. This project, however, has been able to collect and analyse British naval manning statistics.

Looking at the raw overall statistics reveals that impressment accounted for 10 per cent of the men coming into newly commissioned ships.[184] By further factoring for the original recruitment of men who appear in the muster books as 'turned over',[185] it is possible to create a chart that looks substantially different from what most of the historiography has suggested.[186] The data represented in this graph changes the social dynamic of naval manpower from the one that previously dominated the subject, where the majority of men serving were thought to have been there against their will, to a dynamic where not only did the majority of the lower deck consist of volunteers, but more than four out of five men were there of their own will. It is clear that impressment never produced the majority of men that served on the lower deck, a theory that has dominated the history of naval manning. Further, this is also demonstrated by applying the same factoring method to the recruitment of petty officers. Although the un-factored statistics of petty officer recruitment show a higher ratio of turned over men to volunteers than is observed in seamen recruitment, the factored statistics reveal similar recruitment trends between volunteers and pressed men. Impressment was simply not responsible for the majority of men who entered into naval service.[187]

Similarly, the same principle can be applied to the recruitment statistics of individual years. Performing this factoring exercise produces the statistics of original recruitment for men being entered into warships in each year of the war. These numbers can be set into percentages, showing that impressment accounted for 8 per cent of seamen during the first year of the war and grew to 27 per cent in 1801.[188] These figures illustrate that pressed men did not

---

[181] Lewis, *A Social History of the Navy, 1793–1815*, p. 139.

[182] Gradish, *The Manning of the British Navy During the Seven Years' War*, p. 62.

[183] Rogers, *The Press Gang: Naval Impressment and Its Opponents in Georgian Britain*, pp. 3–5.

[184] See Figures 2.4, 2.5, 2.6 and 2.7 for un-factored recruitment statistics for seamen and petty officers.

[185] See Chapter 2 for an in-depth discussion of the factoring process utilised in this research.

[186] See Figures 2.9 and 2.10.

[187] Knight, *The Pursuit of Victory*, pp. 142–143; Rodger, *The Wooden World*, p. 353; Usher Jr., 'Royal Navy Impressment', p. 677.

[188] Note that in 1795 the percentage of seamen that were pressed dropped, likely due to the effects of the Quota Acts.

make up the exceptionally large numbers of men that have been hitherto written about. As to be expected, the ratio of pressed men within Royal Navy ships increased as the war progressed. However, after nine years of warfare, at its height in 1801, impressment accounted for approximately 27 per cent of the seamen on board warships.

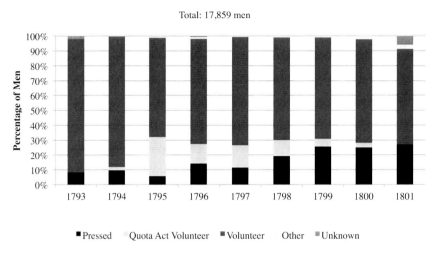

Total: 17,859 men

Figure 4.2 Factored seamen recruitment percentages

Observing the increase of impressment percentages over the course of the nine-year conflict in comparison to the size of the Royal Navy illustrates an interesting trend. The percentages of men conscripted into naval service each year remained relatively steady throughout the war, even though the growth of the Royal Navy slowed significantly after 1798.[189] The logic of many antiquated arguments has suggested that impressment was the primary tool used for naval manning. After 1798, more than half of the seamen entering into newly commissioned ships were turned over. Thus, as the growth of the Royal Navy slowed dramatically, and turned over men became the major means of filling warships with seamen, impressment numbers should have slowed to reflect the reduced growth; as not as many fresh men were needed, attention could have been shifted away from impressment. However, statistics show that impressment numbers saw no major fluctuations throughout the war, with the exception of 1795, when the Quota Acts slowed impressment in naval ports. Impressment rates remained the same because conscription was never the primary tool of naval manning; rather it was used to increase the skill level of the lower deck. Approximately 85 per cent of the men who were impressed between 1793 and 1801 were skilled seamen or petty officers.[190]

---

[189] See Figures 2.3 and 2.6 for Royal Navy growth and un-factored seamen recruitment from 1792 to 1803.

[190] See Figure 4.1 for the skill ratios of pressed seamen and petty officers.

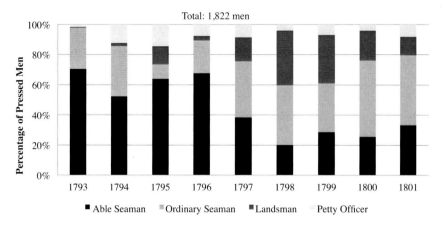

Figure 4.3 Pressed seamen and petty officer ratings

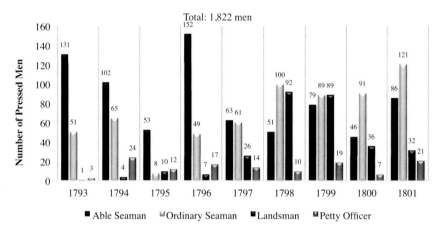

Figure 4.4 Pressed seamen and petty officer ratings

The intake of landsmen by impressment was also exceptionally low; figures for the overall conflict show that only 18 per cent of men taken by impressment were recorded as landsmen. From 1798 onwards, the size of the Royal Navy was in excess of 120,000 men, and accordingly the annual percentage of pressed able seamen falls off in favour of ordinary seamen. To understand the bigger picture of naval recruitment, it is important to take note of these numbers, which stand in relation to a total of 17,859 seamen recorded in this project. That constitutes an average of about 2,000 seamen on newly commissioned ships surveyed in each year, and from that number there is only one landsman pressed in 1793, and only ninety-two pressed in 1798. Impressment during the French Revolutionary Wars was not set up to take in masses of men, but specifically to search for skilled and experienced mariners who were also still young and agile. Most of the historiography has suggested that, although the letter of the law stated that impressment was only allowed for men who used the sea, in reality press gangs took little notice of whom they pressed; rather they worked to a quota or set number of men required to fill the ships available. However, this data illustrates that the end result was the same as the intention, that impressment obtained skilled men for naval wartime service.

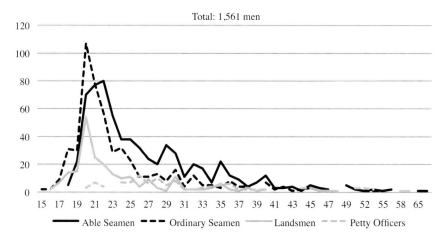

Figure 4.5 Ages of pressed men

The Royal Navy was not simply interested in men with high levels of skill, but men who were also young. Working in the rigging, and being a topman, did not just involve skill, but also required the agility of youth. This data shows that the Royal Navy was not only pressing skilled sailors, but sailors that were also young. The peak age of pressed men occurred at twenty years of age for both landsmen and ordinary seamen and declined very quickly as age increased. It also demonstrates that pressed able seamen peaked at the slightly older age of twenty-two and decreased at a slightly slower rate than ordinary seamen and landsmen, which represents the time it took for a seaman to gain the knowledge and experience necessary to perform at that level of competence. This also explains the lack of interest shown by press gangs in men who were much out of their early twenties.

The historiography has also frequently claimed that press gangs and tenders often engaged in conscripting foreign men unlawfully into the Royal Navy. Between 1793 and 1801, the largest portion of seamen conscripted into the Royal Navy were born in England, totalling 45 per cent. Further, these statistics demonstrate that Ireland and Scotland made up 14 and 11 per cent of pressed men respectively, followed by Wales, which accounted for 5 per cent of pressed men. However, foreign-born men made up 11 per cent of the total men gathered by impressment. To an extent this derives from which locations were deemed as 'foreign' when constructing the database. Many of the men recorded as foreigners in the database would have actually been considered British, as they originated from British territories such as the West

Indies, Canada, the Channel Islands, Gibraltar, the East Indies, and the Isle of Man.[191] Together these account for 23 per cent of the men listed as foreign. To gain a perspective on the topic, take into account pressed Americans, by far the highest percentage of any foreign nationality. Out of almost 18,000 seamen in a survey stretching across nine years of warfare, only 68 of those covered by this database were impressed Americans. When taken as a whole, impressment of foreigners was a rarity, and further it is important to note that after two years of service in a British ship, foreign-born sailors became eligible for impressment.[192] Obviously, when an operation of this size was in motion, people would have been in the wrong place at the wrong time and been mistaken for Britons; or occasionally a captain or a press gang officer may have observed the rules more flexibly than other officers. However, this is by no means the tyrannical and illegal means of manning the Royal Navy that history has portrayed. This is further reinforced by the fact that most pressed nationalities covered by this database are present only in infinitesimal numbers. Clearly, impress officers of the French Revolutionary Wars did not illegally press foreign men to inflate their numbers.

Summation

In function, impressment did not increase the number of seamen in Britain; rather it ensured that the Royal Navy maintained enough skilled manpower to ensure it could function in top form. Impressment exploited the elasticity of Britain's maritime labour resources by ensuring that sailors worked the full twelve months of the year, as they would otherwise in peacetime take two or three months ashore each year.[193] Unlike France, whose maritime population remained relatively steady while its navy grew throughout the eighteenth century, Britain may have inadvertently created a virtuous circle in which wartime demands for seamen created new seamen from landsmen, who remained on the labour market. The result was the creation of an elastic pool of maritime labour, allowing the British manning system, including impressment, to operate effectively.[194] Impressment helped guarantee the success of British seapower by ensuring that the overall skill level of the lower deck remained high enough for British warships to maintain an edge over their adversaries, essentially performing the function that the free labour market could not achieve for the Royal Navy.[195] However, even though the Royal Navy exploited the flexibility of the nation's maritime labour pool, it did not dip to the point of taking in criminals as has been suggested, though

---

[191] Note that the West Indies and East Indies were not entirely British.

[192] Brunsman, p. 355; Lloyd, *The British Seaman, 1200–1860*, pp. 158–159; James Fulton Zimmerman, *Impressment of American Seamen* (New York: Columbia University Press, 1925), pp. 22–23.

[193] Rodger, *The Command of the Ocean*, p. 395; Starkey, 'War and the Market for Seafarers in Britain, 1736–1792', p. 38.

[194] Harding, *Seapower and Naval Warfare, 1650–1830*, pp. 138–139; Knight, *The Pursuit of Victory*, p. 22; Rodger, *The Command of the Ocean*, p. 395.

[195] Rogers, *The Press Gang: Naval Impressment and Its Opponents in Georgian Britain*, p. 31.

Total: 1,695 men

Total: 127 men

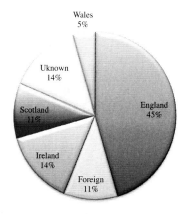

Figure 4.6 Pressed seamen nationalities

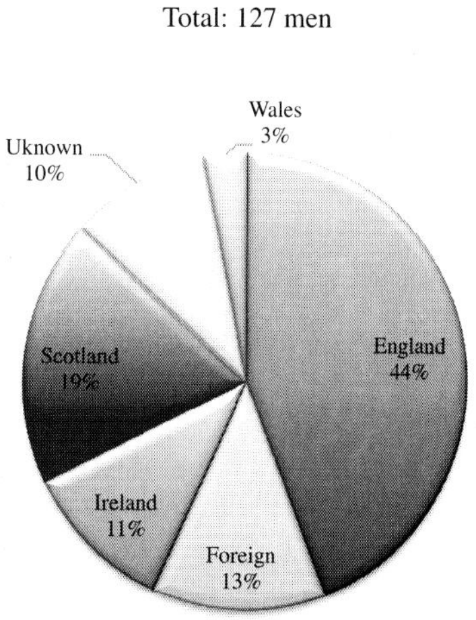

Figure 4.7 Pressed petty officer nationalities

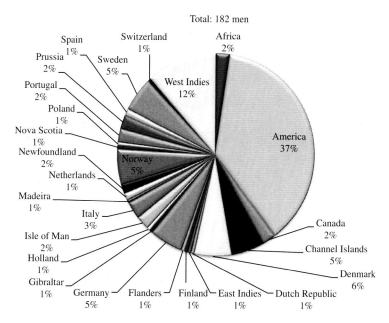

Figure 4.8 Country of birth for pressed foreigners

Note: For simplicity, America, Canada and Germany, as defined in these graphs, are each based on the modern boundaries. References to the Dutch Republic are based on its 1793 government and boundaries.

Total: 182 men

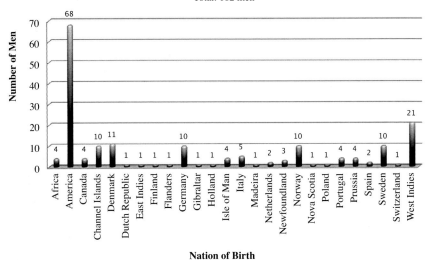

Figure 4.9 Pressed foreigners' nationality

undoubtedly many people would have liked it to take on such a function.[196] Prisoners for debt were welcome into the fleet; however the Navy was not interested in recruiting hardened criminals.[197] Impressment was also not responsible for the desertions and discipline problems as has been claimed; in both situations, volunteer men made up the majority of cases.[198]

Impressment, however, did have down sides; it often drove seamen away, inland and into other land-based occupations, far from shore and the chance of being pressed. This caused a shortage in the supply that affected both the Navy and merchant shipping.[199] Impressment caused individual hardship; an encounter with the press was always a hazard for seamen during wartime, whether on a returning merchant ship or spending time ashore.[200] Though impressment was not the tyrannical and evil implement that history has depicted, on some level it did physically deny men their freedom; however, this was not done on the mass scale suggested. The received history, that masses of men were denied their freedom by press gangs and thrown into a foreign world with harsh conditions and brutal discipline simply does not tally with statistical data, nor does it agree with many leading historians.[201] In fact the men taken by impressment were no strangers to this world; in one

---

[196] Rodger, *The Command of the Ocean*, p. 397.

[197] Bromley, 'The British Navy and Its Seamen after 1688', p. 153.

[198] Byrn, pp. 76, 126, 156–157.

[199] Bromley, 'The British Navy and Its Seamen after 1688', p. 151.

[200] Black, *The British Seaborne Empire*, pp. 121–122; Clayton, p. 161; Earle, *Sailors: English Merchant Seamen, 1650–1775*, pp. 192–193; Oppenheim, p. 108.

[201] For the discipline and harsh conditions view, see Masefield.

manner or another they had in fact chosen it as an occupation, as press gangs were not interested in men with no experience at sea. However, as mentioned previously, press officers undoubtedly made mistakes, and in an operation of such a size, one mistake in every thousand men pressed would have resulted in a fair number of men being unfairly pressed. A critical issue of concern is whether or not a seaman had the knowledge to use the law in his favour if he were pressed wrongly, and if he did have the knowledge would he have had the necessary resources to argue his case successfully. Though seamen could theoretically apply for *habeas corpus* if they were wrongfully pressed, time, money and influence were all on the Admiralty's side.[202] Further, many people, whether wrongfully impressed or not, tried their hand at claiming they were illegally taken. It could have been the case that the cries of those who were wrongfully taken were simply drowned out by the volume of issues facing the Admiralty. Even if a seaman were legally pressed, if he was pressed at sea he risked the possibility of never seeing the wages he had earned on the ship he was pressed from, and in the case of a prolonged voyage this loss could be devastating.[203] Granted this was illegal, and the Admiralty did seek to prosecute merchant masters for such conduct.

Merchants offered seamen substantially higher wages during times of war, due to the problems of supply and demand; a cost that was easily covered by the fact that trade prices saw considerable inflation during wartime.[204] Conveniently this kept seamen in maritime centres looking for merchant berths; however it also goes to show that conscription was not as bad as history has portrayed it. Had naval service been so dire and unbearable then the possibility of impressment in a seaport would have had a devastating effect that would have kept nearly all seamen away. However, the fact that seamen did go to port towns to look for employment in merchant vessels means that the risk of being picked up by a press gang was acceptable. Further, had conditions on board ship been as bad as those often described in the current historiography, the Royal Navy would never have been able to recruit volunteers, as few would volunteer to be placed in a floating prison. Rather, the low impact of impressment on the overall numbers of naval recruitment reflects the opposite, that in fact conditions on board ships of the Royal Navy were not as horrific as those described. Some problems with brutality and bad conditions did surface, such as the previously mentioned experience of the Duke of Cumberland in 1799.[205] Men on press tenders were sometimes held like prisoners and in poor conditions. William Spavens endured thirty-two days in the hold of a press tender before being sent to a warship.[206] The fact that pressed men did not want to be there meant that, on some level, they had to be 'secured' until they could be taken to a warship. This occasionally

---

[202] Rogers, 'Impressment and the Law in Eighteenth-Century Britain', p. 94.
[203] Rediker, p. 145. It is important to note that most modern research suggests that Rediker overstated how common this event was in order to support his argument.
[204] Harding, *Seapower and Naval Warfare, 1650–1830*, p. 135.
[205] *The Naval Chronicle for 1799*, p. 307.
[206] Spavens, p. 27 (46:27).

resulted in mutinies of pressed men who sought their freedom.[207] However in the overall scheme of naval manning operations this was a rarity.

Press gangs and tenders spent their time looking for men with skill and experience at sea, primarily able and ordinary seamen. They also looked for men with a variety of skills that were useful on board a ship. Unlike an infantry company, whose ranks were made up of men with generally the same skill, a ship's company had to be made up of men with different skills and varying proficiencies.[208] This was a result of the fact that when a warship left land, it became its own self-contained world, in which every aspect of ship operation had to be taken care of by the men on board, which ranged from the heat of battle, to the monotony of constant small daily repairs that kept a ship running. Thus, press warrants allowed a broad definition of men who used the sea to be conscripted and press officers sought men of many skills that were useful to the Navy.

Impressment was both hated and supported, and often by the same people. Generally speaking, coverage of impressment by newspapers was relentlessly negative. The reality was and still is that newspapers are printed for sale, and good stories sell papers. Further, as many of the readers of newspapers, especially those based around merchant and maritime centres, would have sympathised with the sailors being pressed, so did the stories that were printed. This fact, the need to sell a story for profit, has had an impact on the entire historiography of naval manning, and for many historians it has served only to unduly colour their research. Lord Sandwich greatly disliked impressment; however, he could see little in the way of other means of manning the Navy. Though interestingly enough, he favoured the traditional method of ships being manned by their own captains, rather than having a centrally focused manning effort.[209]

Some did support impressment, many being naval officers. In 1834, Admiral Sir Thomas Byam Martin defended impressment as the only quick manner of mobilising the fleet and credited the quick mobilisation it made possible with preventing a French intervention in the Netherlands in 1787 and resolving the Nootka Sound incident without major conflict.[210] Some even preferred a harsher system of impress, such as Vice Admiral Nelson, who thought that all ports should be embargoed and every soldier and magistrate in the kingdom should comb the landscape taking up men regardless of protections.[211] Even some newspapers supported impressment, evidenced by *The Morning Post* of 12 March 1803:

> We cannot conclude on this subject without directing the public censure against some Newspapers which daily whine over the pressed men. –"The

207 Clayton, p. 171.
208 Rodger, "'A Little Navy of Your Own Making': Admiral Boscawen and the Cornish Connection in the Royal Navy", pp. 83–87.
209 Rodger, *The Insatiable Earl: A Life of John Montagu, Fourth Earl of Sandwich, 1718–1792*, p. 201.
210 Bromley, *The Manning of the Royal Navy*, pp. 175–177.
211 'Nelson to Henry Addington', 25 October 1802, in White, pp. 310–311.

miseries of war;" "the poor sailors dragged away;" "the Mansion-house surrounded with their wives and daughters, wringing their hands, their eyes streaming with tears, lamenting their relatives torn away by the press-gangs," &c &c. Is, then, the situation of sailors onboard King's ships so deplorable? Are not their wages, food and clothing, far superior to those of most mechanics and labourers? – Where is the cruelty in sending men to the sea who have been bred to it, and live by it; who are never so happy as when they are on it?[212]

Richard Marks, a naval chaplain, supported impressment as a means of spreading education and religion to many who had 'been taken out of a merchant ship, filthy, and so ignorant of God and the Bible, as not to be able to distinguish his letters, or to tell who created and preserved him; and not a few of these have found all the advantages of schools, and clean-liness, and order, and discipline, in the ships of war'.[213] Thus, though little historical work has looked at the supporters of impressment, they certainly did exist.

The function of impressment was to provide the Royal Navy with the necessary skilled and experienced men, especially topmen.[214] The shortage of seamen volunteers was constant, and therefore pressing lasted throughout any given conflict.[215] Impressment was always difficult, and few of those involved actually enjoyed the experience. In the end the Admiralty were keen to enter into deals with merchants' guilds or companies to provide men in lieu of the press, as it provided volunteers without any further expense to the Navy.[216] However, no matter how disliked impressment was, it proved a very potent tool for adding seamen to Britain's warships, and aided the Navy in achieving a high ratio of skilled to unskilled men.[217] Though it has been claimed that landsmen were pressed in large numbers, it was not legal and only anecdotal evidence has been produced to suggest that, as war went on, landsmen were being impressed in great quantity.[218] Further, the statistics of this project show that landsmen only formed 18 per cent of pressed men, and landsmen were eligible for impressment if they 'used the sea' and had skills that were valuable to the Navy. The reality was that the Royal Navy had no desire to recruit men with no use aboard warships.

---

[212] Quoted in Lincoln, p. 66.

[213] Quoted in ibid., p. 125.

[214] Robinson, 'Secret of British Power', p. 6; Rodger, 'Officers and Men', p. 141; Rodger, "'A Little Navy of Your Own Making": Admiral Boscawen and the Cornish Connection in the Royal Navy', p. 84; Usher Jr., 'Royal Navy Impressment', p. 684; Rodger, *The Command of the Ocean*, p. 497.

[215] Usher Jr., 'Royal Navy Impressment', p. 682.

[216] Rodger, *The Command of the Ocean*, p. 443.

[217] Starkey, 'War and the Market for Seafarers in Britain, 1736–1792', p. 37; Usher Jr., 'Royal Navy Impressment', p. 681.

[218] Rodger, *The Wooden World*, pp. 150–151; Rodger, 'Officers and Men', p. 141; Starkey, 'War and the Market for Seafarers in Britain, 1736–1792', p. 37.

In the end, impressment may have been an evil, but it was a lesser evil.[219] Seamen accepted naval conscription as unavoidable;[220] evidenced by the fact that in all of the grievances of the mutineers at Spithead and the Nore in 1797, impressment was not mentioned.[221] In his own memoirs, William Spavens showed no resentment of the press.[222] The British fleets of the French Revolutionary Wars were not manned by impressed men, rather pressed men formed a supplement to a mainly volunteer force, and functioned to raise the overall skill level of the lower deck. Though successful, impressment was also problematic, especially in the public's eye. The problems it caused and stresses that accompanied it meant that in reality, though it was necessary and often supported, impressment had no real friends.[223] In the end, seamen were conscripted into the Royal Navy by press gangs because their skills were one of Britain's most prized military assets.[224]

[219] Baugh, *British Naval Administration in the Age of Walpole*, pp. 149, 159–161; Bromley, 'The British Navy and Its Seamen after 1688'; Lloyd, *The British Seaman, 1200–1860*, pp. 149–151; Rodger, *The Wooden World*, p. 151.
[220] Rodger, *The Command of the Ocean*, p. 499.
[221] Ibid., p. 447.
[222] Spavens, p. 12.
[223] Rodger, *The Command of the Ocean*, p. 500.
[224] Usher Jr., 'Royal Navy Impressment', p. 680.

5

The Quota Acts

At the beginning of 1795 Britain was in a precarious position in a war that was quickly expanding. The separation from the European continent offered by the English Channel greatly benefited the British Isles. However, the narrow sea was by no means an insurmountable obstacle for potential invaders, as Britain had seen several invasions over its history; the last of which, led by William III, was only removed from 1795 by just over a century. Nevertheless, this narrow strip of sea did offer Britain breathing room, as moving armies across the Channel was complicated and costly.[1] This allowed Britain to prioritise its naval forces above its army in a manner that continental powers could not.[2] It was the Royal Navy that provided the wooden walls that protected Britain, and in 1795 its primary mission was to guard against invasion, as it had been for nearly 400 years.[3] At the end of the eighteenth century Britain stood as the dominant European naval power, in large part due to the ability of the Royal Navy to employ more seafarers than its rivals.[4]

British naval forces had grown rapidly over the eighteenth century, and by the end of 1794, after only two years of mobilisation, the wartime Royal Navy was nearly twice the size it had been half a century earlier in the midst of the War of Austrian Succession, topping 85,000.[5] More importantly, British maritime activity had undergone remarkable expansion in the second half of the eighteenth century.[6] The strength of the merchant marine was essential for naval supremacy, as the mariners who were trained in seaborne trade formed the pool from which the Royal Navy manned its fleets.[7] Seamen proved to be the nation's most important form of labour, and serving in

[1] Brewer, p. 12.
[2] Black, *The British Seaborne Empire*, p. 121.
[3] Rodger, 'Sea-Power and Empire, 1688–1793', p. 169.
[4] Starkey, 'War and the Market for Seafarers in Britain, 1736–1792', p. 25.
[5] See Figure 2.3; Duffy, *Parameters of British Naval Power, 1650–1850*, p. 7; Rodger, *The Command of the Ocean*, pp. 442, 636–639.
[6] Palmer and Williams, p. 97; Starkey, 'War and the Market for Seafarers in Britain, 1736–1792', pp. 26, 40–41.
[7] Lincoln, p. 78.

British warships they formed the nation's largest workforce.[8] Upon the declaration of war, Britain found itself in a race against its adversaries to mobilise its fleets; a race in which manning was a key issue. As there were never enough men to fully man the merchant marine and Royal Navy at the same time, the manning problem can be divided into three distinct issues. First, the Navy was in competition with merchant sea trade to recruit as many seamen as possible. Second, the Navy was forced to recruit landsmen to make up the difference between the skilled mariners it could recruit and the numbers it needed to put warships to sea. Third, the Royal Navy had to reduce wastage – the discharging and rerecruiting of seamen – as much as possible.[9]

The extreme growth of the Royal Navy between peace and war meant that the flexibility of the maritime labour market was taken to its limit well before naval forces reached their maximum mobilisation, necessitating the intake of landsmen. Finding seamen put the Royal Navy under great pressure during wartime, but the problem was too short-lived to bring about dramatic change from the traditional system of accepting volunteers and using impressment to bolster the number of highly skilled men.[10] The only major innovation to this system was the Quota Acts of 1795 and 1796.[11] The very nature of naval recruiting, the fact that it was only problematic during wartime and the necessary scale and organisation were unlike anything else in eighteenth-century Britain, made the entire process rather *ad hoc*.[12] The problem did produce some minor political changes to help with naval manning; one of which was an Act passed in April 1795 that allowed magistrates to issue warrants to search for able-bodied persons who were 'idle or disorderly'.[13]

The Royal Navy drew on manpower from a world-leading merchant fleet, even though there were never enough skilled seafarers to man a fully mobilised navy and the merchant trading fleets at the same time, creating a fundamental shortage of seamen.[14] Further, naval manning and mobilisation took time, as the bulk of warships were decommissioned during peacetime, and maintained only at a basic level to keep them preserved.[15] It took time

[8]   Ibid., p. 5.
[9]   Rodger, *The Wooden World*, pp. 149–150.
[10] Harding, *The Evolution of the Sailing Navy, 1509–1815*, p. 141; Joanna Innes, 'The Domestic Face of the Military-Fiscal State: Government and Society in Eighteenth-Century Britain', in *Insurrection: The British Experience 1795–1803*, ed. Roger Wells (Gloucester: Alan Sutton, 1983), p. 12.
[11] Harding, *Seapower and Naval Warfare, 1650–1830*, p. 270; Christopher Oprey, 'Schemes for the Reform of Naval Recruitment' (unpublished MA thesis, University of Liverpool, 1961), p. 88.
[12] Innes, p. 119.
[13] 35 Geo. III c. 34. Also see: F.W. Brooks, 'Naval Recruiting in Lindsey, 1795–7', *English Historical Review* XLIII, no. 170 (1928): p. 232; Emsley, 'The Recruitment of Petty Offenders During the French Wars, 1793–1815', p. 200.
[14] Black, *Naval Power: A History of Warfare and the Sea from 1500*, p. 104; Duffy, *Soldiers, Sugar and Seapower: The Expeditions to the West Indies and the War against Revolutionary France*, p. 20; Harding, *Seapower and Naval Warfare, 1650–1830*, p. 270.
[15] Glete, p. 174; Rodger, '"A Little Navy of Your Own Making": Admiral Boscawen and the Cornish Connection in the Royal Navy', p. 83. See also Rodger, 'Mobilizing Seapower in the Eighteenth Century'.

to commission the large numbers of ships necessary to fight a protracted war, which in turn meant that the Navy's need for men was ever growing throughout the duration of open hostility. The manning process had to be slow; otherwise if the Royal Navy had taken all of the men it needed at once, it would have proved devastating to merchant trade.[16]

Britain's naval forces experienced considerable success during the first two years of the French Revolutionary Wars. The French Navy had taken heavy losses during the siege of Toulon, where British and Spanish forces occupying the port destroyed a significant portion of the dockyard facilities and stores, along with nine ships-of-the-line; a further thirteen ships-of-the-line were captured, dealing the French Mediterranean fleet a crippling blow.[17] Similarly, in the summer of 1794 Howe's action of the Glorious First of June resulted in the loss of seven ships-of-the-line and over 5,000 French sailors killed or captured.[18] These two victories early in the war gave the Royal Navy breathing room to fully mobilise the British fleets. Naval growth during the initial years of the French Revolutionary War was enormous, as the Royal Navy went from a pre-war figure of 17,361 borne on the books to 83,891 by the end of 1794.[19] Manning the Navy was a problem of national security and was perceived to be so within the British government, and soon after the beginning of hostilities with France, Britain began to experience difficulty in finding the necessary seamen to mobilise the fleets.[20] The labour pool that both the Royal Navy and merchant sea trade drew their manpower from was quickly beginning to dry up, and a new means of introducing men to naval service needed to be devised.[21] Of all of the problems that faced the Royal Navy in the opening years of warfare, manning the fleets proved the greatest.[22] This problem was further amplified when the war on the continent began to go badly for Britain.[23] Beginning in 1795, one by one Britain's continental allies began to make peace with France, and the Revolutionary government attempted to overcome naval setbacks by adding the weight of foreign navies to their own. In Britain this became painfully evident in January 1795 when France invaded the United Provinces and captured the ice-bound Dutch fleet.[24] This put even more pressure on Britain to bolster its naval force in

---

[16] Duffy, 'The Foundations of British Naval Power', p. 70; Duffy, *Parameters of British Naval Power, 1650–1850*, p. 7.

[17] Rodger, *The Command of the Ocean*, pp. 426–427; Duffy, *The Younger Pitt*, p. 189. For a detailed description of the Toulon campaign see Bernard Ireland, *The Fall of Toulon: The Last Opportunity to Defeat the French Revolution* (London: Weidenfeld and Nicolson, 2005).

[18] Black, *The British Seaborne Empire*, p. 150; Rodger, *The Command of the Ocean*, pp. 429–430.

[19] TNA: PRO 30/8/248, 'Account of Seamen …', f. 29; Rodger, *The Command of the Ocean*, pp. 442, 636–639.

[20] Black and Woodfine, p. 18; Clowes, p. 155; Lincoln, p. 5; Lloyd, *The Nation and the Navy: A History of Naval Life and Policy*, p. 157.

[21] Lewis, *A Social History of the Navy, 1793–1815*, p. 116.

[22] Duffy, 'The Foundations of British Naval Power', p. 67.

[23] Duffy, 'World-Wide War and British Empire, 1793–1815', pp. 189–191.

[24] Ibid., p. 189.

the Channel, as it was the nation's greatest defence against invasion.[25] The Quota Acts were an attempt to alleviate the pressure brought on by the need for continued naval growth.

Currently, little academic study has gone into the Quota Acts, though many historians, especially in reference to the naval mutinies of 1797, have addressed them in some manner. As it stands, only three studies of the Quota Acts exist, an article by F.W. Brooks, a Masters dissertation by Christopher Oprey, and a publication of primary source material edited by Clive Emsley, A.M. Hill and M.Y. Ashcroft.[26] The first to appear, in 1928, was the article by Brooks, which consists of a case study of the Quota Acts in Lindsey, North Lincolnshire. It gives a breakdown of the technical nature of the County Quota Acts, including the process that was laid out for counties to divide the quotas among parishes, and how the parishes in Lindsey handled the burden of raising men. Brooks also detailed how magistrates took on the responsibility of manning, and what type of men were recruited in Lindsey, and alluded to the type of men the County Acts recruited in general. Christopher Oprey's 1961 Masters dissertation, though unpublished, is the most extensive study of the Acts to date, and addresses the application of the Quota Acts in England, using returns from Lancashire, Kent, Essex, Nottinghamshire and London. Like Brooks, Oprey used local returns to form his arguments about the national results. However, he drew his conclusions from a larger sample. Oprey tended not to commit himself to figures, but rather suggested that the 1795 County Act for England and Wales was successful in achieving the overall quota. Finally, the Emsley, Hill and Ashcroft study consists of the returns for the North Riding of Yorkshire, as well as statistics from Kent, Leicestershire, Lincolnshire, Northumberland, Nottinghamshire and Sussex. Emsley provided an introduction to the work, which analyses the data within along with statistics from other counties, while Hill and Ashcroft provided an edited transcript of the returns from the North Riding of Yorkshire. Though it contains less analysis than the other two studies, for the historian it proves perhaps the most useful, as it is a source of easily accessible source material.

All three of these studies are highly useful for a historian looking into the intricacies of the Quota Acts, and accurately depict the Acts as they pertain to the areas studied in each. The Emsley publication and the Oprey dissertation suffer from dissemination problems. The first is a publication of the North Yorkshire County Record Office that is not well-known and difficult to obtain, while the second, being an unpublished Masters dissertation, is virtually unknown to the academic community and only obtainable through the University of Liverpool, where only one copy exists. The Brooks article,

[25] Rodger, 'Sea-Power and Empire, 1688–1793', p. 169.
[26] Brooks, 'Naval Recruiting in Lindsey, 1795–7'; Clive Emsley, A.M. Hill and M.Y. Ashcroft, eds, *North Riding Naval Recruits: The Quota Acts and the Quota Men, 1795–1797* (Northallerton: North Yorkshire County Council, 1978); Oprey.

though published in an eminent journal, is not a well-known article and unlikely to attract attention from more than an adamant researcher. All three works concentrate on the County Acts; however none of the three devote time to the Port Quota Act, as it is not within the bounds of their respective studies. All three also base their conclusions on manuscript data and do not fall into the trap of relying heavily on traditional portrayals of the Royal Navy. This has ensured that their work has remained current and useful, despite their age, where the works of many scholars have become dated as new research emerges. Notably Oprey is probably the most dated of the three, as his views on naval manning outside of the Quota Acts derived from an antiquated interpretation of the Royal Navy.

A New System of Naval Manning

In 1795, Pitt's government, desperate for men, enacted the Quota Acts.[27] Though Britain's continental allies were beginning to crumble under the weight of Revolutionary France, there was still some relief in the fact that the Royal Navy possessed more than 115 ships-of-the-line, providing Britain with formidable naval strength on paper.[28] However, at the start of the war the Royal Navy could only put a fraction of these vessels to sea, as peacetime manpower had slipped below 20,000 men and the previous war had demon-strated that fully mobilising the Navy would require more than 100,000 men. This demand for men, combined with the dwindling supply of skilled mariners, encouraged the government to look for an alternative means of recruiting men for sea service, and gave rise to the Quota Acts.[29]

The Quota Acts were most likely the brainchild of Charles Middleton, who was a Lord Commissioner of the Admiralty during the opening years of the war.[30] The idea for a quota system had been proposed by Middleton a decade earlier in December of 1785, as a means of introducing landsmen into the fleet and thus quickening mobilisation. The administration of Middleton had also been responsible for the relatively smooth transition of the Royal Navy from peace to war, as he had ensured that good stocks of naval supplies were available and that warships not in commission were kept in good condition.[31] The idea behind a quota system was not original to Middleton, however, as county quotas had been used in the 1690s to raise men.[32] Though not implemented a decade earlier, the idea of a manning system based on quotas reappeared again in a manning debate in the House of Commons, which began on 2 February 1795.[33]

---

[27] Brunsman, p. 355; Knight, *The Pursuit of Victory*, p. 143.

[28] Lloyd, *The Nation and the Navy: A History of Naval Life and Policy*, p. 157.

[29] N.A.M. Rodger, 'Mutiny or Subversion? Spithead and the Nore', in *1798: A Bicentenary Perspective*, ed. Thomas Bartlett (Dublin: Fourcourts Press Ltd, 2003), p. 559.

[30] Note that although Middleton left the Admiralty Board early in 1795, he was close to Pitt and therefore in a position to get his ideas adopted.

[31] Emsley *et al.*, *North Riding Naval Recruits*, p. 7.

[32] Rodger, *The Command of the Ocean*, p. 208.

[33] Oprey, pp. 128–129.

Inspiration for the Quota Acts was born out of the idea that merchants and other local interest groups could aid in manning the Royal Navy, thus alleviating pressure on naval administration and national government. This had been successful on a small scale in the past, as in 1759 when the Bristol Merchant Venturers raised 200 men for the Royal Navy to aid and ensure that convoys were properly protected.[34] The London Corporation endorsed a bounty scheme in 1793 that produced 1,901 men for naval service over a period of a couple of months.[35] Also in 1793, many maritime towns and cities, such as the town of Scarborough, voted to raise money to supplement the King's bounty for naval volunteers by adding a further three guineas for able seamen, two guineas for ordinary seamen, and one and a half guineas for landsmen.[36] In early 1795, the East India Company was busy raising 3,000 men for naval service.[37] Merchants and local government officials were willing to take the burden of naval manning, largely because the Royal Navy was more integrated into the domestic economy than its counterpart, the Army, due to the relationship between merchants and the Navy.[38] This demonstrated that local interests would, if so motivated, actively involve themselves in naval manning, helping to alleviate some of the burden faced by naval administration and increasing the flow of men into British warships.

The idea quickly made its way into law, and three Quota Acts emerged in 1795,[39] two in March and one in April.[40] The two Acts that were passed in March were the County Quota Act, which applied to England and Wales, and the Port Quota Act, which applied to the ports of England, Wales and Scotland. The County Quota Act that was passed in April addressed Scottish counties. Two additional County Acts, one directed toward England and Wales and the other applying to Scotland, followed these in November of 1796.[41] The 1795 quotas called for English and Welsh counties to raise 9,420 men, Scottish counties to raise 1,814 men, and ports of England, Wales and Scotland to raise 19,866 men.

The 1795 County Acts were principally designed to recruit landsmen into the Navy.[42] Their focus was to get volunteers from the inland counties, which provided a relatively untapped source of manpower for the Navy. The quotas were set in proportion to the population of the counties. The 1795 County Acts required the English county of Rutland to provide twenty-three men, and Yorkshire to provide 1,081.[43] The counties each then subdivided

---

[34] Bromley, 'The British Navy and Its Seamen after 1688', pp. 150–151.

[35] Oprey, pp. 57–58.

[36] Emsley *et al.*, *North Riding Naval Recruits*, p. 27.

[37] Bromley, 'The British Navy and Its Seamen after 1688', pp. 150–151.

[38] Black, *Naval Power: A History of Warfare and the Sea from 1500*, p. 104.

[39] 35 Geo. III c.5 (English and Welsh Counties); 35 Geo. III c.9 (English, Welsh and Scottish Ports); 35 Geo. III c.29 (Scottish Counties).

[40] Emsley, *British Society and the French Wars, 1793–1815*, pp. 52–53; Kemp, p. 162.

[41] 37 Geo. III c.4 (English and Welsh Counties); and 37 Geo. III c.5 (Scottish Counties).

[42] Oprey, pp. 147–148.

[43] 35 Geo. III c.5.

the quotas by parishes, where the actual process of recruiting took place. The Acts each provided that parishes would raise funds to pay bounties that supplemented the standard King's bounty in order to attract recruits, and further that parishes not producing the set number of men had to pay a fine that equated to the local bounty plus an additional £10.0.0 per man short of the quota. This money was to be placed with the County treasurer and used for the purpose of hiring substitutes. The provisions laid out in the Acts were to be met by 1 July 1795 and money left over after recruiting substitutes was to be sent to the Treasury.[44]

There were specific regulations as to the men allowed to join, which were provided in the twenty-third clause of the 1795 County Act for England and Wales. This made it clear that no man was to be received who was not able-bodied and fit, with no illness or infirmity that would render them unfit to serve. Further, no men would be accepted who looked to the regulating officer to be of less than sixteen or of greater than forty-five years of age. The Acts would not accept any articled clerks, apprentices without consent of their master, men of the coal trade, or deserters from the Army or Navy. Finally, they would not accept any poor man, who was not a seafarer, and who had two or more children in wedlock. Men enrolled under the Act were to serve for the duration of the war and three months beyond if required.[45] These regulations were repeated in the four Acts that followed as well. The recruits taken under the Acts were to be volunteers, as there was no means of compulsion mentioned anywhere in the Acts, only the means to raise the funds to pay bounties.[46] Bounties raised within the counties and parishes were the motivation for recruits to join, and combined with the King's bounty, amounted to a handsome financial sum. The two County Acts that were passed in November 1796 differed from the 1795 County Acts only in that the England and Wales quota was divided, providing some men for the Army and some for the Navy, while in Scotland volunteers were given the option to choose either the Army or the Navy.[47] The Acts reduced the quotas in England and Wales to 6,146 men, and slightly increased the Scottish quota of 2,219.

The exception to the County Acts was the Port Quota Act, which had additional clauses.[48] As the name implies, this Act was directed toward the ports of England, Scotland and Wales, and sought to place the responsibility of manning on merchant sea trade, ship owners, and the economies that revolved around them.[49] The Act placed quotas on seaports that ranged from 5,704 men in London to three men each for Preston Pans and Scilly. This Act

[44] TNA: T 1/758/77–85, 'Account of Fines received … for not raising Volunteers of the Navy, 1795'. This document shows that the Counties of Derby, Essex and Nottingham paid £2,982, £1,129 and £975 respectively; Oprey, p. 143; Brooks, 'Naval Recruiting in Lindsey, 1795–7', pp. 232, 235.
[45] 35 Geo. III c.5. See also Emsley *et al.*, *North Riding Naval Recruits*, pp. 143–145.
[46] Rodger, 'Mutiny or Subversion? Spithead and the Nore', p. 555.
[47] 37 Geo. III c.4; 37 Geo. III c.5; Brooks, 'Naval Recruiting in Lindsey, 1795–7', p. 236.
[48] 35 Geo. III c.9.
[49] Rodger, *The Command of the Ocean*, p. 443.

differed from the County Acts in two core ways. The second clause of the Act allowed that men deemed able seamen by the Port Commissioners and approved by the Regulating Officer would be taken as equal to and in lieu of two landsmen. Further the Act placed the financial burden of raising money for bounties on the port community by setting an embargo on outgoing trade until the quota of men were recruited.

The British Navy had to continue to grow if it was to maintain superiority over France and its rapidly growing naval assets. The Navy's voracious appetite for men continued as the upward trend of naval mobilisation continued sprouting new ideas concerned with naval recruiting. In January and February of 1795 the issue of naval recruitment escalated to the point that government petitioned the authorities in the principal seaports and asked them to consult with local merchants and ship owners to find more effective ways of increasing the number of seamen.[50] A driving force behind the implementation of the Quota Acts was the concept that they would put more of the responsibility of naval recruiting onto local authorities. This was intended to take the pressure of naval recruiting from the shoulders of those working on the national stage and spread it among local government offices such as magistrates, deputy-lieutenants, and constables.[51] This also sought to ease the friction caused by the system of impressment by placing the responsibility and power of naval manning on local authorities, thus defusing many of the problems associated with naval recruiting, while spreading the administration of naval manning over a larger workforce.

Other options for naval recruiting, such as seafarer registration, had also proved inadequate or impractical for the Royal Navy. Under the absolutist Bourbon monarchy, France had implemented the *système des classes*, later renamed the *Inscription Maritime* by Revolutionary France, which required 'any man who has sufficient experience to be able to work a ship' to register with the French government.[52] Those men would then serve one year in three with the French Navy and in return receive a certain list of benefits as registered mariners.[53] A British system of volunteer registration was attempted at the end of the seventeenth century, but it never delivered on its promises, either to the seafarers who registered or to the Navy as a source of men, and was ultimately scrapped. The system never really worked correctly in France either. The Crown rarely honoured its promises to the men registered and a lack of enforcement meant that many men never registered. When war did actually break out, the system broke down completely, as one-third of France's seamen were never enough to man the fleets, causing the system to turn into a form of compulsion that simply swept up everyone who had registered.[54]

---

[50]   Lincoln, p. 85.
[51]   Brooks, 'Naval Recruiting in Lindsey, 1795–7', pp. 231–232; Emsley *et al.*, 'The Impact of War and Military Participation on Britain and France', pp. 62–63; Oprey, p. 128.
[52]   Armel De Wismes, 'The French Navy under Louis XIV', in *Louis XIV and Absolution*, ed. Ragnhild Marie Hatton (London: Macmillan Press Ltd, 1976), p. 428.
[53]   Cormack, pp. 24–25; Harding, *Seapower and Naval Warfare, 1650–1830*, p. 136.
[54]   Rodger, *The Wooden World*, p. 151.

The Quota Acts

The Quota Acts were implemented as a means of increasing naval manpower. At the end of 1794, approximately 85,000 men were serving in the Royal Navy, a number that had grown from just under 17,000 only two years earlier. However, after two years of naval intake, the supply of seafarers in Britain began to run out, a problem further aggravated by the fact that British merchant sea trade could not be sacrificed for naval manpower. Out of this rose the two County Quota Acts of 1795 and later the two of 1796. Prior to this, naval recruiting had concentrated in seaside areas. Although many of the volunteers who entered the Royal Navy were indeed landsmen with no experience at sea, to a great extent they were landsmen from areas near the sea, as there were no recruiting officers operating in areas well away from seafaring communities. The County Quota Acts were principally designed to recruit landsmen into the Navy, and in 1796 into the Army as well. Their focus was to get volunteers from the inland counties, which provided an untapped source of manpower. They attracted volunteers with financial reward in the form of locally raised bounties, which were added to the King's bounty. In many cases the Acts also offered the possibility of a better life, where at least naval service came with the guarantee of being fed every day. It also appealed to younger men, who likely did not have the ties to hold them to a particular location, such as a wife and children. The two 1795 County Acts sought to raise 11,234 men to aid in naval expansion; most of these would have been expected to be landsmen. Members of Parliament had no illusions of landlocked counties providing masses of skilled seamen, but rather saw the opportunity of gaining an additional supply of unskilled men without putting naval administration under any significantly larger strain.

The Port Quota Act of 1795, on the other hand, was intended to find skilled seamen, and called for a total of 19,866 men. As the name implies, the Act was directed at commercial ports, and involved an embargo that was placed on outgoing shipping of individual ports until they raised their quota.[55] The Port Quota Act also specified that an able seaman counted as the equivalent of two men toward the quota. Thus if every man the Act recruited was indeed a highly skilled able seaman, it would have had the effect of putting almost 10,000 skilled seamen into the Royal Navy. It also put the pressure of raising bounties necessary for recruitment on the backs of local maritime interests, which naturally were in the proper place to recruit skilled seamen.

History has not been kind to the Quota Acts. Generally speaking most historians have been quick to find flaws in the Acts, often based on misconceptions surrounding their design, purpose, and outcome. Much of the misconception can be attributed to the lack of research on the topic. Historians have also been quick to blame social and administrative problems within the Royal Navy on the Quota Acts, and the Acts have been regarded by most as the main suspect in the great mutinies of 1797. To an extent, this has

---

[55] 35 Geo. III c.9.

been the result of the unpopularity of the Acts at the time they were implemented by officers and men serving in the Royal Navy. Understandably, naval
officers wanted more skilled men; however they were faced with unskilled
landsmen that the Acts recruited in large numbers. As these landsmen had,
for the most part, little or no experience of the seafaring world, they became
an easy scapegoat for the social and labour problems that occurred during
the years following the Quota Acts, which were seen as having introduced
corruption into the lower deck of the Navy.

On some level this is slightly surprising, as contemporaries and historians
alike believed that one of the major problems of naval recruiting was the fact
that it fell on the maritime population, and forced them to take up an unfair
portion of the burden of war. Though unskilled men entered the Navy from
virtually all walks of life, it was necessary that approximately two-thirds or
more of the seamen complement of warships be made up of able and ordinary
seamen. This meant that the hammer fell heaviest on a relatively narrow band
of the population, in particular the maritime areas of the south and east
coasts of England. Further, impressment, which was the most controversial
form of recruitment, took place almost solely in naval and merchant ports
and at sea. Many historians have stated that naval conscription should have
been extended to the general population.[56] Though they were not a form
of compulsion, the Quota Acts did exactly that. They required every county
of England, Wales and Scotland to provide men for naval service, and also
tapped into all of the portside communities. The Acts therefore fulfilled the
desire to reach beyond the coastline in search of men for the Royal Navy.
However, these aspirations were not those of naval officers, but rather of men
who generally saw the Navy from the shoreline. Naval officers knew they
needed skilled men, with years of knowledge at sea, without whom the Navy
could not get its ships to sea, much less successfully carry out complex operations such as battle and blockade.

History has also addressed the Quota Acts as a primitive form of
conscription.[57] Labelling the Acts in this manner has formed a dubious
cloud around the entire topic. The idea of a 'primitive form of conscription'
is most likely a reference to the relationship between the Navy and the
Cinque Ports in the thirteenth and fourteenth centuries, where these ports
provided ships and the men for England in times of war, loosely based on
a quota.[58] Michael Lewis argued that the men were not volunteers 'because
various geographical quotas had to be found'.[59] Lewis was not alone in this

---

[56] Harding, *Seapower and Naval Warfare, 1650–1830*, pp. 139–140; Lewis, *History of the British Navy*, p. 184.

[57] Harding, *Seapower and Naval Warfare, 1650–1830*, pp. 139–140; Lewis, *A Social History of the Navy, 1793–1815*, p. 86; Lloyd, *The British Seaman, 1200–1860*, p. 195.

[58] N.A.M. Rodger, *The Safeguard of the Sea: A Naval History of Britain, 660–1649* (New York: W.W. Norton & Company, 1997), pp. 131–142. See also N.A.M. Rodger, 'The Naval Service of the Cinque Ports', *English Historical Review* CXI, no. 442 (1996).

[59] Lewis, *A Social History of the Navy, 1793–1815*, p. 117.

claim, as other historians, before and since, have adopted it.[60] John Masefield went as far as to say the men recruited by the Quota Acts came unwillingly.[61] The fact that geographical regions were given quotas of men to raise for the Navy does not mean the men were forced into service, whether the location was a landlocked county or a Cinque Port. The Quota Acts themselves provided no method for compulsion, only a means to raise money to pay bounties.[62]

Lewis further misunderstood the means of recruitment under the Quota Acts in his references to how substitutes were recruited. Lewis stated that after the men were 'picked' they were given an opportunity to recruit a substitute to serve in the Navy in their place.[63] This again is supported by the assumption that men taken in by the Quota Acts were virtually pressed, only that magistrates rather than naval officers and press gangs performed the act. This concept is wholly incorrect. As mentioned earlier, parishes that could not raise their quota paid a fine, usually £10.0.0 above the local bounty. This money was then used to attract volunteers from different parts of the given county or even neighbouring counties. Thus, neither the Quota men nor the substitutes were conscripted, and there was further no need for a substitute system to function as stated by Lewis, as the men were volunteers and thus had no need to seek a substitute for their service.

Historians, such as Lewis, as well as eighteenth-century contemporaries, blamed the Quota Acts for introducing large numbers of landsmen into the fleet, which included men with educations or, worse, men of dubious character, such as prisoners or revolutionaries.[64] This assumption made Quota men even less desired than the landsmen who volunteered on a regular basis.[65] Quota men were considered by some naval officers to have been of poor quality for service in the Navy, and virtually useless on board a warship.[66] Further, historians have claimed that the men introduced by the Quota Acts included a large number of revolutionaries, who sowed discontent into the fleet.[67]

The Quota Acts have also been depicted as offering very large bounties that caused social friction on the lower deck of British warships, as well as introducing corruption into the fleet.[68] Some of these bounties have been stated as being of £70.0.0 or more.[69] Undoubtedly, the Quota Acts raised the

---

[60] Lloyd, *The British Seaman, 1200–1860*, p. 195; Masefield, p. 55.

[61] Masefield, p. 55.

[62] Rodger, 'Mutiny or Subversion? Spithead and the Nore', p. 555.

[63] Lewis, *A Social History of the Navy, 1793–1815*, pp. 94, 118, 303.

[64] Ibid., p. 123.

[65] Rodger, 'Mutiny or Subversion? Spithead and the Nore', p. 555.

[66] W.M. James, *The Naval History of Great Britain During the French Revolutionary and Napoleonic Wars, 1797–1799*, vol. II (London: Conway Maritime, 2002), p. 65.

[67] Wells, p. 81.

[68] Clowes, pp. 155–156; Lewis, *A Social History of the Navy, 1793–1815*, p. 122.

[69] Kemp, p. 164; Lloyd, *The British Seaman, 1200–1860*, p. 198.

bounties received for naval service, as they attracted volunteers primarily with monetary incentive. On some level this obviously caused friction on the lower deck, as landsmen with far less skill than experienced seamen received higher bounties than seamen recruited just a few months earlier. Michael Lewis's argument stated that Quota men were not patriotic at all, unlike the 'hardy sailor', but rather were greedy and served only because of the money offered by the bounty, often being debtors who used the bounty to pay their way out of prison.[70] Going even further, Peter Kemp stated that these men were mostly vagrants and prisoners that magistrates could happily get rid of for long periods of time.[71] Overall, history has painted a bleak image of the men recruited by the Quota Acts, due greatly to a lack of serious research on the subject.

The Quota Acts are probably most noted as one of the major causes behind the naval mutinies of 1797. Once the mutinies were over, authorities sought somewhere to place the blame for the incidents. The Quota Acts were convenient and disliked by many naval officers and were therefore an easy target for contemporaries to concentrate their frustrations upon. Subsequently, many historians have followed in these footsteps.[72] Most of the historiography has claimed that the Quota Acts introduced a social revolution into the fleet, primarily by introducing a new kind of recruit. Described by John Brewer, this new type of recruit was 'younger, better educated, less inured to the traditional rigors of naval life, and unprepared to accept unreasonable manifestations of authority'.[73] Brewer also stated that by the time of the 1797 mutinies, '100,000 of the 120,000 to 135,000 strong naval force had been recruited in the preceding three years, primarily products of the Quota Acts'.[74] Other historians have stated that the superior intellect of the Quota men allowed them to 'infuse a secret leaven of discontent into the ranks of the seamen'.[75] The 'transient and heterogeneous' nature of Quota men has been used as a reason why the mutinies at the Nore were so unsuccessful and contentious in comparison with the mutiny at Spithead.[76] Oddly enough, one of the main arguments against the Quota Acts claims that seamen were not sophisticated enough for a mutiny of such a grand nature.[77] This argument claims that, rather, seamen were rough men, made by the sea, and further had little knowledge of the fact that the standard of life on land had risen greatly since the last reorganisation of the Navy in the mid-seventeenth century.[78] William James described the type of

---

[70] Lewis, *A Social History of the Navy, 1793–1815*, p. 290.

[71] Kemp, p. 164.

[72] Rodger, 'Mutiny or Subversion? Spithead and the Nore', p. 555. See also Brunsman, pp. 355–356; Conrad Gill, *The Naval Mutinies of 1797* (Manchester: University of Manchester Press, 1913).

[73] Brewer, p. 136.

[74] Ibid.

[75] Wells, p. 90.

[76] Rogers, *The Press Gang: Naval Impressment and Its Opponents in Georgian Britain*, p. 108.

[77] Lewis, *A Social History of the Navy, 1793–1815*, p. 125.

[78] Kemp, p. 163; G.E. Manwaring and Bonamy Dobrée, *The Floating Republic: An Account of the*

Quota man responsible for the mutinies as a kind of criminal mastermind who was clever at evading the law and manipulating others into carrying out his business:

> He was generally a plausible fellow, with a smattering of learning and a knowledge of the world; two qualities which ranked him very high in the estimation of the unsophisticated sailor. He sang a good song, or at all events, he told a good story, and became, in time, the oracle of the forecastle. He knew his business (that which had brought him on ship-board) too well to practice on so circumscribed a spot; and therefore, as no one witnessed, no one believed, any harm of him. He was perhaps a dabbler of politics, and certainly, from the nature of his profession, a 'bit of a lawyer'. He therefore could expound acts of parliament to the sailors. In doing this, he read what he pleased, and explained how he pleased; told them where they were wronged, and pointed out how they might get redressed.[79]

The defence provided in these arguments suggests that the mariner, though able to master wind, sail and sea, was not smart or educated enough to realise how bad his life and working conditions actually were, and thus the introduction of those who were capable of such knowledge had an effect similar to introducing a flame to gunpowder.

The introduction of intelligence to the lower deck has not been the only failure that history has assigned to the Quota Acts in regard to the 1797 mutinies. The Quota Acts have also been blamed for introducing unrest into the Navy in the form of Irish dissidents, particularly United Irishmen working in French interests.[80] Generally speaking these interpretations of history suggest that the seamen of the Royal Navy were, on the whole, good and patriotic Britons. However, the introduction of the Quota Acts produced what appeared to be the perfect opportunity for French agents to enter the Royal Navy unnoticed. Once among the men of the lower deck they sowed discontent and eventually caused or at least fuelled the events that led to the large-scale mutinies. It has also been argued that the mutinies were an extension of an English peace movement, and the purpose of the mutinies was not so much to produce better conditions and pay for the seamen, but rather to drive Britain out of the war, possibly even beginning another English revolution.[81] Outside influence is the common thread which binds the majority of the attacks on the Quota Acts together, as it proved a convenient

Mutinies at Spithead and the Nore 1797 (London: Geoffrey Bles, 1935), p. 248.

[79] James, *The Naval History of Great Britain During the French Revolutionary and Napoleonic Wars, 1797–1799*, p. 65.

[80] Ian R. Christie, *Wars and Revolutions: Britain 1760–1815* (London: Edward Arnold, 1982), pp. 239–240; Rodger, 'Mutiny or Subversion? Spithead and the Nore', p. 556; E.P. Thompson, *The Making of the English Working Class* (London: Penguin Books, 1991), pp. 183–188; Wells, p. 84.

[81] Wells, pp. 81–150. See also Rodger, 'Mutiny or Subversion? Spithead and the Nore', p. 556; Neale, pp. 138–144. Note, many of the leaders of the mutinies have been pointed to by historians as Quota men; however it has since been disproved.

and seemingly logical argument both in the years immediately following the 1797 mutinies and for historians who have subsequently written about them.[82] To a great extent this derives from the fact that officers and seamen alike were not fond of the men the Quota Acts produced for naval service.[83] Their dislike for these men undoubtedly stemmed from the fact that they were, generally speaking, unfamiliar with the sea and until they gained some experience proved cumbersome in their new environment; however this was little different from the unskilled landsmen who volunteered for naval service on a regular basis.

Much of the history that has been written has negatively labelled the Quota Acts, blaming them for many of the problems that surfaced in the Royal Navy following their introduction. However, few of these accusations hold water, and most require great leaps of faith as they are based mostly on assumption with little or no hard evidence pointing to the Quota Acts. The reasons for placing blame on the Quota Acts seem to be based around convenience, both as a source of manning which was disliked by naval officers who were on the receiving end of recruiting efforts, and because they allow for explanations other than the simple fact that seamen were competent, understood their situation, and were capable of organising what today would be called a labour strike over grievances between employee and employer. However, although convenience, speculation and assumption have assigned many unproven shortfalls to the Quota Acts, hard evidence in the form of manuscript research can reveal some truth about how the Acts actually performed.

Statistics of the Quota Acts

The best sources for gauging the results of naval recruitment are muster books of warships, particularly the musters of ships as they first went to sea with complete crews, from which data relating to the recruitment of men can be gathered and compiled. The data shows that when considering the overall scope of Royal Navy recruiting between 1793 and 1801, the Quota Acts provided approximately 9 per cent of seamen and 2 per cent of petty officers entering warships.[84] This proves that the Quota Acts did have a substantial effect on overall recruiting numbers in respect to the nine years of the French Revolutionary Wars. Further, in 1795, 1796 and 1797 Quota men made up approximately 26 per cent, 13 per cent, and 15 per cent respectively of the seamen recruited into naval service. In these years, especially 1795, the Quota Acts accounted for a substantial portion of seamen who entered the Royal Navy. Though these figures are broad and sweeping they do illustrate that regardless of whom the Quota Acts recruited they did have a significant impact on the overall numbers.

---

[82] Thompson, pp. 183–184; Wells, p. 84.
[83] Lewis, *A Social History of the Navy, 1793–1815*, p. 124; Lloyd, *The British Seaman, 1200–1860*, p. 200.
[84] See Figures 2.9 and 2.10.

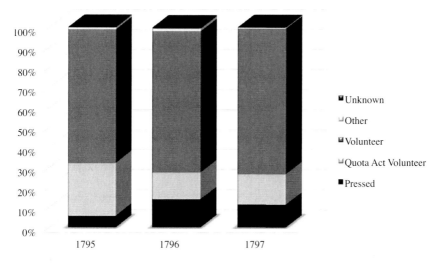

Figure 5.1 Factored seamen recruitment, 1795–1797

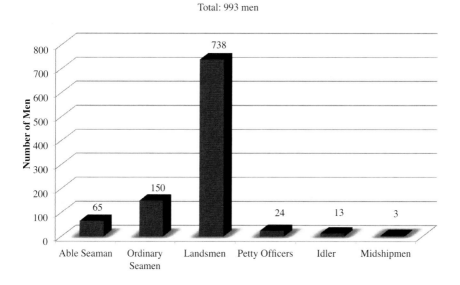

Figure 5.2 Quota Act recruits

Total: 993 men

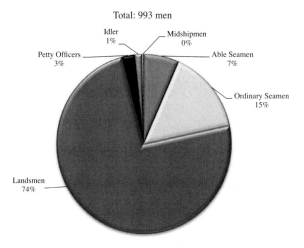

Figure 5.3 Overall Quota Act recruitment percentages

Although similar in nature and motivation, the County Acts and the Port Act were designed to attract different types of men into naval service. Overall numbers show that out of 993 men recruited by the Quota Acts that fell within this database, there were 738 landsmen, 150 ordinary seamen, 65 able seamen, 24 petty officers, 13 idlers, and 3 midshipmen. This sample illustrates that the five Acts combined produced around 74 per cent landsmen, 15 per cent ordinary seamen, only 7 per cent able seamen, and a further 3 per cent were petty officers. It seems clear that about one in four men who entered as a volunteer under the Quota Acts had some level of skill and experience at sea, while the remaining three-quarters were landsmen. By observing the dates that the men appeared on board ship, it can be deduced whether they were the product of the 1795 Quota Acts or those of 1796. Of the 993 Quota men surveyed in this sample, 774 were the product of the 1795 Acts and 219 came from the 1796 Acts. Seventy-eight per cent of the Quota men in this sample were therefore the result of the 1795 Acts, leaving 22 per cent coming out of the 1796 Acts. This may also suggest that the overall outcome of the Acts was similar, with the 1796 Acts producing less than a third as many men as those of 1795. Looking at the differences in the men each set of Acts produced also shows how the two years differed in the type of men they recruited.

Once the product of the 1795 Acts made it to their respective ships they were rated: 72 per cent were landsmen, 18 per cent ordinary seamen, 7 per cent able seamen, 2 per cent petty officers, and 1 per cent were idlers. The 1796 Acts produced 84 per cent landsmen, 5 per cent ordinary seamen, 4 per cent able seamen, 5 per cent petty officers, and 2 per cent idlers. This shows that the 1795 Acts were more successful in both overall numbers as well as in the ratio of skilled men to landsmen that they produced. Notably, the 1795 Acts also included the Port Quota Act, which sought skilled seamen, and therefore boosted the 1795 intake of experienced mariners. However, this

Total: 774 men

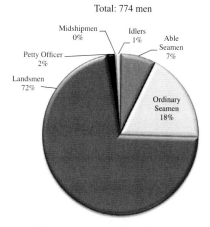

Total: 219 men

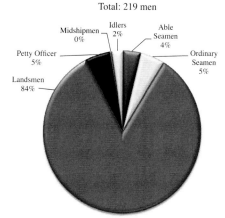

Figure 5.4 Muster data for the 1795 Quota Acts

Figure 5.5 Muster data for the 1796 Quota Acts

also suggests that as a means for recruiting skilled seamen, and replacing impressment as a form of acquiring able seamen, the Acts were a failure.

The Quota Acts can be further broken down into the County Acts and the Port Act. The County Acts were designed to pull in landsmen from areas previously untapped by naval recruiting efforts. From the returns of the 1795 County Quota Acts of Kent, Leicestershire, Lindsey, Northumberland, Nottinghamshire and Sussex, a survey accounting for 1,059 men, it is evident that 83 per cent, 880 men, were considered landsmen.[85] The remaining 179 men were listed as some form of seaman, a number that possibly includes watermen and boatmen who may well have been rated as ordinary seamen. Thus, less than 17 per cent of men brought in by the County Quota Acts seem to have had any experience at sea, which essentially seems to be what was expected. The County Acts have been blamed for bringing large numbers of criminals, vagrants and undesirables into the Royal Navy. However, from these returns it seems clear that the men who volunteered under the Quota Acts represent a cross-section of lower-class trades, and there is little evidence of any of the men being criminals or vagrants.[86] From the returns it seems apparent that the majority of the men were 'village lads with decent reputations,'[87] which is not how history has reported the Quota Acts. In fact, the only historians who have said that the County Quota Acts did not bring in large numbers of criminals and vagrants are those few who have studied the actual returns, primarily Brooks and Emsley, or work based on their research.

[85] Emsley *et al.*, *North Riding Naval Recruits*, pp. 16–18.
[86] Ibid., p. 11.
[87] Brooks, 'Naval Recruiting in Lindsey, 1795–7', p. 239; Emsley *et al.*, *North Riding Naval Recruits*, pp. 11, 16–18.

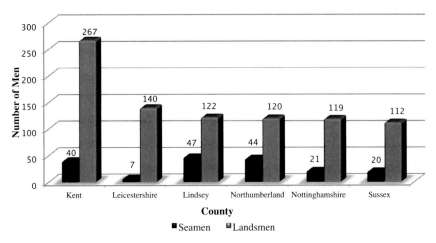

Figure 5.6 1795 County Quota Acts returns

Unlike the County Acts, the Port Quota Acts were designed to gain volunteer seamen for the Royal Navy, and rewarded ports for recruiting skilled seamen by allowing them to count each able seaman as two landsmen in their quotas. Therefore, as few as 2,852 men could have fulfilled London's quota of 5,704 men, had they all been able seamen. In reality it was unlikely for port quotas to be filled entirely by seamen; however the motivation for ports to find skilled seafarers was high. Examining the returns for Britain's largest merchant port, the Port of London, produces statistics that can shed some light on the Port Quota Acts.[88] Out of a total return of 3,894 men, London produced 627 able seamen, 747 ordinary seamen, and 2,523 landsmen. Thus only 16 per cent of the men were able seamen and another 19 per cent were rated as ordinary seamen, while 65 per cent were landsmen. The intake of skilled seafarers for the Port Quota Acts is nearly double when compared to the above six-county survey, in which only 17 per cent of men were considered to have 'sea experience', some of whom would not have been rated as able or ordinary seamen.

Looking deeper into the statistics of the Port of London returns reveals the previous occupations of men recruited under the Act. Out of 3,894 men who entered under the Port Quota Act for London, 207 different occupations were listed as the previous 'callings' of the volunteers. Of these, 22 per cent were listed as some form of seaman. Another 12 per cent were listed as labourers, followed by 5 per cent as shoemakers, 4 per cent as servants, 4 per cent as carpenters, and the list continues with smaller percentages.[89] As with the County Acts and as expected, these are in fact a cross-section of the lower-class trades of the time. Of the 627 men who volunteered as able

---

[88] TNA: ADM 7/361, 'Account of Men Raised ... Port of London by Virtue of the Act 35th Geo III, Cap 9'.
[89] See Figure 5.11.

seamen, nineteen different callings were given, of which 90 per cent were listed as seamen, 4 per cent as shipwrights, 1 per cent as sailmakers, and 1 per cent as watermen. Thus, the vast majority of men who volunteered as able seamen listed callings that were directly related to their level of experience. It seems that only 4 per cent listed callings outside of what would have been considered seafaring jobs, such as carpenters,[90] weavers, butchers, clerks, and so on. The men who were entered as ordinary seamen, however, came from more diverse backgrounds, and eighty-eight different callings were given, of which only 38 per cent were listed as seamen. Nine per cent were listed as labourers, 5 per cent as carpenters, 3 per cent as fishermen, 3 per cent as watermen, and 3 per cent as weavers, with the list continuing to smaller divisions. It would seem likely that many of these men were in fact part-time seamen, likely having spent some time at sea and then working ashore or possibly taking to sea seasonally or as the opportunity presented, filling the rest of their time with jobs on land. Of the 2,523 men who entered as landsmen only seventeen men had their calling listed as seamen. These men had likely only recently taken to the sea, as nine were under twenty and only one was above thirty. Labourers were the largest listed calling for landsmen, accounting for 16 per cent, followed by a very diverse listing, which included 7 per cent shoemakers, 6 per cent servants, 5 per cent carpenters, 5 per cent tailors, 4 per cent weavers, 3 per cent clerks, 2 per cent bakers, and a very wide range of occupations totalling 191 different callings that ranged from book binders and coal heavers to silk weavers and watch makers.[91]

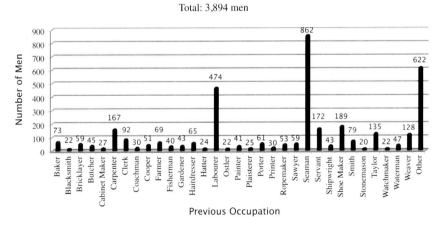

Figure 5.7 Callings for Port Quota men from London

[90] Note that carpenters may well have been seafaring men, but, with no distinction as such documented, I have chosen to list the occupation as non-seafaring.

[91] Aside from the presence of seamen, the previous occupations for men that entered under the Port Quota for London match up very closely with those from the British Army. Stephen Brumwell, *Redcoats: The British Soldier and War in the Americas, 1755–1763* (Cambridge: Cambridge University Press, 2002), p. 370.

It is also important to note that the London returns counted both able and ordinary seamen as two landsmen, whereas the Port Quota Act states that only able seamen could be counted as two landsmen. Therefore, they counted 623 able seamen and 748 ordinary seamen as 2,742 men for the Port of London, combined with 2,522 landsmen to equal 5,264 men recruited under the Port Quota Acts as volunteers.[92] It would further seem that there was no problem encountered in doing so, as no manuscript documentation has yet been found that questions or contradicts this action; and further research into the returns of other ports may find a similar trend. It is also highly interesting to observe that the Port of London also claimed 220 seamen who were pressed between 26 March and 14 September 1795, which counted on the books as 440 men, bringing the London total to exactly the quota placed on the port of 5,704 men. This illustrates that, although the Port Quota Act actively sought to produce skilled men, it failed to produce the necessary quantity for the Royal Navy to maintain a desired ratio of one-third able seamen, one-third ordinary seamen, and one-third landsmen. Though, in comparison to the total returns of the Quota Acts, the percentages of able and ordinary seamen increased substantially. However, it was not nearly enough to ensure that able and ordinary seamen remained above two-thirds of the total number of seamen on board warships, as landsmen still made up 65 per cent of the men recruited under the Port Quota Act in London.

The Quota Acts primarily drew in landsmen for naval service,[93] who, like most men serving in the eighteenth-century Royal Navy, were quite young. Sixty-seven per cent of the men who entered under the 1795 Quota Acts and 70 per cent of the men from the 1796 Acts were twenty-five years of age or younger, with the peak ages being twenty in 1795 and nineteen in 1796. Similarly the returns from the Port of London show that 54 per cent of the men were twenty-five or under, with the peak age being twenty. The counties of Kent, Leicestershire, Lindsey, Northumberland, Nottinghamshire and Sussex had peak ages of twenty, twenty-one, eighteen, eighteen, eighteen and twenty respectively, all of which illustrates the youth of Quota men.[94]

Contrary to what some historians have stated,[95] these men were actually useful on board Royal Navy ships. Much of a warship's rigging led to a deck where mainly unskilled men could do the heavy job of pulling and heaving as long as they had a highly experienced man to lead them in the task.[96] Young landsmen were also trainable to an extent, and

---

[92] It is important to note that the arithmetic in ADM 7/361, 'Account of Men Raised … Port of London' is incorrect, which was discovered after creating a digital database from the document. The actual number of men entered was 627 able seamen, 747 ordinary seamen, and 2,523 landsmen.

[93] Emsley *et al.*, *North Riding Naval Recruits*, p. 12.

[94] Ibid., p. 19.

[95] Oprey, p. 4. Oprey claimed that landsmen were useless on board ship, and that the Royal Navy's shortage was qualitative rather than quantitative.

[96] Rodger, 'Officers and Men', p. 138; Rodger, '"A Little Navy of Your Own Making": Admiral Boscawen and the Cornish Connection in the Royal Navy', p. 83.

Total: 981 men

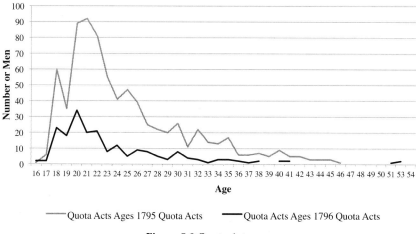

Figure 5.8 Quota Acts ages

Total: 3,890 men

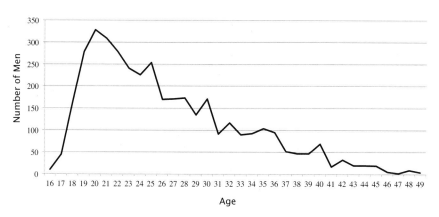

Age

Figure 5.9 Ages for Port of London returns

they learned the tasks necessary of their position on board naval ships and thus were successfully integrated into ships' companies.[97] The Royal Navy was actually good at integrating unskilled men into its service, mainly by spreading raw recruits as evenly as possible across the fleets, ensuring that they rarely exceeded one-third of the seamen within a ship's company.[98] The landsmen that the Quota Acts attracted were also not hardened criminals, revolutionaries, or attorneys,[99] they were simply

---

[97] Emsley *et al.*, *North Riding Naval Recruits*, p. 151; Emsley, *British Society and the French Wars, 1793–1815*, p. 53; Kemp, p. 164.

[98] Emsley, 'The Recruitment of Petty Offenders During the French Wars, 1793–1815', p. 36.

[99] Out of 3,897 men recruited in London only one was listed as an attorney.

men in need of jobs and came from a cross-section of the lower-class trades.[100] Recruiting landsmen ultimately proved one of the ways to relieve the supply and demand problem faced by the Royal Navy after two years of warfare.[101]

As monetary reward was the only mechanism available to attract volunteers, the Quota Acts did produce large bounties. Logically this makes sense, as the Acts came two years into the war and the King's bounty of £5.0.0 for able seamen, £2.10.0 for ordinary seamen, and £1.10.0 for landsmen was proving insufficient to attract the number of volunteers necessary. Essentially the Royal Navy had to increase beyond its maximum size from the previous war, in effect pushing well beyond 100,000 men. The Quota Acts have been blamed for producing very large bounties, which in turn caused social friction within the lower deck,[102] and some of these bounties have been claimed by historians to have exceeded £70.0.0.[103] Technically the Admiralty put restrictions on the port bounties, which were not allowed to rise above that offered by the Port of London: £26.5.0 for able seamen, £21.0.0 for ordinary seamen, and £15.15.0 for landsmen, exclusive of the King's bounty.[104] The use of high bounties to attract volunteers can be seen in a recruiting poster, dated April 1795, from the Port of Stockton which reads, 'The Largest Bounties ever given … Volunteers wanted for the Royal Navy, under management of the Merchants and Ship-owners'.[105] The poster goes on to state that able seamen will receive £31.5.0, ordinary seamen £23.10.0, and landsmen £17.5.0, all inclusive of the King's bounty. Brooks's study of the Quota Acts in Lindsey found that bounties paid there were generally between £30.0.0 and £35.0.0, and that most substitutes recruited after the deadline received £30.0.0 or less.[106] Bounties were indeed much larger than they had been prior to the Quota Acts, with landsmen receiving three times what an able seaman would have received weeks earlier.[107] However, the restrictions put in place on bounties produced by ports made it unlikely that an able seaman would have received more than £31.5.0 inclusive of the King's bounty. Although there were no such restrictions put in place on the County Acts, it is unlikely that they would have been much higher, as there was no motivation to raise such large bounties. Any evidence that Quota men received more than £50.0.0 is yet to be found.[108]

---

[100] Neale, p. 133.
[101] Earle, 'English Sailors, 1570–1775', p. 91.
[102] Clowes, pp. 155–156; Lewis, *A Social History of the Navy, 1793–1815*, p. 122.
[103] Kemp, p. 164; Lloyd, *The British Seaman, 1200–1860*, p. 198.
[104] TNA: ADM 7/361, 'Account of Men Raised … Port of London by Virtue of the Act 35th Geo III, Cap 9'; Oprey, p. 177.
[105] 'Recruiting Poster, 2nd April 1795', *The Mariner's Mirror* VIII, no. 2 (1922): p. 23.
[106] Brooks, 'Naval Recruiting in Lindsey, 1795–7', pp. 235–236.
[107] Emsley *et al.*, *North Riding Naval Recruits*, p. 12.
[108] Oprey, pp. 176–177.

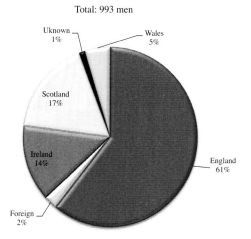

Total: 993 men

Figure 5.10 Quota Act nationalities

The Quota Acts and the Great Mutinies

The Quota Acts have most often been mentioned by historians in reference to the Spithead and Nore mutinies of 1797. For many historians, and indeed most contemporaries, the explanation of the 1797 mutinies has been that they were the result of outside influence, and the Quota Acts served as the obvious change in naval recruiting that introduced it into the Royal Navy.[109] One of the leading theories has been the introduction of large numbers of Irish men into the fleets by the Quota Acts.[110] In fact, Irishmen made up 19 per cent of the overall number of men in the Royal Navy from 1793 to 1801,[111] and only 14 per cent of men who entered under all five of the Quota Acts. None of the Quota Acts applied to Ireland and recruiting for Quota volunteers never took place in Ireland. The Irish men who did join under the Act were men with the same callings as the rest of the Quota men, and were likely working in English, Scottish and Welsh towns when the Quota Acts were passed. Further, Irish men in the fleet broke down into similar skill ratios to the rest of the seamen, as 30 per cent were able seamen, 30 per cent ordinary seamen, and a slightly larger number were landsmen at 40 per cent. Emsley, Hill and Ashcroft's study of the County Acts shows that only 3 per cent of Quota men from those six counties were Irish. Therefore, if Irish dissidents, such as United Irishmen, entered the service and were responsible for the 1797 mutinies, it would seem unlikely that their source of recruitment would have been the Quota Acts, as statistically they were more likely to enter through the standard recruitment methods of volunteering and impressment.

[109] Rodger, 'Mutiny or Subversion? Spithead and the Nore', p. 555.
[110] Thompson, pp. 183–185.
[111] See Figure 2.21.

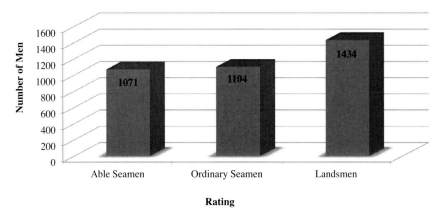

Total: 3,690 men

Figure 5.11 Rating of Irish seamen in the Royal Navy
Source: Emsley *et al.*, *North Riding Naval Recruits*, p. 15.

Though it has been claimed that many of the mutiny leaders were Quota men, all but Richard Parker have proved to come from sources other than the Quota Acts.[112] Parker, on the other hand, was definitely a Quota man recruited for the Port of Edinburgh. At the time of recruitment, Parker was in a debtors' prison and it appears that he volunteered under the Quota Acts, using the bounty to pay his debts.[113] Parker however was not a landsman, but a highly valued experienced seaman, and had served in the Royal Navy during the American War as a petty officer. It appears that he was well educated by sailors' standards, as he kept a school in Exeter for a period of time between the wars. The Royal Navy regularly accepted men from debtors' prisons, who then used the bounty to pay their debts. Labelling this man a criminal in a modern context would be unfair, as debtors are rarely locked away in this age.[114] Therefore, rather than a hardened criminal, Parker was in fact a man who had found himself in a bad financial situation and saw a solution in naval service, where he had skills that were in high demand. Criminals and vagrants were explicitly excluded in the Quota Acts.[115]

It is only practical to consider that Quota men were responsible for the Spithead and Nore mutinies if one believes that the delegates were actually straw men, put in place to conceal the true leaders, or that the true leader was somehow a master criminal genius who covered his tracks so well as to

[112] Brunsman, p. 356; Lewis, *A Social History of the Navy, 1793–1815*, p. 125; Rodger, 'Mutiny or Subversion? Spithead and the Nore', p. 555.
[113] Timothy Jenks, 'Naval Engagements: Patriotism, Cultural Politics, and the Royal Navy, 1793–1815' (unpublished PhD thesis, University of Toronto, 2001), p. 136; Lloyd, *The British Seaman, 1200–1860*, p. 201; Manwaring and Dobrée, p. 121.
[114] Lewis, *A Social History of the Navy, 1793–1815*, p. 126.
[115] Rodger, *The Command of the Ocean*, p. 443.

leave no evidence at all of his existence.[116] As stated by N.A.M. Rodger, this is an example of a conspiracy theory in the purest form, 'in which the absence of evidence only serves to prove the fiendish cunning of the conspirators'.[117] Ultimately, the most feasible candidate for a straw man is Richard Parker, who was likely not the 'true leader' of the Nore mutiny, and was in fact an undoubted Quota man. Further, of all the men officially accused of mutiny at court martial in 1797, only forty-three out of 462 were Quota men, plus another forty who may have been Quota volunteers based on their dates of entry into the fleet.[118] In the end, the men on board belonged to a complex hierarchy, in which skilled seamen and petty officers took the lead, which was in fact confirmed by the men who made up the leaders of the 1797 mutinies.[119] If Quota men were responsible for the 1797 mutinies, which most evidence contradicts, then they were in the position to act because they were men familiar with the sea with years of experience, and in a position to lead the lower deck because of their seniority as seamen and petty officers, not because they were revolutionaries or educated men not familiar with the Navy and its ways. Therefore, the line of reasoning that Quota men were somehow responsible for unrest in the fleet resulting in the 1797 mutinies is, in fact, a defunct argument, for which no hard evidence exists. The only means by which the Quota Acts may have been an added factor in the 1797 mutinies was in the friction that they caused within the lower deck over late-coming landsmen having received higher bounties than many prime seamen who volunteered in 1793 and 1794. However, this theory is a far cry from the introduction of educated dissidents into the fleet.

Summation

In the end, the Quota Acts did perform the function for which they were intended, as from the beginning of 1795 to the end of 1797 the Royal Navy grew in total strength by over 36,000 men. Best estimates suggest that the 1795 Acts raised up to 31,000 men, with 1796 seeing far less success.[120] A glimpse of the large numbers recruited and the financial impact on local economies can be seen in the account of London which paid £98,074 in bounties from 31 March to 10 October 1795, and £44,509 from 11 October 1795 to 10 October 1796,[121] with the amount of the King's bounty paid to London volunteers in 1796 amounting to only £19,739.[122] This illustrates that the Quota Acts were no small instrument for manning the Royal Navy, but

---

[116] Manwaring and Dobrée, pp. 16–17. See also Rodger, 'Mutiny or Subversion? Spithead and the Nore', p. 558.

[117] Rodger, 'Mutiny or Subversion? Spithead and the Nore', p. 558.

[118] Ibid., pp. 558–559.

[119] Lincoln, p. 9; Rodger, 'Officers and Men', pp. 137–138.

[120] Rodger, 'Mutiny or Subversion? Spithead and the Nore', p. 560; Rodger, *The Command of the Ocean*, p. 444; Wells, p. 83.

[121] TNA: PC 1/36/102, 'Sums paid for Bounties and Expenses to Seamen, 2 November 1796'.

[122] TNA: T 1/796/69–70, 'Account of Bounties and Expenses, 5 January 1796 – 5 January 1797'.

were in fact a major operation that required high levels of administrative work to maintain.

The Quota Acts were far from the perfect answer to the problems faced in manning the fleet, yet they had many positive aspects. Significantly, they took the strain of naval manning from the heads of those working on the national stage and spread it among local government agencies such as magistrates, deputy-lieutenants and constables;[123] though the Quota Acts still certainly experienced friction. Ship owners and traders in Whitehaven, Cumberland doubted the wisdom of the Acts, claiming that there were not enough mariners to fill the quota and that many landsmen would have to be taken to do so, and that the Acts would undoubtedly result in damage to the coal trade.[124] A letter to William Pitt from Thomas Bunter in Lancaster stated that the problem of manning should be that of the Royal Navy as, in his opinion, they had made naval service unbearable for seamen and forcing an embargo on shipping to man the fleet would only hurt merchants who were already hard pressed to make ends meet.[125] A further petition from Scarborough called the Port Act impractical and claimed that it would greatly harm trade.[126] A letter from a lieutenant in the Impress Service at Plymouth claimed that the proper way to man the Navy would be by making all mariners register with the Royal Navy to then be called up as needed.[127] These examples illustrate that there was indeed opposition to the Quota Acts from those with both naval and private interests.

However, the Quota Acts also saw a great deal of support. In February 1795 Samuel Jones and Mark Hartford, Wardens of the Society of Merchants in Bristol, wrote:

> The Committee of the Society of Merchants have met this Morning on the Subject of the Bill now depending in Parliament for the continuing the Embargo till the required Number of Men are raised in each Port; and they have desired that We will as Wardons of the Society acquaint you that if meets their Approbation: and their full Confidence that the most vigorous Exertions will be made for promoting the Purposes of the Bill ...[128]

This letter and many more like it show that many societies of merchants were much more comfortable with the idea of providing men for the Royal Navy, rather than having press gangs, which were unpredictable by the nature of their task, conscripting men from their ports and ships. Many supporters were comfortable with this style of manning because the quotas were set up

---

[123] Emsley *et al.*, 'The Impact of War and Military Participation on Britain and France', pp. 62–63.

[124] Emsley *et al.*, *North Riding Naval Recruits*, p. 9.

[125] TNA: PRO 30/8/249, 'Thomas Bunter to Pitt', 17 February 1795, f. 37.

[126] 'A Petition from Scarborough against a Quota Bill', in Emsley *et al.*, *North Riding Naval Recruits*, p. 24.

[127] TNA: PRO 30/8/249, 'Andrew Launders to Pitt', 4 February 1795, f. 250.

[128] TNA: PRO 30/8/249, 'Samuel Jones and Mark Hartford to Pitt', 24 February 1795, f. 31.

in proportion to the size of the county or the port. Evidence of this can be seen in a column of the *Sheffield Iris* on 3 April 1795:

> The Assessment to support the present levy may in some instances be severely felt; but it is certainly fair that the country at large should contribute to an object which is of national importance; and if this mode of raising men be more expensive it is infinitely more just and honourable, and more consistent with the free and generous sentiments of Britain than the odious measure of pressing.[129]

This illustrates that the Quota Acts were seen by many as a satisfactory manner of manning the Royal Navy, especially if it served to reduce or replace impressment.

Historians who have used manuscript evidence have concluded that the men recruited by the Quota Acts were actually decent people, who were generally village lads with good reputations or common men in need of jobs.[130] To a great extent the success of the 1795 Quota Acts can be attributed to the harvest of 1794,[131] which had failed, and resulted in climbing bread prices and increased unemployment. As the Acts went into action the following spring they resulted in many men who had never seen the sea, much less served on a ship, rushing into naval service.[132] Essentially this worked in the Royal Navy's favour, as it proved a success in alleviating the supply and demand problem faced at the time.[133] Further, the Navy was good at integrating skilled and unskilled men, so the high ratio of landsmen found in the Quota recruits was dealt with by spreading them as thinly as possible among the fleet.[134] The men integrated well and learned the tasks necessary of their position on board warships, aiding in their transition to naval life.[135] The men even developed *esprit de corps* once they arrived on board ship, evidenced by a letter home from Robert Ackdrill who was saddened to leave the ship he was assigned to for another and stated that he was sorry to be transferred from his ship, 'for if I was to go aboard twenty I would not find a better'.[136] The Quota men were also not criminals; however there were undoubtedly debtors who viewed the Quota bounties as a new lease on life, and the Navy was happy to take prisoners for debt if they had seafaring skills.[137] Though they accepted debtors, the Royal Navy was adamant about

---

[129] *Sheffield Iris*, 3 April 1795 quoted in Emsley *et al.*, *North Riding Naval Recruits*, p. 9.

[130] Brooks, 'Naval Recruiting in Lindsey, 1795–7', p. 239.

[131] Rodger, 'Mutiny or Subversion? Spithead and the Nore', p. 555.

[132] Brooks, 'Naval Recruiting in Lindsey, 1795–7', p. 238; Emsley *et al.*, *North Riding Naval Recruits*, pp. 10–11; Rodger, 'Mutiny or Subversion? Spithead and the Nore', p. 559.

[133] Earle, 'English Sailors, 1570–1775', p. 91.

[134] Starkey, 'War and the Market for Seafarers in Britain, 1736–1792', p. 30.

[135] Emsley *et al.*, *North Riding Naval Recruits*, p. 151; Emsley, *British Society and the French Wars, 1793–1815*, p. 53; Kemp, p. 164.

[136] Letter transcribed in Brooks, 'Naval Recruiting in Lindsey, 1795–7', pp. 239–240.

[137] Bromley, 'The British Navy and Its Seamen after 1688', p. 153.

ensuring that the men were not criminals, especially thieves. It is possible that magistrates would have made the Quota bounties look as appealing as possible to the poor who would have been a financial drain on the local area;[138] however in a time of high unemployment these people could have hardly been considered criminals.

Though most of what has been written about the Quota Acts has labelled them a failure,[139] they were actually successful. They were an attempt to bolster the Royal Navy's manpower while avoiding the problems that arose with impressment. The Quota Acts attempted to supplement the intrusive nature of impressment with an inclusive system that supported the power of local government, merchants, and societies. Politically this met with great success, as local authorities were eager to take on the responsibility and raised money vigorously to pay the bounties of Quota volunteers. The friction between naval recruitment and maritime centres across Britain eased. A key piece of evidence for this is the fact that there were virtually no appeals against recruiting officers, which suggests that the recruiting process went smoothly.[140] In a debate on 18 October 1796, Pitt remarked that the Acts of 1795 had been highly successful, and the statement went unchallenged by the opposition.[141] The apparent success, or at least the possibility of further success, moved Henry Dundas, 1st Viscount Melville, to propose a manning scheme in 1805 based on the 1795 Port Quota Act, where merchant ship owners would have had to provide a proportionate number of seamen based on ship tonnage. However, Melville's impeachment in 1806 caused him to leave office, and his plan, which may possibly have been far more successful than the Port Quota Act, never saw fruition.[142]

There were certainly problems with the Quota Acts. First and foremost was that they could not recruit enough skilled seafarers to sustain the Navy, as the returns for London, Britain's largest port, resulted in only 35 per cent of men with some level of skill at sea. Considering all of the Quota Acts, it is evident that only 23 per cent of the men who volunteered had any level of skill at sea. This ratio was far too low to allow the Royal Navy to rely solely on this as a form of recruitment. If the Royal Navy was to ensure that one-third of its crews consisted of able seamen and another third were ordinary seamen, then it would have to rely on other forms of recruitment, specifically impressment. As competition to replace impressment, the Quota Acts never really compared. Impressment and the Quota Acts sought two different types of men. Impressment sought skilled mariners from the only source from which they could be found, the sea, whereas the Quota Acts sought to tap new sources of manpower, mainly the inland counties. Though the Port

---

[138] Brewer, p. 51.

[139] Lewis, *A Social History of the Navy, 1793–1815*, p. 127; McCord and Brewster, 'Some Labour Troubles', p. 380.

[140] Brooks, 'Naval Recruiting in Lindsey, 1795–7', p. 238.

[141] Ibid., pp. 237–238; William Cobbett, *Cobbett's Parliamentary History of England: From the Norman Conquest in 1066 to the Year 1803*, 36 vols, vol. XXXIII (London, 1818), pp. 1209–1222.

[142] Rodger, *The Command of the Ocean*, p. 497.

Quota Act did specifically seek seamen, it did not guarantee them and in the end could not deliver the ratios necessary to replace impressment as a means of improving the skill level of the Royal Navy's lower deck.

Ultimately, the Quota Acts did help the Royal Navy boost its fleets to full mobilisation. From the beginning of 1795 to the end of 1797, the Royal Navy grew by just over 36,000 men at a time when finding yet more men to serve in the Royal Navy was becoming ever more difficult. The combination of high bounties and a bad harvest in 1795 ensured that the Quota Acts were successful in producing numbers for naval growth, even if the majority of the men came from inland counties having never set foot on a ship. The Quota Acts were one tool among many at Britain's disposal for achieving its naval manpower goals, and in two years helped to boost the size of the Royal Navy dramatically. However, just like impressment, this scheme had drawbacks, and ultimately proved not to be a suitable source of naval manpower; in 1796 it failed, as a good harvest saw lower unemployment, combined with the fact that many counties and parishes struggled to raise the money to pay bounties the second year. Recruiting seamen into naval service was not, nor had it ever been, simple or easily handled. In the end, the Quota Acts did not and could not replace impressment, as impressment was not intended to man the fleet, but rather to supplement its skill level. However, the contribution of the Quota Acts bolstered overall naval numbers and allowed the Royal Navy to maintain a numerical advantage over its foes.

Conclusion

Between 1660 and 1815, the British Royal Navy grew from a seasonal force of around 20,000 men to employing over 145,000 men and being mobilised year-round during war. During the half-century leading up to the French Revolutionary Wars, the number of seamen employed during peacetime nearly doubled, from just under 54,000 in 1738 to over 98,000 in 1791.[1] However, although the Navy required a full seven times more men in 1810 than it had in 1665, the impact on naval administration and the seafaring population of Britain was far greater, as keeping the fleet commissioned throughout the year transformed the manpower problem, as well as many aspects of naval administration. The recruitment of large numbers of men required a streamlined administrative system that raised men more efficiently, yet did not tie down more naval resources than absolutely necessary. This was critically important during the early phases of war, when many ships had to be commissioned quickly.

The introduction of the Impress Service during the Seven Years' War was the most significant step toward a centralised manning process. This system began a change where officers serving aboard warships became less involved in manning their ships, and relied more on naval administration to fulfil this crucial role. The fact that naval manning became more centralised with each successive war during the eighteenth century suggests that this process, at least in the eyes of naval administrators, was more efficient and effective than relying on ships' officers to man their own vessels. However, without statistics we have no solid evidence of how successful naval manning procedures were, nor do we know very much about the men of the lower deck, in particular, how they were recruited.

The examination of ships' muster books, as this book has demonstrated, is crucial to the study of the lower deck of the British Navy during the eighteenth century, and prior to this, there has been no serious study of naval manning that focuses on this period.[2] The primary reason for a lack of a statistical study has been technology, as without access to the computer technology of recent years, any serious study of ships' musters would have

---

[1] Starkey, 'War and the Market for Seafarers in Britain, 1736–1792', p. 29.
[2] Rodger, *The Command of the Ocean*, p. 442.

been impossibly labour-intensive, and further, the results that could have been produced would have been limited compared to how data can be produced utilising computer technology.

The lack of a statistical study has left significant gaps within the historiography of naval manpower, as without the necessary quantitative data, the value of qualitative judgements has been uncertain. These judgements were biased by the fact that only extraordinary events were recorded, while common occurrences went unrecorded. The vast majority of work on naval manning procedures has concentrated so heavily on impressment that it has neglected the form and function of the other means of naval manning. The impressment discussion has also drawn heavily on source material from the 1830s, a time when naval manning practices were vilified in order to support political arguments.[3] Many historians have dealt with the topic in exemplary form, especially considering the information that they had available. However, fully understanding a subject that dealt with so many men without statistical data has proved virtually impossible. Further, each additional work on the social history of the lower deck has generally, though not always, amplified the problem, as these works were built on the findings of previous historians. Using statistics from a relatively large-scale study of ships' muster books, this book sheds new light on the social history of the lower deck by providing a statistical basis for further work.

The key findings behind this book, recruitment statistics, resolve many of the problems found within the historiography. Using a factoring process to approximate the original recruitment of turned over men, this research project has demonstrated that roughly four out of five men on the lower deck were volunteers, whereas the historiography has previously portrayed a ratio that is nearly the opposite, suggesting that between 50 and 75 per cent of men were impressed. This data also demonstrates that most seamen of the lower deck were young, generally in their early twenties, while petty officers were only slightly older, most being in their late twenties or early thirties. More than half of the men were English by birth, and only 19 per cent were Irish, again challenging a historiography that suggested that one-third to half of the men in the Royal Navy were Irish.

The importance of volunteers to the eighteenth-century Royal Navy is undeniable, and this research has demonstrated that the number of volunteers serving in British warships was two or three times higher than had been previously considered, and must have played a significant part in the lack of disorder faced by the Navy when manning its fleets for war. There was ample motivation for volunteers to serve on warships. Bounties provided a handsome bonus for joining, and prize money helped to close the gap that existed between naval and merchant pay during wartime.[4] For many men, life aboard a naval vessel offered the hope of advancement, where life

---

[3] Ibid., p. 492.
[4] Benjamin and Thornberg, 'Organization and Incentives', p. 338.

ashore did not.[5] The Navy's system of promotion provided incentive for both recruitment and retention.[6] For an unskilled labourer, this provided opportunities that were well beyond those that were available ashore. For ordinary and able seamen, the prospect of promotion to petty officer positions, with increased pay and higher prize returns, provided motivation. The result of the Royal Navy's compensation and incentive system was the clear influx in the number of volunteers with each respective war throughout the eighteenth century.[7]

However, even though volunteers turned out in large numbers, the fact that labour-intensive sailing vessels demanded large numbers of experienced seamen, combined with the intense competition for the limited supply of men with maritime skill, meant that the Royal Navy could not recruit enough skilled men by relying solely upon volunteers.[8] Therefore, press gangs were necessary, though rather than functioning to primarily increase the quantity of men in the Navy, they served to bolster the quality of naval manpower as a whole. Beyond this, press gangs never covered the entire country in search of seamen; rather they operated predominantly in and around major naval and merchant centres. Even with the Impress Service, naval recruitment was restricted to spheres of operation that centred on areas where seamen could reliably be found,[9] and the areas adjacent to the Royal Dockyards at Chatham, Portsmouth and Plymouth tended to be the focus of heavy naval recruitment.[10] Volunteers, however, came from many places, both inside and outside of the areas where the Impress Service operated, driven by their motivations, patriotic or otherwise, to serve King and country at sea.

Impressment existed specifically to recruit skilled seamen, who were a commodity prized in both the Royal Navy and merchant seafaring, and thus press gangs and tenders of the Impress Service spent their time searching for able and ordinary seamen. Merchants were forced to offer high wages in order to ensure that they had enough men to sail their vessels, and conveniently for the Royal Navy this drew skilled seamen to maritime centres looking for merchant berths, and allowed press gangs ashore to find the men they sought. However, the fact that men came in search of merchant berths, knowing full well that they stood a chance of being pressed, meant that naval impressment and service was not the dire and unbearable affair that many historians have claimed. Had impressment actually been a horrific experience, then seamen would not have ventured into maritime centres to seek merchant berths, as the reward for success would not have been worth the risk of running into a press gang. Further, had naval conditions been as bad as they have often been described, volunteers would not have turned out in such prolific numbers.

[5]   Lambert, p. 55.
[6]   Benjamin and Thornberg, 'Organization and Incentives', p. 338.
[7]   Gradish, *The Manning of the British Navy During the Seven Years' War*, p. 71.
[8]   Rogers, *The Press Gang: Naval Impressment and Its Opponents in Georgian Britain*, p. 4.
[9]   Lavery, *Royal Tars: The Lower Deck of the Royal Navy, 875–1850*, pp. 205–206.
[10] Starkey, 'War and the Market for Seafarers in Britain, 1736–1792', p. 32.

Even with the very large number of volunteers, there were never enough skilled volunteers to fully man the fleets, and naval impressment therefore lasted throughout every eighteenth-century conflict.[11] Impressment existed to provide the Navy with the necessary skill and experience to increase the overall proficiency of the lower deck. To this end, impressment sought the most highly skilled men, especially topmen who were essential to sailing and manoeuvring large square rigged vessels.[12] Though it has been claimed that large numbers of landsmen were impressed, only anecdotal evidence has been produced to suggest that unskilled men were either targeted by press gangs or pressed in great quantities.[13] As this project has shown, landsmen made up only 18 per cent of pressed men, and many of these men had skills valuable to ships at sea. The Royal Navy had no desire to actively recruit men with no use aboard a warship.

Impressment may have been an evil, but it was a lesser evil,[14] and seamen accepted it as unavoidable.[15] Evidence can be drawn from the fact that it was never mentioned in the grievances of the seamen involved in the great mutinies of 1797.[16] The Royal Navy of the French Revolutionary and Napoleonic Wars was not manned by conscripted men, rather impressment supplemented a primarily volunteer force, and was used specifically to raise the skill level of the lower deck. Though impressment was successful in providing skilled men for naval service, it was problematic, especially in the public's eye. The problems and social friction that accompanied impressment meant that although it was certainly necessary and often supported, it had no real friends, especially amongst the officers charged with carrying it out.[17] However, no matter how much it was disliked, impressment proved a potent tool for increasing the number of skilled men in naval service, and helped Britain achieve a high ratio of skilled to unskilled men.[18] The Royal Navy sought to press seamen into service because their skills made them one of Britain's most prized military assets.[19]

The Quota Acts attempted to alleviate the social friction caused by impressment by taking the pressure of naval manning from the Royal Navy and spreading it among local authorities, such as magistrates,

---

[11] Usher Jr., 'Royal Navy Impressment', p. 682.

[12] Robinson, 'Secret of British Power', p. 6; Rodger, 'Officers and Men', p. 141; Rodger, '"A Little Navy of Your Own Making": Admiral Boscawen and the Cornish Connection in the Royal Navy', p. 84; Usher Jr., 'Royal Navy Impressment', p. 684; Rodger, *The Command of the Ocean*, p. 497.

[13] Rodger, *The Wooden World*, pp. 150–151; Rodger, 'Officers and Men', p. 141; Starkey, 'War and the Market for Seafarers in Britain, 1736–1792', p. 37.

[14] Baugh, *British Naval Administration in the Age of Walpole*, pp. 149, 159–161; Bromley; Lloyd, *The British Seaman, 1200–1860*, pp. 149–151; Rodger, *The Wooden World*, p. 151.

[15] Rodger, *The Command of the Ocean*, p. 499.

[16] Ibid., p. 447.

[17] Ibid., p. 500.

[18] Starkey, 'War and the Market for Seafarers in Britain, 1736–1792', p. 37; Usher Jr., 'Royal Navy Impressment', p. 681.

[19] Usher Jr., 'Royal Navy Impressment', p. 680.

deputy-lieutenants, and constables.[20] In this capacity, the Acts were generally supported, as they set manning quotas based on population of counties and ports. The Quota Acts recruited large numbers of unskilled landsmen, which worked only because the Royal Navy was proficient at spreading unskilled men evenly across the fleet, allowing them to integrate with skilled men.[21] In the end, these men merged well into crews and learned the skills necessary to their position aboard warships.[22] Further evidence exists that these men developed *esprit de corps* once they arrived aboard their ships, and men like Robert Ackdrill found it difficult to leave once they had settled into a ship's company.[23] The men recruited by the Quota Acts were not the criminals or local delinquents that have been reported by historians,[24] but rather they were decent people, generally village lads, with good reputations, who were simply in need of employment.[25]

Though some have branded the Quota Acts as a failure,[26] they actually were a limited success. They allowed the Navy to expand during a time when the pool of available manpower was being stretched to its limits.[27] However, although they provided men for the Royal Navy, they did not provide the skilled men that were so desperately needed aboard warships. The Quota Acts could not be counted on as a replacement for impressment, as even in the Port of London only 35 per cent of the men recruited had any level of sea skill, and when looking at the overall results of all five Quota Acts across 1795 and 1796, the proportion dropped to 23 per cent. This ratio proved far too low to supply warships with the necessary skilled men. As a means of replacing impressment, the Quota Acts failed, even though they did provide the Navy with a substantial number of men, and came at a time when the Royal Navy increased its size by about 36,000 men, between 1795 and 1797.

The men of the lower deck were predominantly young men, under thirty. Just over half of the seamen and petty officers were born in England, and 72 per cent had enough experience to be rated as ordinary seamen, able seamen, or petty officers. Four out of five of these men were volunteers. If we consider that in 1801, the height of the French Revolutionary Wars, almost 132,000 men were serving in the Royal Navy, then statistics tell us that 75 per cent, or approximately 99,000, of these men were either seamen or petty officers. As the men serving in 1801 were most likely recruited in the previous three years, these statistics suggest that approximately 12,870 were petty officers,

---

[20] Emsley *et al.*, 'The Impact of War and Military Participation on Britain and France', pp. 62–63.
[21] Starkey, 'War and the Market for Seafarers in Britain, 1736–1792', p. 30.
[22] Emsley *et al.*, North Riding Naval Recruits, p. 151; Emsley, *British Society and the French Wars, 1793–1815*, p. 53; Kemp, p. 164.
[23] Letter transcribed in Brooks, 'Naval Recruiting in Lindsey, 1795–7', pp. 239–240.
[24] Bromley, p. 153.
[25] Brooks, 'Naval Recruiting in Lindsey, 1795–7', p. 239.
[26] Lewis, *A Social History of the Navy, 1793–1815*, p. 127; McCord and Brewster, 'Some Labour Troubles', p. 380.
[27] Earle, 'English Sailors, 1570–1775', p. 91.

31,680 were able seamen, 28,710 were ordinary seamen, and 25,740 were landsmen. Though the end of the war experienced the highest levels of impressment,[28] we can state that approximately 67,488 of the estimated 99,000 seamen and petty officers were volunteers, while approximately 24,453 were pressed. Volunteers undoubtedly played the leading role on the lower deck of the Royal Navy.

Although this project is the first statistical study of the lower deck that examines more than just a single snapshot in time of the Royal Navy, the data produced within it only breaks the surface of what can be done with a comprehensive statistical study. Data produced in this study clearly casts doubt on the findings of previous historians, especially where they are concerned with recruitment. Had historians such as Michael Lewis had access to this type of data, it would surely have altered their findings. Therefore perhaps this study calls for a new look at social history, if not to re-write it, perhaps simply to update some of the already exceptional work produced in the past. New research in the discipline has already been undertaken, which is beginning to do just that, by examining the social histories of the midshipmen and marines,[29] and future projects examining the social history of the Royal Navy's officer corps may potentially alter our perception of the quarter deck.[30] Perhaps, this project fits well within this new drive toward social history and statistics. It also seems inconceivable, from the point of view of this individual study, that these research projects have closed the door on the subject of social history of the Royal Navy; rather to the contrary it seems more likely that they have unlocked new doors for future projects to further exploit these findings, as there are certainly many questions that this work was not able to address. Additionally, historians examining these findings will undoubtedly be able to expand the subject with questions that at present have not even been asked.

Readers of this work will also undoubtedly have found mistakes within it, which, as the sole author, I take full responsibility for. The process of examining and entering over 700,000 data entries for over 27,000 men, from handwritten documents that are over 200 years old, could not conceivably be done without a few minor errors along the way. Eighteenth-century spelling, especially when dealing with the places of birth, proved an exceptional challenge, and most of the mistakes I found and corrected came from this. Though I have spent many hours trying to uncover any inconsistencies within the database, I have no doubt that some still exist. However, I have done my best to ensure that such mistakes have not affected the overall statistics. Further, as this research is based on a 'sample' of Royal Navy

[28] By averaging statistics for 1799 to 1801, this data demonstrates that in the Royal Navy of 1801 approximately 16 per cent of petty officers and 26 per cent of seamen were pressed, while 76 per cent of petty officers and 67 per cent of seamen were volunteers.

[29] Samantha Cavell, *Midshipmen and Quarterdeck Boys in the British Navy, 1771–1831* (Woodbridge: The Boydell Press, 2012); Zerbe, *Birth of the Royal Marines*.

[30] Evan Wilson, at the University of Oxford, is currently in the midst of a doctoral project that uses statistics to examine the social background of officers.

manpower, its conclusions must be taken as such. The sample, by statistical standards, is sound and can be applied to the Royal Navy of the French Revolutionary Wars indicatively. This research also looks to complement, rather than replace, qualitative studies of the Royal Navy, as quantitative and qualitative research function best together rather than standing alone.

As technology develops, and the ability of computers to recognise handwritten script becomes ever better, a future study that examines every man entered into a Royal Navy record book is not inconceivable, and could produce solid statistics that stretch across a couple of centuries of naval history. It is also possible to apply these techniques to similar studies on the militaries of other nations, providing that the necessary source material exists. It is clear, examining the historiography, that the British Navy has been the recipient of far more historical study than any of its European contemporaries, especially during the era of sail. Perhaps this emanates from both the success of British sea forces of the time, as well as the very large and easily accessible collections of British naval records. However, these new statistical studies would certainly benefit from comparative studies of other nations.

Over the eighteenth century, the Royal Navy became the dominant power of the Atlantic, if not the world. By the French Revolutionary and Napoleonic Wars, Britain's ability to float a naval force that could fight simultaneously against the navies of all of Europe and the United States, throughout the Atlantic World, and across the globe, was a direct result of the Navy's ability to effectively man its warships. This became especially important as a war of attrition set in and rival nations were effectively crippled by a shortage of seamen, further combined with losses to the Royal Navy, which took a heavy toll on their supply of skilled seamen. Britain's supply of skilled mariners came as a direct result of the strength of British merchant sea trade, which trained the men necessary to fulfil the needs of a wartime Navy, as well as kept merchant sea trade functioning during wartime.[31] Britain's ability to meet its manpower needs without recourse to significant financial or administrative disruption was a critical factor in its dominance at sea.[32] Seamen were a precious commodity to both the Royal Navy and merchant trade, who knew their value, and aboard warships they expected naval officers to treat them with fairness and respect.[33] As the French Revolutionary and Napoleonic Wars wore on, Britain stood alone, an island nation, against all of Europe; its Navy stood as its primary bulwark of defence, while British merchants took advantage of naval dominance and kept the nation supplied. For Britain, it was seamen, mostly young and volunteers, who made naval success possible and proved to be the lifeblood of both the Navy and nation.[34]

---

[31] Starkey, 'War and the Market for Seafarers in Britain, 1736–1792', p. 25.

[32] Harding, *Seapower and Naval Warfare, 1650–1830*, p. 140.

[33] Rodger, *The Command of the Ocean*, p. 489.

[34] R.J.B. Knight, *Britain against Napoleon: The Organisation of Victory, 1793–1815* (London: Allen Lane, 2013).

Bibliography

Manuscript Sources

1. The National Archive

Admiralty Records

ADM 1/5120/20, 'Bowry to Stephens', 5 January 1792, f. 190.

ADM 7/361, 'Account of Men Raised … Port of London by Virtue of the Act 35th Geo III, Cap 9'.

ADM 7/567, 'Admiralty Miscellanea, 1754–1806', ff. 22, 27.

ADM 7-967, 'Instructions to Officers Raising Men, 1807'.

ADM 8/69 to ADM 8/101, Admiralty List Books, 1793 to 1821.

ADM 12, Admiralty: Digests and Indexes.

ADM 36/11162, Muster-table: HMS *London*, 1 September 1793 to 31 October 1793.

ADM 36/11329, Muster-table: HMS *Lady Taylor*, 1 July 1793 to 31 August 1793.

ADM 36/11353, Muster-table: HMS *Prince*, 10 June 1795 to 31 July 1795.

ADM 36/11383, Muster-table: HMS *L'Oiseau*, 1 March 1794 to 30 April 1794.

ADM 36/11393, Muster-table: HMS *Castor*, 1 March 1795 to 30 April 1795.

ADM 36/11563, Muster-table: HMS *La Trompeuse*, 1 August 1794 to 30 September 1794.

ADM 36/11603, Muster-table: HMS *Melampus*, 10 April 1793 to 30 June 1793.

ADM 36/11663, Muster-table: HMS *Sans Pareil*, 1 July 1795 to 31 August 1795.

ADM 36/11685, Muster-table: HMS *Blenheim*, 13 November 1794 to 28 December 1794.

ADM 36/11741, Muster-table: HMS *Leviathan*, 1 April 1793 to 31 May 1793.

ADM 36/11816, Muster-table: HMS *Minotaur*, 2 February 1794 to 31 March 1794.

ADM 36/11872, Muster-table: HMS *L'Aimable*, 1 April 1793 to 31 May 1793.

ADM 36/11930, Muster-table: HMS *Janus*, 4 December 1796 to 4 February 1797.

ADM 36/12132, Muster-table: HMS *Vengeance*, 1 September 1795 to 31 October 1795.

ADM 36/12237, Muster-table: HMS *Standard*, 7 April 1795 to 30 June 1795.

ADM 36/12255, Muster-table: HMS *Overyssel*, 1 November 1796 to 31 December 1796.

ADM 36/12261, Muster-table: HMS *Ethalion*, 6 September 1797 to 29 October 1797.

ADM 36/12456, Muster-table: HMS *Eugenie*, 14 October 1797 to 30 December 1797.

ADM 36/12492, Muster-table: HMS *Amelia*, 1 November 1797 to 31 December 1797.

ADM 36/12535, Muster-table: HMS *Polyphemus*, 1 September 1794 to 31 October 1794.

ADM 36/12571, Muster-table: HMS *Ruby*, 1 August 1799 to 20 September 1799.

ADM 36/12659, Muster-table: HMS *St. Fiorenzo*, 23 June 1795 to 31 August 1795.

ADM 36/12688, Muster-table: HMS *Tribune*, 8 May 1797 to 31 July 1797.

ADM 36/12754, Muster-table: HMS *Montague*, 1 September 1796 to 31 October 1796.

ADM 36/12825, Muster-table: HMS *Impetueux*, 10 October 1796 to 28 December 1796.

ADM 36/12976, Muster-table: HMS *Chapman*, 1 November 1793 to 31 December 1793.

ADM 36/12994, Muster-table: HMS *Raileur*, 8 August 1798 to 7 October 1798.

ADM 36/12995, Muster-table: HMS *Resolution*, 3 August 1799 to 31 October 1799.

ADM 36/13005, Muster-table: HMS *Veteran*, 1 June 1797 to 31 July 1797.

ADM 36/13092, Muster-table: HMS *Magnanime*, 1 January 1795 to 28 February 1795.

ADM 36/13122, Muster-table: HMS *Seahorse*, 10 November 1794 to 31 December 1794.

ADM 36/13129, Muster-table: HMS *La Babet*, 14 April 1795 to 30 June 1795.

ADM 36/13164, Muster-table: HMS *La Nymphe*, 1 July 1796 to 31 August 1796.

ADM 36/13184, Muster-table: HMS *Thames*, 1 February 1797 to 31 March 1797.

ADM 36/13294, Muster-table: HMS *La Topaze*, 1 October 1795 to 30 November 1795.

ADM 36/13333, Muster-table: HMS *Solebay*, 1 January 1798 to 28 February 1798.

ADM 36/13366, Muster-table: HMS *Arrow*, 1 February 1797 to 30 April 1797.

ADM 36/13457, Muster-table: HMS *L'Espiegle*, 1 November 1794 to 31 December 1794.

ADM 36/13472, Muster-table: HMS *Harpy*, 1 July 1796 to 31 August 1796.

ADM 36/13506, Muster-table: HMS *Swift*, 1 March 1794 to 30 April 1794.

ADM 36/13507, Muster-table: HMS *Pylades*, 20 March 1797 to 31 May 1797.

ADM 36/13517, Muster-table: HMS *Spy*, 1 November 1795 to 31 December 1795.

ADM 36/13520, Muster-table: HMS *Scourge*, 12 October 1796 to 30 November 1796.

ADM 36/13942, Muster-table: HMS *Patterell*, 1 July 1794 to 31 August 1794.

ADM 36/13965, Muster-table: HMS *Imogen*, 31 August 1801 to 19 October 1801.

ADM 36/13967, Muster-table: HMS *Hunter*, 8 July 1801 to 31 August 1801.

ADM 36/13968, Muster-table: HMS *Gannet*, 3 July 1800 to 26 August 1800.

ADM 36/14012, Muster-table: HMS *San Josef*, 28 December 1800 to 10 February 1801.

ADM 36/14075, Muster-table: HMS *Windsor Castle*, 1 September 1799 to 31 October 1799.

ADM 36/14114, Muster-table: HMS *Quebec*, 4 February 1799 to 30 April 1799.

ADM 36/14305, Muster-table: HMS *Magnificent*, 1 September 1798 to 31 October 1798.

ADM 36/14357, Muster-table: HMS *Dreadnought*, 29 June 1801 to 31 August 1801.

ADM 36/14414, Muster-table: HMS *Carysfort*, 22 May 1801 to 30 June 1801.

ADM 36/14496, Muster-table: HMS *Tigre*, 1 September 1798 to 31 October 1798.

ADM 36/14594, Muster-table: HMS *Northumberland*, 1 July 1798 to 14 July 1798.

ADM 36/14606, Muster-table: HMS *Bourdelois*, 1 June 1800 to 31 July 1800.

ADM 36/14715, Muster-table: HMS *Resistance*, 1 July 1801 to 31 August 1801.

ADM 36/14719, Muster-table: HMS *La Victorieuse*, 1 February 1796 to 31 March 1796.

ADM 36/14726, Muster-table: HMS *Donegal*, 1 October 1801 to 30 November 1801.

ADM 36/14729, Muster-table: HMS *Alarm*, 1 March 1798 to 30 April 1798.

ADM 36/14871, Muster-table: HMS *Déterminée*, 1 January 1801 to 28 February 1801.

ADM 36/14875, Muster-table: HMS *Swallow*, 1 January 1796 to 29 February 1796.

ADM 36/14892, Muster-table: HMS *Severn*, 1 September 1799 to 31 October 1799.

ADM 36/14908, Muster-table: HMS *Selby*, 1 December 1798 to 31 January 1799.

ADM 36/14953, Muster-table: HMS *Jason*, 1 September 1800 to 31 October 1800.

ADM 36/14990, Muster-table: HMS *Volage*, 1 January 1799 to 28 February 1799.

ADM 36/15012, Muster-table: HMS *La Sophie*, 1 November 1799 to 31 December 1799.

ADM 36/15034, Muster-table: HMS *Pheasant*, 1 August 1798 to 30 September 1798.

ADM 36/15064, Muster-table: HMS *Intrepid*, 1 May 1797 to 30 June 1797.

ADM 36/15136, Muster-table: HMS *Shark*, 1 December 1799 to 31 January 1800.

ADM 36/15138, Muster-table: HMS *La Constance*, 1 November 1799 to 31 December 1799.

ADM 36/15138, Muster-table: HMS *Renard*, 1 November 1799 to 31 December 1799.

ADM 36/15175, Muster-table: HMS *De Ruyter*, 6 June 1801 to 31 August 1801.

ADM 36/15199, Muster-table: HMS *Amphion*, 1 July 1797 to 31 August 1797.

ADM 36/15302, Muster-table: HMS *Leyden*, 1 December 1800 to 31 January 1801.

ADM 36/15317, Muster-table: HMS *Belleisle*, 2 February 1801 to 30 April 1801.

ADM 36/15332, Muster-table: HMS *Raven*, 1 January 1801 to 28 February 1801.

ADM 36/15356, Muster-table: HMS *Vanguard*, 1 March 1798 to 30 April 1798.

ADM 36/15404, Muster-table: HMS *Wasp*, 1 September 1801 to 31 October 1801.

ADM 36/15592, Muster-table: HMS *Deseree*, 1 November 1800 to 31 December 1800.

ADM 36/15623, Muster-table: HMS *Narcissus*, 3 November 1801 to 31 January 1802.

Home Office Papers
HO 44/42, Press Warrant issued to Philip D'Auvergne, Prince of Bouillon of HM Floating Battery the *Nonsuch*, 1 July 1794, ff. 314–317.

HO 69/6, Press Warrant issued to Philip D'Auvergne, Prince of Bouillon, of HMS *Bravo*, 14 December 1795

Privy Council Papers
PC 1/36/102, 'Sums paid for Bounties and Expenses to Seamen, 2 November 1796'.

Public Record Office Special Collections
PRO 30/8/248, Navy Office papers relating to seamen and mariners.

PRO 30/8/249, Letters on Manning the Navy.

PRO 30/8/250/1, Essays, propositions &c on Manning the Navy.

Treasury
T 1/758/77–85, 'Account of Fines received … for not raising Volunteers of the Navy, 1795'.

T 1/796/69–70, 'Account of Bounties and Expenses, 5 January 1796 – 5 January 1797'.

2. National Maritime Museum
CRK/16/20, Admiralty to Lord Nelson, 10 October 1801.
E/4559, 'Infallible Project for the Speedy Manning of the Royal Navy, 1745'.
HSR/H/1, 'Whitehall Council Chamber Letter to Port Counties, 7 April 1692'.
KEI/45/2, 'Signed but undated order to press men from Merchant Ships'.
MEL/5, 'John Robinson Letter to Commission of Excise and Customs, 25 June 1779'.
MID 7/3/1, 'Memorial on Supplying the Navy with Seamen', 1787.
MID 7/3/2, 'Expense of the Impress Service in the American War of Year 1775 to 1783'.
PBB/7521, 'Proclamation for the Encouragement and Increase of Seamen, 1706'.
PBH/3190, 'Recruitment Poster for the *Pallas*'.
PLT/56, Press Warrant issued to William Affleck of HMS *Alligator*, 20 December 1794.

Printed Primary Sources

Baugh, Daniel, ed. *Naval Administration, 1715–1750*, Publications of the Navy Records Society. London: Navy Records Society, 1977.
Bromley, J.S., ed. *The Manning of the Royal Navy: Selected Public Pamphlets, 1693–1873*, Publications of the Navy Records Society. London: Navy Records Society, 1974.
Choate, Jean, ed. *At Sea under Impressment: Accounts of Involuntary Service Aboard Navy and Pirate Vessels, 1700–1820*. Jefferson, NC: McFarland, 2010.
Cobbett, William. *Cobbett's Parliamentary History of England: From the Norman Conquest in 1066 to the Year 1803*. Vol. XX. 36 vols. London, 1814.
—*Cobbett's Parliamentary History of England: From the Norman Conquest in 1066 to the Year 1803*. Vol. XXXIII. 36 vols. London, 1818.
Dann, John C., ed. *The Nagle Journal: A Diary of the Life of Jacob Nagle, Sailor, from the Year 1775 to 1841*. New York: Weidenfeld and Nicolson, 1988.
Emsley, Clive, A.M. Hill and M.Y. Ashcroft, eds. *North Riding Naval Recruits: The Quota Acts and the Quota Men, 1795–1797*. Northallerton: North Yorkshire County Council, 1978.
Hattendorf, John B., R.J.B. Knight, A.W.H. Pearsall, N.A.M. Rodger and Geoffrey Till, eds. *British Naval Documents, 1204–1960*, Publications of the Naval Records Society. Aldershot: Ashgate, 1993.
Hay, Robert. *Landsman Hay: The Memoirs of Robert Hay, 1789–1847*. London: R. Hart-Davis, 1953.
Lowry, James. *Fiddlers and Whores: The Candid Memoirs of a Surgeon in Nelson's Fleet*, ed. John Millyard. London: Chatham, 2006.
Merriman, R.D., ed. *Queen Anne's Navy: Documents Concerning the Administration of the Navy of Queen Anne, 1702–1714*, Publications of the Navy Records Society. London: Navy Records Society, 1961.

The Naval Chronicle for 1799. London: Joyce Gold, 1799.

'Recruiting Poster, 2nd April 1795'. *The Mariner's Mirror* VIII, no. 2 (1922): p. 23.

Robinson, William. *Jack Nastyface: Memoirs of an English Seaman*. London: Chatham Publishing, 2002.

Rodger, N.A.M, ed. *The Naval Miscellany, Volume V*, Publications of the Navy Records Society. London: Navy Records Society, 1984.

Spavens, William. *Memoirs of a Seafaring Life: The Narrative of William Spavens, Pensioner on the Naval Chest at Chatham*, ed. N.A.M. Rodger. Bath: Folio Society, 2000.

Syrett, David. *The Rodney Papers: Selections from the Correspondence of Admiral Lord Rodney, Volume II, 1763–1780*, Publications of the Navy Records Society. Aldershot: Ashgate, 2007.

White, Colin, ed. *Nelson: The New Letters*. Woodbridge: The Boydell Press, 2005.

Secondary Sources

Books

Adkins, Roy, and Lesley Adkins. *Jack Tar: Life in Nelson's Navy*. London: Little, Brown, 2008.

Baugh, Daniel. *British Naval Administration in the Age of Walpole*. Princeton: Princeton University Press, 1965.

Baynham, Henry. *From the Lower Deck*. London: Hutchinson & Co., 1969.

Black, Jeremy. *The British Seaborne Empire*. New Haven, Conn.: Yale University Press, 2004.

—*Naval Power: A History of Warfare and the Sea from 1500*. Basingstoke: Palgrave Macmillan, 2009.

Black, Jeremy, and Philip Woodfine, eds. *The British Navy and the Use of Naval Power in the Eighteenth Century*. Leicester: Leicester University Press, 1988.

Blake, Nicholas, and Richard Russell Lawrence. *The Illustrated Companion to Nelson's Navy*. London: Chatham Publishing, 1999.

Bonnett, Stanley. *The Price of Admiralty: An Indictment of the Royal Navy, 1805–1966*. London: Robert Hale Ltd, 1968.

Brewer, John. *The Sinews of Power: War, Money and the English State, 1688–1783*. London: Unwin Hyman, 1989.

Brumwell, Stephen. *Redcoats: The British Soldier and War in the Americas, 1755–1763*. Cambridge: Cambridge University Press, 2002.

Bullocke, J.G. *Sailors' Rebellion: A Century of Naval Mutinies*. London: Eyre and Spottiswoode, 1938.

Byrn, John D. *Crime and Punishment in the Royal Navy: Discipline on the Leeward Islands Station, 1784–1812*. Aldershot: Scolar Press, 1989.

Callender, Geoffrey. *The Naval Side of British History*. London: Christophers, 1925.

Capp, Bernard. *Cromwell's Navy: The Fleet and the English Revolution, 1648–1660*. Oxford: Clarendon, 1989.

Cavell, Samantha. *Midshipmen and Quarterdeck Boys in the British Navy, 1771–1831*. Woodbridge: The Boydell Press, 2012.

Christie, Ian R. *Wars and Revolutions: Britain 1760–1815*. London: Edward Arnold, 1982.

Clayton, Tim. *Tars: The Men Who Made Britain Rule the Waves*. London: Hodder & Stoughton, 2007.

Clowes, W. Laird. *The Royal Navy: A History from the Earliest Times to the Present*. Vol. IV. London: Chatham Publishing, 1997.

Colley, Linda. *Britons: Forging the Nation, 1707–1837*. London: Pimlico, 1994.

Cookson, J.E. *The British Armed Nation, 1793–1815*. Oxford: Oxford University Press, 1997.

Cormack, William S. *Revolution and Political Conflict in the French Navy, 1789–1794*. Cambridge: Cambridge University Press, 1995.

Crewe, Duncan. *Yellow Jack and the Worm: British Naval Administration in the West Indies, 1739–1748*. Liverpool: Liverpool University Press, 1993.

Davies, David. *A Brief History of Fighting Ships*. New York: Carroll & Graf Publishers, 2002.

Davies, J.D. *Gentlemen and Tarpaulins: The Officers and Men of the Restoration Navy*. Oxford: Clarendon Press, 1991.

Davis, Ralph. *The Rise of the English Shipping Industry in the Seventeenth and Eighteenth Centuries*. 2nd edn. Newton Abbot: David and Charles, 1972.

Duffy, Michael. *Soldiers, Sugar and Seapower: The Expeditions to the West Indies and the War against Revolutionary France*. Oxford: Clarendon Press, 1987.

—*The Younger Pitt*. Harlow: Longman, 2000.

—ed. *Parameters of British Naval Power, 1650–1850*. Exeter: University of Exeter Press, 1998.

Duffy, Michael, and Roger Morriss, eds. *The Glorious First of June 1794*. Exeter: University of Exeter Press, 2001.

Dull, Jonathan R. *The French Navy and the Seven Years' War*. Lincoln, Neb.: University of Nebraska Press, 2005.

Earle, Peter. *Sailors: English Merchant Seamen, 1650–1775*. London: Methuen, 1998.

Ehrman, John. *The Navy in the War of William III, 1689–1697: Its State and Direction*. Cambridge: Cambridge University Press, 1953.

Elliott, Marianne. *Partners in Revolution: The United Irishmen and France*. New Haven, Conn.: Yale University Press, 1982.

Emsley, Clive. *British Society and the French Wars, 1793–1815*. London: Macmillan, 1979.

Gill, Conrad. *The Naval Mutinies of 1797*. Manchester: University of Manchester Press, 1913.

Glete, Jan. *Navies and Nations: Warships, Navies, and State Building in Europe and America, 1500–1860*. Vol. I. Stockholm: Almqvist & Wiksell International, 1993.

Gradish, Stephen. *The Manning of the British Navy During the Seven Years' War*. London: Royal Historical Society, 1980.

Guy, Alan J. *Oeconomy and Discipline: Officership and Administration in the British Army 1714–63*. Manchester: Manchester University Press, 1985.

Harding, Richard. *The Evolution of the Sailing Navy, 1509–1815*. London: St. Martin's Press, 1995.

—*Seapower and Naval Warfare, 1650–1830*. London: Routledge, 1999.

—*The Emergence of Britain's Global Naval Supremacy: The War of 1739–1748*. Woodbridge: The Boydell Press, 2010.

Hill, Richard. *The Prizes of War: The Naval Prize System in the Napoleonic Wars, 1793–1815*. Stroud: Sutton Publishing Ltd, 1998.

Hore, Peter. *The Habit of Victory: The Story of the Royal Navy, 1545 to 1945*. London: Pan Books, 2006.

Hutchinson, J.R. *The Press-Gang Afloat and Ashore*. London: Eveleigh Nash, 1913.

Ireland, Bernard. *The Fall of Toulon: The Last Opportunity to Defeat the French Revolution*. London: Weidenfeld and Nicolson, 2005.

James, W.M. *The Naval History of Great Britain During the French Revolutionary and Napoleonic Wars, 1793–1796*. Vol. I. London: Conway Maritime, 2002.

—*The Naval History of Great Britain During the French Revolutionary and Napoleonic Wars, 1797–1799*. Vol. II. London: Conway Maritime, 2002.

Jenks, Timothy. *Naval Engagements: Patriotism, Cultural Politics, and the Royal Navy, 1793–1815*. Oxford: Oxford University Press, 2006.

Kemp, Peter. *The British Sailor: A Social History of the Lower Deck*. London: J.M. Dent & Sons Ltd, 1970.

Kindleberter, Charles P. *Mariners and Markets*. Hertfordshire: Harvester Wheatsheaf, 1992.

Knight, R.J.B. *The Pursuit of Victory: The Life and Achievement of Horatio Nelson*. London: Allen Lane, 2005.

—*Britain against Napoleon: The Organisation of Victory, 1793–1815*. London: Allen Lane, 2013.

Lambert, Andrew D. *War at Sea in the Age of Sail, 1650–1850*. Smithsonian History of Warfare. Washington, DC: Smithsonian Books, 2005.

Land, Isaac. *War, Nationalism, and the British Sailor, 1750–1850*. New York: Palgrave Macmillan, 2009.

Lavery, Brian. *Nelson's Navy: The Ships, Men and Organisation, 1793–1815*. Annapolis: Naval Institute Press, 2005.

—*Royal Tars: The Lower Deck of the Royal Navy, 875–1850*. London: Conway, 2010.

—ed. *Shipboard Life and Organisation, 1731–1815*, Publications of the Navy Records Society. Aldershot: Ashgate, 1998.

Lewis, Michael. *History of the British Navy*. Harmondsworth: Penguin Books, 1957.

—*Napoleon and His British Captives*. London: Allen & Unwin, 1962.

—*A Social History of the Navy, 1793–1815*. London: Chatham Publishing, 2004.

Lincoln, Margarette. *Representing the Royal Navy: British Sea Power, 1750–1815*. Aldershot: Ashgate, 2002.

Lloyd, Christopher. *The Nation and the Navy: A History of Naval Life and Policy*. London: Cresset Press, 1954.

—*The British Seaman, 1200–1860*. London: Collins, 1968.

Mahan, A.T. *The Influence of Sea Power upon the French Revolution and Empire: 1793–1812*. Vol. I. London: Sampson Low, 1892.

—*The Influence of Sea Power upon History, 1660–1783*. Gretna: Penguin Publishing Company, 2003.

Manwaring, G.E., and Bonamy Dobrée. *The Floating Republic: An Account of the Mutinies at Spithead and the Nore 1797*. London: Geoffrey Bles, 1935.

Marcus, G.J. *Heart of Oak: A Survey of British Sea Power in the Georgian Era*. London: Oxford University Press, 1975.

Masefield, John. *Sea Life in Nelson's Time*. London: Methuen & Co., 1905.

Morriss, Roger. *Naval Power and British Culture, 1760–1850: Public Trust and Government Ideology*. Aldershot: Ashgate, 2003.

—ed. *The Channel Fleet and the Blockade of Brest, 1793–1801*, Publications of the Navy Records Society. Aldershot: Ashgate, 2001.

—*The Foundations of British Maritime Ascendancy: Resources, Logistics and the State, 1755–1815*. Cambridge: Cambridge University Press, 2011.

Neale, Jonathan. *The Cutlass and the Lash: Mutiny and Discipline in Nelson's Navy*. London: Pluto Press, 1985.

Oppenheim, Michael. *The Maritime History of Devon*: Exeter: University of Exeter, 1968.

Padfield, Peter. *Maritime Supremacy and the Opening of the Western Mind*. New York: The Overlook Press, 1999.

Rediker, Marcus. *Between the Devil and the Deep Blue Sea: Merchant Seamen, Pirates and the Anglo-American Maritime World, 1700–1750*. Cambridge: Cambridge University Press, 1987.

Rickard, Gillian. *Kent Enrolments under the Navy Act, 1796*. Canterbury: Author, 1996.

Rodger, N.A.M. *The Wooden World: An Anatomy of the Georgian Navy*. London: Collins, 1986.

—*The Insatiable Earl: A Life of John Montagu, Fourth Earl of Sandwich, 1718–1792*. London: HarperCollins, 1993.

—*The Safeguard of the Sea: A Naval History of Britain, 660–1649*. New York: W.W. Norton & Company, 1997.

—*The Command of the Ocean: A Naval History of Britain, 1649–1815*. First American edition. New York: W.W. Norton & Company, 2005.

Rogers, Nicholas. *Crowds, Culture, and Politics in Georgian Britain*. Oxford: Clarendon Press, 1998.

—*The Press Gang: Naval Impressment and Its Opponents in Georgian Britain*. London: Continuum, 2007.

Rommelse, Gijs. *The Second Anglo-Dutch War, 1665–1667*. Hilversm: Verloren, 2006.

Smith, Adam. *An Inquiry into the Nature and Causes of the Wealth of Nations*. 2nd edn. London: Encyclopaedia Britannica, Inc., 1990.

Talbott, John E. *The Pen and Ink Sailor: Charles Middleton and the King's Navy, 1778–1813*. Naval Policy and History. London: Frank Cass, 1998.

Thompson, E.P. *The Making of the English Working Class*. London: Penguin Books, 1991.

Vickers, Daniel, and Vince Walsh. *Young Men and the Sea: Yankee Seafarers in the Age of Sail*. New Haven, Conn.: Yale University Press, 2005.

Wells, Roger A.E., ed. *Insurrection: The British Experience 1795–1803*. Gloucester: Alan Sutton, 1983.

Wilkinson, Clive. *The British Navy and the State in the Eighteenth Century*. Woodbridge: The Boydell Press, 2004.

Willis, Sam. *Fighting at Sea in the Eighteenth Century: The Art of Sailing Warfare*. Woodbridge: The Boydell Press, 2008.

Zerbe, Britt. *The Birth of the Royal Marines, 1664–1802*. Woodbridge: The Boydell Press, 2013.

Zimmerman, James Fulton. *Impressment of American Seamen*. New York: Columbia University Press, 1925.

Articles and Chapters

Aldridge, David. 'The Navy as Handmaid for Commerce and High Policy, 1680–1720.' In *The British Navy and the Use of Naval Power in the Eighteenth Century*, ed. Jeremy Black and Philip Woodfine, pp. 51–69. Leicester: Leicester University Press, 1988.

Anderson, Olive. 'The Establishment of British Supremacy at Sea and the Exchange of Naval Prisoners of War, 1689–1783.' *English Historical Review* LXXV, no. 294 (1960): pp. 77–89.

Baugh, Daniel. 'Maritime Strength and Atlantic Commerce: The Uses of "a Grand Marine Empire".' In *An Imperial State at War: Britain from 1689 to 1815*, ed. Lawrence Stone, pp. 185–223. London: Routledge, 1994.

—'The Eighteenth-Century Navy as a National Institution, 1690–1815.' In *The Oxford Illustrated History of the Royal Navy*, ed. J.R. Hill and Bryan Ranft, pp. 120–160. Oxford: Oxford University Press, 1995. Reprint, 2002.

Benjamin, Daniel K., and Christopher Thornberg. 'Comment: Rules, Monitoring, and Incentives in the Age of Sail.' *Explorations in Economic History*, no. 40 (2003): pp. 195–211.

—'Organization and Incentives in the Age of Sail.' *Explorations in Economic History*, no. 44 (2007): pp. 317–341.

Bromley, J.S. 'The British Navy and Its Seamen after 1688: Notes for an Unwritten History.' In *Charted and Uncharted Waters*, ed. Sarah Palmer and David Williams, pp. 148–163. Queen Mary College, London: Trustees of the National Maritime Museum, 1981.

Brooks, F.W. 'Naval Recruiting in Lindsey, 1795–7.' *English Historical Review* XLIII, no. 170 (1928): pp. 230–240.

Colley, Linda. 'The Apotheosis of George III: Loyalty, Royalty and the British Nation, 1760–1820.' *Past and Present*, no. 102 (1984): pp. 94–129.

—'Whose Nation? Class and National Consciousness in Britain, 1750–1830.' *Past and Present*, no. 113 (1986): pp. 97–117.

—'The Reach of the State, the Appeal of the Nation: Mass Arming and Political Culture in Napoleonic Wars.' In *An Imperial State at War*, ed. Lawrence Stone, pp. 165–184. London: Routledge, 1994.

Conway, Stephen. 'The Politics of British Military and Naval Mobilization, 1775–83.' *English Historical Review* CXII, no. 449 (1997): pp. 1179–1201.

—'The Mobilization of Manpower for Britain's Mid-Eighteenth Century Wars.' *Historical Research* LXXVII, no. 197 (2004): pp. 377–404.

Cookson, J.E. 'The English Volunteer Movement of the French Wars, 1793–1815.' *The Historical Journal* XXXII, no. 4 (1989): pp. 867–891.

Davids, Karel. 'Seamen's Organizations and Social Protest in Europe, 1300–1825.' In *Before the Unions: Wage Earners and Collective Action in Europe, 1300–1850*, ed. Catharina Lis, Jan Lucassen and Hugo Soly. Cambridge: Cambridge University Press, 1994.

Davis, Ralph. 'English Foreign Trade, 1700–1774.' In *The Growth of English Overseas Trade in the Seventeenth and Eighteenth Centuries*, ed. W.E. Minchinton, pp. 99–120. London: Methuen & Co., Ltd, 1969.

Duffy, Michael. 'The Foundations of British Naval Power.' In *The Military Revolution and the State, 1500–1800*, ed. Michael Duffy, pp. 49–85. Exeter: University of Exeter Press, 1980.

—'The Establishment of the Western Squadron as the Linchpin of British Naval Strategy.' In *Parameters of British Naval Power, 1650–1850*, ed. Michael Duffy, pp. 60–81. Exeter: University of Exeter Press, 1992.

—'World-Wide War and British Empire, 1793–1815.' In *The Oxford History of the British Empire: The Eighteenth Century*, ed. P.J. Marshall, pp. 184–207. Oxford: Oxford University Press, 1998.

Earle, Peter. 'English Sailors, 1570–1775.' In *"Those Emblems of Hell?" European Sailors and the Maritime Labour Market, 1570–1870*, ed. Paul van Royen, Jaap Bruijn and Jan Lucassen, pp. 73–92. St John's, Newfoundland: International Maritime Economic History Association, 1997.

Emsley, Clive. 'The Recruitment of Petty Offenders During the French Wars, 1793–1815.' *The Mariner's Mirror* CXVI, no. 3 (1980): pp. 199–208.

—'Behind the Wooden Walls: The British Defences against Invasion, 1803–1805.' In *A Great and Glorious Victory: New Perspectives on the Battle of Trafalgar*, ed. Richard Harding. Barnsley: Seaforth Publishing, 2008.

Emsley, Clive, James Walvin and Gwyn A. Williams. 'The Impact of War and Military Participation on Britain and France.' In *Artisans, Peasants and Proletarians, 1760–1860: Essays Presented to Gwyn A. Williams*, ed. Clive Emsley, James Walvin and Gwyn A. Williams, pp. 57–80. London: Croom Helm Ltd, 1985.

Foy, Charles R. 'Hidden Lives: Elderly Cooks, Powder Boys, and Fugitive Slaves among Eighteenth-Century Anglo-American Naval Crews.' In *New Interpretations in Naval History: Selected Papers from the Fifteenth Naval History Symposium*, ed. Maochun Miles Yu, pp. 266–278. United States Naval Academy: Naval Institute Press, 2007.

Frykman, Niklas. 'Seamen on Late Eighteenth-Century European Warships.' *International Review of Social History* LIV, no. 1 (2009): pp. 67–93.

Gradish, Stephen. 'Wages and Manning: The Navy Act of 1758.' *English Historical Review* XCIII, no. 366 (1978): pp. 46–67.

Hubley, Martin. "'The Most Outrageous Set of People That Ever Lived": Desertion, Identity and Irish Seamen of the Royal Navy in North America, 1745–1815.' In *The British Empire and Its Contested Pasts*, ed. Robert J. Blyth and Keith Jeffery, pp. 169–195. Dublin: Irish Academic Press, 2009.

Hubley, Martin, and Thomas Malcomson. "'The People, from Being Tyrannically Treated, Would Rejoice in Being Captured by the Americans": Mutiny and the Royal Navy During the War of 1812.' In *The Apathetic and the Defiant: Case Studies of Canadian Mutiny and Disobedience, 1812 to 1919*, ed. Craig Leslie Mantle, pp. 31–83. Kingston, Ontario & Toronto: Dundurn Press & Canadian Defence Academy Press, 2007.

Innes, Joanna. 'The Domestic Face of the Military-Fiscal State: Government and Society in Eighteenth-Century Britain.' In *Insurrection: The British Experience 1795–1803*, ed. Roger Wells, pp. 96–127. Gloucester: Alan Sutton, 1983.

La Goff, T.J.A. 'Naval Recruitment and Labour Supply in the French War Effort, 1755–59.' In *New Aspects in Naval History: Selected Papers from the 5th Naval History Symposium*. Annapolis: Naval Institute Press, 1985.

MacFarlane, Helen, and Paul Mortimer-Lee. 'Inflation over 300 Years.' *Bank of England Quarterly Bulletin*, May (1994): pp. 156–162.

McCord, Norman, and David E. Brewster. 'Some Labour Troubles of the 1790s in North East England.' *International Review of Social History* XIII (1968): pp. 366–383.

McCranie, K.D. 'The Recruitment of Seamen for the British Navy, 1793–1815: "Why Don't You Raise More Men?"' In *Conscription in the Napoleonic Era: A Revolution in Military Affairs?* ed. Donald J. Stoker, Frederick C. Schneid and Harold D. Blanton, pp. 84–101. London: Routledge, 2009.

Middleton, Richard. 'Naval Administration in the Age of Pitt and Anson, 1755–1763.' In *The British Navy and the Use of Naval Power in the Eighteenth Century*, ed. Jeremy Black and Philip Woodfine, pp. 109–127. Leicester: Leicester University Press, 1988.

Neal, Larry. 'The Cost of Impressment During the Seven Years' War.' *The Mariner's Mirror* LXIV, no. 1 (1978): pp. 45–56.

O'Brien, P.K., and S.L. Engerman. 'Exports and the Growth of the British Economy from the Glorious Revolution to the Peace of Amiens.' In *Slavery and the Rise of the Atlantic System*, ed. Barbara L. Solow, pp. 177–209. Cambridge: Cambridge University Press, 1991.

Palmer, Sarah, and David M. Williams. 'British Sailors, 1775–1870.' In *"Those Emblems of Hell?" European Sailors and the Maritime Labour Market, 1570–1870*, ed. Paul van Royen, Jaap Bruijn and Jan Lucassen, pp. 93–118. St John's, Newfoundland: International Maritime Economic History Assoication, 1997.

Pares, R. 'The Manning of the Navy in the West Indies, 1702–63.' *Transactions of the Royal Historical Society* XX (1937): pp. 31–60.

Peitsch, Roland. 'Ships' Boys and Youth Culture in Eighteenth-Century Britain: The Navy Recruits of the London Marine Society.' *The Northern Mariner* XIV, no. 4 (2004): pp. 11–24.

Phillips, Carla Rahn. 'Maritime Labour in Early Modern Spain.' In *The Market for Seamen in the Age of Sail*, ed. Lewis R. Fischer, pp. 1–25. St John's, Newfoundland: International Maritime Economic History Association, 1994.

—'The Life Blood of the Navy: Recruiting Sailors in Eighteenth-Century Spain.' *The Mariner's Mirror* LXXXVII, no. 4 (2001): pp. 420–445.

Robinson, Dwight E. 'Secret of British Power in the Age of Sail: Admiralty Records of the Coasting Fleet.' *The American Neptune* XLVIII, no. 1 (1988): pp. 5–21.

Rodger, N.A.M. 'Devon Men and the Navy, 1689–1815.' In *The New Maritime History of Devon*, ed. Michael Duffy *et al.*, I, pp. 209–215. London: Conway Maritime Press, 1992.

—'Shipboard Life in the Georgian Navy, 1750–1800: The Decline of the Old Order?' In *The North Sea: Twelve Essays on Social History of Maritime Labour*, ed. Lewis R. Fischer, Harald Hamre, Poul Holm and Jaap Bruijn, pp. 29–39. Stavanger: Stavanger Maritime Museum, 1992.

—'The Naval Service of the Cinque Ports.' *English Historical Review* CXI, no. 442 (1996): pp. 636–651.

—'Officers and Men.' In *Maritime History: The Eighteenth Century and the Classic Age of Sail*, ed. John B. Hattendorf, II, pp. 137–144. Malabar: Krieger Publishing Company, 1997.

—'"A Little Navy of Your Own Making": Admiral Boscawen and the Cornish Connection in the Royal Navy.' In *Parameters of British Naval Power, 1650–1850*, ed. Michael Duffy, pp. 82–92. Exeter: University of Exeter Press, 1998.

—'Sea-Power and Empire, 1688–1793.' In *The Oxford History of the British Empire: Vol. 2, The Eighteenth Century*, ed. P.J. Marshall, pp. 169–183. Oxford: Oxford University Press, 1998.

—'Mutiny or Subversion? Spithead and the Nore.' In *1798: A Bicentenary Perspective*, ed. Thomas Bartlett, pp. 549–564. Dublin: Fourcourts Press Ltd, 2003.

—'Mobilizing Seapower in the Eighteenth Century.' In *Essays in Naval History, from Medieval to Modern*, ed. N.A.M. Rodger, Section IX, pp. 1–9. Farnham: Ashgate Publishing, 2009.

Rogers, Nicholas. 'Liberty Road: Opposition to Impressment in Britain During the American War of Independence.' In *Jack Tar in History: Essays in the History of Maritime Life and Labour*, ed. Colin Howel and Richard J. Twomey, pp. 53–75. Fredericton, New Brunswick: Acadiensis Press, 1991.

—'Vagrancy, Impressment and the Regulation of Labour in Eighteenth-Century Britain.' In *Unfree Labour in the Development of the Atlantic World*, ed. Paul E. Lovejoy and Nicholas Rogers, pp. 102–113. London: Cass, 1994.

—'Impressment and the Law in Eighteenth-Century Britain.' In *Law, Crime and English Society*, ed. Norma Laundau, pp. 71–94. Cambridge: Cambridge University Press, 2002.

Rossam, Matthias van, Lex Heerma van Voss, Jellel van Lottum and Jan Lucassen. 'National and International Labour Markets for Sailors in European, Atlantic and Asian Waters, 1600–1850.' In *Maritime History as Global History*, ed. Maria Fusaro and Amélia Polónia, pp. 47–82. St John's, Newfoundland: International Maritime Economic History Association, 2010.

Royen, Paul van. 'Mariners and Markets in the Age of Sail: The Case of the Netherlands.' In *The Market for Seamen in the Age of Sail*, ed. Lewis R. Fischer, pp. 47–57. St John's, Newfoundland: International Maritime Economic History Association, 1994.

Scammell, G.V. 'Mutiny in British Ships, c. 1500–1750.' In *Seafaring, Sailors and Trade, 1450–1750: Studies in British and European Maritime and Imperial History*, ed. G.V. Scammell, pp. 337–354. Aldershot: Ashgate Publishing, 2003.

—'War at Sea under the Early Tudors: Some Newcastle-Upon-Tyne Evidence.' In *Seafaring, Sailors and Trade, 1450–1750: Studies in British and European Maritime and Imperial History*, ed. G.V. Scammell, pp. 179–205. Aldershot: Ashgate Publishing, 2003.

Starkey, David J. 'War and the Market for Seafarers in Britain, 1736–1792.' In *Shipping and Trade, 1750–1950: Essays in International Maritime Economic History*, ed. Lewis R. Fischer and Helge W. Nordvik, pp. 25–42. Pontefract: Lofthouse Publications, 1990.

—'Quantifying British Seafarers, 1789–1828.' In *Maritime Labour: Contributions to the History of Work at Sea, 1500–2000*, ed. Richard Gorski, pp. 83–103. Amsterdam: Aksant Academic Publishers, 2007.

Stout, Neil R. 'Manning the Royal Navy in North America, 1763–1775.' *American Neptune* XXIII, no. 3 (1963): pp. 174–185.

Syrett, David. 'The Organization of British Trade Convoys During the American War, 1775–83.' *The Mariner's Mirror* LXII (1976): pp. 169–181.

Usher Jr., Roland G. 'Royal Navy Impressment During the American Revolution.' *The Mississippi Valley Historical Review* XXXVII, no. 4 (1951): pp. 673–688.

Vale, Brian. 'The Conquest of Scurvy in the Royal Navy, 1793–1800: A Challenge to the Current Orthodoxy.' *The Mariner's Mirror* XCIV, no. 2 (2008): pp. 160–175.

Western, J.R. 'The Volunteer Movement as an Anti-Revolutionary Force, 1793–1801.' *English Historical Review* LXXI, no. 281 (1956): pp. 603–614.

Willis, Sam. 'The High Life: Topmen in the Eighteenth-Century Navy.' *The Mariner's Mirror* XC, no. 2 (2004): pp. 152–166.

Wismes, Armel De. 'The French Navy under Louis XIV.' In *Louis XIV and Absolution*, ed. Ragnhild Marie Hatton, pp. 243–262. London: Macmillan Press Ltd, 1976.

Woodfine, Philip. '"Proper Objects of the Press": Naval Impressment and Habeas Corpus in the French Revolutionary Wars.' In *The Representation and Reality of War, the British Experience: Essays in Honour of David Wright*, ed. Keith Dockray and Keith Laybourn, pp. 39–60. Stroud: Sutton Publishing, 1999.

Theses

Brunsman, Denver Alexander. 'The Evil Necessity: British Naval Impressment in the Eighteenth-Century Atlantic World.' Unpublished PhD thesis, Princeton University, 2004.

Cavell, Samantha. 'A Social History of Midshipmen and Quarterdeck Boys in the Royal Navy, 1761–1831.' Unpublished PhD thesis, University of Exeter, 2010.

Dacam, John H. '"Wanton and Torturing Punishments": Patterns of Discipline and Punishment in the Royal Navy, 1783–1815.' Unpublished PhD thesis, University of Hull, 2009.

Dancy, Jeremiah. 'British Naval Manpower During the French Revolutionary Wars, 1793–1802.' Unpublished DPhil thesis, University of Oxford, 2012.

Hubley, Martin. 'Desertion, Identity and the Experience of Authority in the North American Squadron of the Royal Navy, 1745–1812.' Unpublished PhD thesis, University of Ottawa, 2009.

Jenks, Timothy. 'Naval Engagements: Patriotism, Cultural Politics, and the Royal Navy, 1793–1815.' Unpublished PhD thesis, University of Toronto, 2001.

Mercer, Keith. 'North Atlantic Press Gangs: Impressment and Naval-Civilian Relations in Nova Scotia and Newfoundland, 1749–1815.' Unpublished PhD thesis, Dalhousie University, 2008.

Oprey, Christopher. 'Schemes for the Reform of Naval Recruitment.' Unpublished MA thesis, University of Liverpool, 1961.

Usher Jr., Roland G. 'The Civil Administration of the British Navy During the American Revolution.' Unpublished PhD thesis, University of Michigan, 1942.

Zerbe, Britt. '"That Most Useful Body of Men": The Operational Doctrine and Identity of the British Marine Corps, 1755–1802.' Unpublished PhD thesis, University of Exeter, 2010.

Electronic Sources

Ayshford, Pam, and Derek Ayshford. 'The Ayshford Complete Trafalgar Roll.' Brussels: SEFF, 2004. CD-ROM.

Marioné, Patrick. 'The Complete Navy List of the Napoleonic Wars', Brussels: SEFF, 2003. CD-ROM.

Index

Swallow, 7
Swift, 7
Tigre, 7
Wasp, 8, 80
Windsor Castle, 8
Sixpenny Office, 20, 68, 70
Smith, Sir Sidney, 103
Somerset, 84
Southampton, 21, 97, 138
Spavens, William, 66, 124, 126–8, 143, 145, 153, 156
Spithead, 3, 5, 79, 156, 161, 163, 167–9, 179–81, 183
Suffolk, 84
surgeon, 98–9
Sussex, 84, 103, 160, 173, 176
Sweden, 151
système des classes, 129, 164

Thompson, John, 1st Baron Haversham, 56
Torbay, 5
Toulon, 61, 130, 159
Trafalgar, 65, 67
Treasury, 23, 163

United States of America, 105, 116–17

volunteer movement, 56, 59, 93, 118
volunteers, 9, 13, 24, 31–9, 41–2, 52, 57–9, 63, 65–7, 76–92, 96–7, 99, 101–11, 113–14, 116, 121, 127–8, 131–2, 140–1, 152–3, 156, 164, 171–2, 174, 189

Wales, 10, 50, 52, 59, 85, 114, 149, 160, 162–3, 166
Wars
  French Revolutionary Wars, 8, 11, 13, 19, 25–8, 39, 55, 58, 61, 75, 78, 81, 83, 90, 95, 105, 107, 109, 115, 120, 123, 131, 139–41, 148, 150, 156, 159, 170, 186, 190
  Napoleonic Wars, 58, 65, 123–4, 126, 130
  Second Dutch War, 19
  Seven Years' War, 4, 13, 19–23, 25, 30–1, 57, 66–8, 74–6, 97, 102, 109, 112–13, 115, 118, 124, 126, 129, 133, 136–8, 143, 146, 186, 188
  War of American Independence, 14, 24–6, 58, 67, 138–9, 143
  War of Austrian Succession, 18–19, 97, 109, 138, 157
  War of the Grand Alliance, 14–5
watermen, 112, 173, 175
West Indies, 15, 17, 19, 33, 60, 64, 71, 75, 95, 108, 112, 116, 124, 132, 144, 150, 152, 158
Whitehaven, 21, 97, 138, 182
William III, 14–17, 126, 157
Winchester, 21, 138
Wrexham, 97

Yarmouth, 21, 138
York, 12
Yorkshire, 97, 160, 162